ALSO BY MICHAEL H. COLES

2016

Naval Occasions 1939 through 1956

"Vividly narrated and subtly observed, Coles's essays bring to life ten key naval actions from World War II and the Cold War."

"...this collection added insights and details to a number of events that I had vaguely 'known' about but not really understood."

2018

A Boyhood in Wartime Britain

"Author Coles neatly balances scrupulous scholarship in a memoir with a deeply personal perspective. This book is destined to take its place among the finest up-close accounts of life during World War II."

"Mr. Coles has written a poignant historical account of World War II, remembered from his childhood viewpoint."

LUCKY,
NOT SMART

MICHAEL H. COLES

Published by Devonport Press

ISBN: 9781701892514

COVER ART

HMAS *Sydney* in Korean waters, 1951, taken from a painting by Ray Honisett, used by permission from the Australian War Memorial. HMAS *Sydney* was part of the British Commonwealth contribution to the United Nations' defense of South Korea against the 1950-53 attack by Communist North Korea. She was of the same class and virtually identical to HMS *Ocean*, a carrier that also fought in the Korean War and plays a significant role in this book.

DEDICATION

This book is dedicated to the memory of our mother, who provided my brother and me with the gift of unconditional love; our father who patiently and affectionately taught us so many useful and varied skills; to my two amazing wives who (sequentially) gave me love, security and confidence sufficient to take on the world; to my large and amazing family who continuously inspire and delight me; and finally to Lt.(O) Reginald Simmonds, RN (Retd.), without whose skill and watchfulness I might not have survived to write this book.

ACKNOWLEDGMENTS

Great thanks are due to several people without whose help and support this book would never have been written. First, my neighbor and good friend Academy Award-winning writer Janet Roach who has given me constant encouragement to keep writing, and who has generously read and critiqued my many drafts. Second, my kind neighbor Robert Lypsite, *New York Times* sports reporter who read my earlier book: *A Boyhood in Wartime Britain*, and urged me to write a sequel. That first moment facing a keyboard always requires a strong push to get one going, and it was Robert who provided it. Also another huge thank you to Marilyn Shames who, to my great good fortune, continues ready to edit my work, always doing it gently enough so that I never feel the pain of the whip. And lastly, my lovely wife Edie who set me off down the writing path many years back: the day I first heard her introduce me as "My husband, the writer."

TABLE OF CONTENTS

PREFACE i

Chapter 1 LEARNING BECAUSE THE LAW REQUIRED IT 1

Chapter 2 LEARNING TO BE THE MASTER OF MY FATE – THE CAPTAIN OF MY SOUL..................................21

Chapter 3 LEARNING THAT I ABSOLUTELY NEVER WANTED TO BE A FARMER......................................31

Chapter 4 LEARNING TO LOVE THE SEA AND BOATS...........57

Chapter 5 BEFORE BECOMING A NAVAL PILOT: LEARNING TO BE A NAVAL OFFICER......................65

Chapter 6 LEARNING TO BE A NAVAL AVIATOR 71

Chapter 7 LEARNING DURING A SMALL WAR, WITH REAL BOMBS AND REAL BULLETS...........113

Chapter 8 A FIRST TIME VISITOR LEARNING ABOUT AMERICA, UP CLOSE..173

Chapter 9 LEARNING WHILE FLYING IN THE PEACETIME NAVY 195

Chapter 10 LEARNING ABOUT THE MAGIC OF AN ENCHANTED EVENING.....................................211

Chapter 11 LEARNING TO BE A FLYING INSTRUCTOR 225

Chapter 12 LEARNING BY TEACHING.......................................235

Chapter 13 LEARNING DURING A CIVIL WAR, WITH REAL WEAPONS 261

ABOUT THE AUTHOR 285

PREFACE

During the summer of 1986 Michael stood with a small group of his Harvard Business School classmates on the steps of the school's Baker Library. They had been celebrating the 25th Anniversary of their graduation from The Business School and were basking in the satisfaction of their shared successes. With commendable lack of restraint, his class had long before christened itself "The Fabulous Class of 1961", and such title had played a prominent role in their celebrations. Now, stressing the fact that he had no desire to rain on their parade, Michael turned to his nearby classmates and suggested that it could be a good time to make a modest sacrifice to whatever gods might still be keeping watch over them. "Why don't we" he said, "march slowly down the steps of this famous Library chanting softly, so as not to disturb any onlookers: "Lucky, not smart'." Then they could turn around and walk back up (thus demonstrating stamina beyond their years), chanting the same thing. He's not sure whether any gods were propitiated, or whether anyone in his little group felt any better, but he did feel glad to have provided the opportunity to say what, in his case was certainly true: he would never lay claim to being smart, but he will admit to having been mostly very, very lucky.

A timeline may be helpful. Michael was born in England and, until the age of eighteen was educated at various private schools there. At his own insistence, however, he did not go on to college. Age eighteen marked the end of his conventional education so far as professionals would recognize it. Leaving school, he joined the Royal Navy, trained as a naval pilot, flew combat missions during the Korean War, and later served as a flight instructor. After eight years in the Navy he entered Harvard Business School. In 1961 he graduated with honors and was hired as an Associate by Goldman, Sachs & Co. In 1968 he became a Partner, in 1975 he became Chairman of Goldman, Sachs International Corp. and in 1985 he retired to become a Limited Partner in the firm.

In retirement he devoted himself to a number of not-for-profit organizations, continued to improve his education, acquired his own airplane, and recaptured his flying skills. He has always hoped that his later life not-for-profit work would represent some kind of a "thank you" to the nation that has given him so much, including his citizenship there.

During his naval service he was fortunate to meet and marry Joan Collins, an extraordinary American woman who changed his life in many ways, but most of all by teaching him the meaning of true love while encouraging him to return to education and to apply to Harvard Business School. She also gave him the ultimate gift, their five wonderful children who in turn have produced nineteen exceptional grandchildren. Tragically, Joan died in her late sixties. However, he was fortunate enough to fall in love again, with Edie Langner, an outstanding medical doctor. This marriage represented a second stroke of great fortune. Edie has added extraordinary luster to his life and has given him and his large family enormous love, support and happiness.

The following pages are devoted largely to the many years of his adulthood during which learning, in the fullest sense of the word, provided the principal focus of his life. He leaves it to readers to decide whether all that education made him any smarter, but he hopes that when they have read the book, they will share his sense of having truly led a very lucky life.

The narrative you will be reading also describes the process, largely a matter of chance, whereby a young Englishman became increasingly enamored with America, and the American people. Michael's naval service provided what, for the time, was an unusual opportunity for an Englishman to visit the United States, meet and get to know its people and become familiar with its customs. Strangers will sometimes ask him if he is English. He will reply by saying that he was born and largely educated there, but add proudly that he is now an American.

MAP OF GREAT BRITAIN

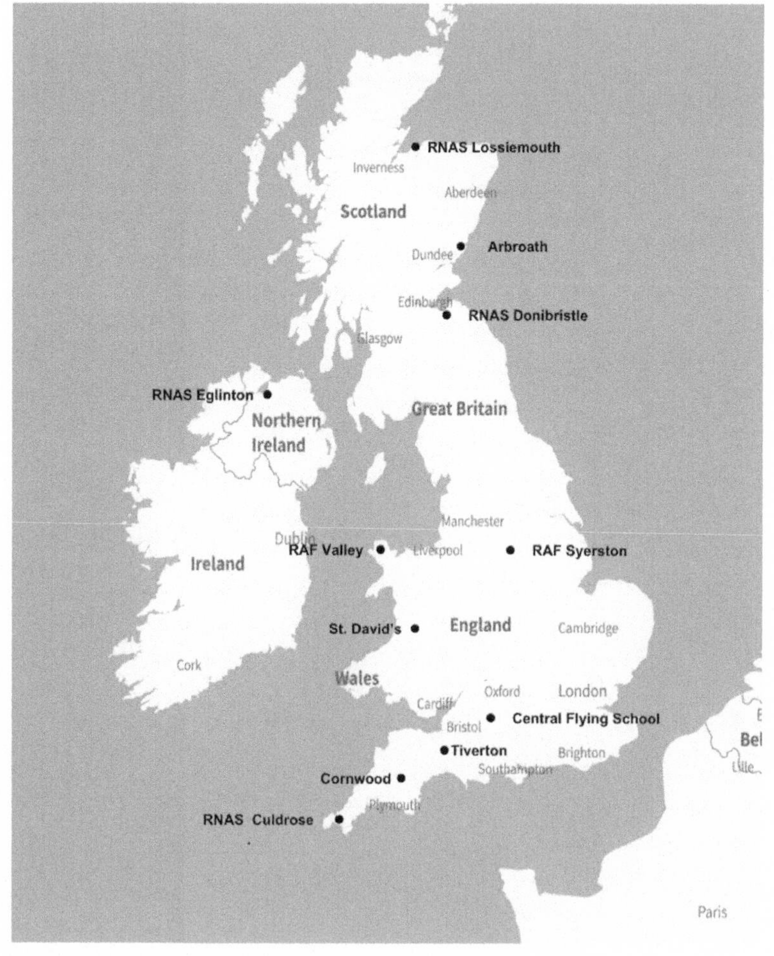

Chapter 1

LEARNING BECAUSE THE LAW REQUIRED IT

The British Education Act of 1944 provided compulsory State-funded schooling for all children up to the age of 15. Such was the basis for this chapter heading: until I was 15 I had to be in school or risk arrest for truancy. However, like many things British at the time, long held class distinctions created a sharp divide between those who could afford private schools and those who had to rely on the state system. And certainly, in the 1940's and 1950's, the best definition of who belonged where was one of accent. It might have been possible to find a lower-class accent in a private school, although very unlikely; the owner of an upper-class accent in a state school would be pressured to get rid of it quickly, just to survive. I think my parents would have sacrificed anything to ensure I had as good an education as they could find, and I was fortunate that they could afford the related costs of a private school (although I often wondered how). So although the education described here was probably a financial struggle, my inherited accent enabled me to appear as if I was there by right.

JOSEPHINE AND DEREK COLES (1930)

"I think my parents would have sacrificed anything to ensure I had as good an education as they could find, and I was fortunate that they could afford the related costs of a private school (although I often wondered how)."

The end of World War II caught me roughly halfway through my formal education. Like most boys of my background, I had gone away to boarding school at the age of eight and would remain there for as long as my parents considered it necessary and could manage the expense. The school that I was entrusted to up to the age of thirteen (known as a "Prep School" - not to be confused with similarly titled American establishments catering to older boys) was located deep in the countryside north west of London, and thus safe from German bombing. Victory in Europe Day (VE Day) happened when I was thirteen, and due to transition from Prep School to the Public School my parents had selected for me. Public School, the next stage on the British education ladder, was by no means public: it required payment of fees, and in most cases entrance was selective.

My father had attended Uppingham, a middle ranking Public School located north of London. He had been an outstanding Rugby player there and I suspect had always harboured hopes that I would follow in his footsteps. As in many aspects of my younger life, he was to be grievously disappointed.

My mother, who had visited Uppingham once, deemed it unsuitable for either of her two sons on the grounds that the lavatories smelled bad. They probably did: in those days most boys' boarding schools (maybe girls' schools too) had bad smelling lavatories, not unexpected in 19th Century buildings. Fortunately, factors outside our control decided the matter. For the British the end of the war did not mean the end of shortages of all kinds; in fact, in many respects, things actually got worse as the country elected a Socialist government and then came to grips with the truly sad state of its post-war economy.

During the early years of the war my father had served in the London Fire Service, and later transferred to the War Office where he was involved in officer selection. Although he had been a successful stockbroker before the war, for some reason he had always really wanted to be a farmer. When the war ended he hastened to acquire the farm in Devonshire he had been hankering for during the previous five years. It was located in Cornwood, a small village on the southern edge of Dartmoor, in the county of Devonshire. There was no way that the meagre gas ration allowed during the early years of peace would enable my parents to travel all the way from Devonshire to Uppingham in order to see me. Accordingly they selected Blundell's, a school with a standing similar to that of Uppingham, but located in the same county as our new home. My brother Tony, then seven, initially went to the Cornwood village school, but eventually went to Blundell's also.

BLUNDELL'S SCHOOL

"Blundell's can best be described as a minor regional public school. It had no Etonian pretensions, but rather saw itself as a provider of superior education to the West of England squierachy. For three centuries it had existed happily as a modest grammar school serving the local gentry."

Blundell's can best be described as a minor regional public school. It had no Etonian pretensions, but rather saw itself as a provider of superior education to the West of England squierachy. For three centuries it had existed happily as a modest grammar school serving the local gentry. Then, at the end of the nineteenth century when the example of Arnold at Rugby School began to percolate around the Public school system, it developed grand ideas, raised a quite substantial amount of endowment money, and moved to much larger quarters a couple of miles out of town. The new buildings consisted of the normal classrooms, "Big School" (assembly hall), library, gymnasium etc., with some half dozen boarding "houses" in which the boys (no girls then, or for several decades thereafter) studied, slept and ate. One of the funders of this move was my great grandfather John Coles who had grown up nearby, gone to work in London's financial district, done well in life and, to my eternal embarrassment, had provided money for a number of the expanding school's requirements, but most notably for me, at the time a budding scientist, The Coles Physics Laboratory.

JOHN COLES, Esq. J.P 1833-1919

"...my great grandfather John Coles who had grown up nearby, gone to work in London's financial district, done well in life and, to my eternal embarrassment, had provided money for a number of the expanding school's requirements, but most notably for me, who had to spend quite a lot of time in there, The Coles Physics Laboratory."

In 1945 there were two routes to making the transition from prep school to public school: Common Entrance or Scholarship. Common Entrance was a written exam covering all the normal subjects expected of adolescent boys. All the boys at my prep school, other than the Scholarship candidates, would take it at age thirteen and their grades would be considered when seeking admittance to the public school of their choice. The brightest boys, those in the sixth form, were sometimes encouraged to sit for a scholarship. This was an endowment at a particular public school that provided an annual stipend, which in those days, actually paid quite a lot of the school fees. But the point wasn't supposed to be the money. None of the parents with sons at my prep school, possibly excepting my own, would ever admit to anything quite so crass as an interest in money–it was more the prestige.

Not being in the sixth (highest) form at my prep school, I really wasn't supposed to be a candidate, but some of my teachers thought I might have a shot, particularly since Blundell's did not have the cachet of Harrow or Eton. So, in the summer of 1945 my mother and I went down to Blundell's by train and spent the night in the school sanitarium so that I would be in place to take the exam the next day. While there we visited Francis House, where I would board, and met the matron, who looked after the boys' domestic needs. My mother asked about the uniform, which included a dark gray suit. She was told that it could be obtained either new or second hand from the school clothing shop and, in view of the fact that clothing was still rationed and boys grew rapidly, during the war (and months following) most boys had bought second-hand suits. My mother told her that I had a perfectly good dark blue suit, and would it be all right if I wore that. "Oh yes," said the Matron. "I'm sure under the circumstances it will be fine." I could not believe my ears: I, who dreaded being "different", was to be locked into an eternity of high visibility as my blue suit shimmered among the clerical grays of the other three hundred and fifty or so pupils. Was there no end to this perfidy? Besides which, as I pointed out to my mother, there was no such blue suit. No, she admitted, but my cousin Jeremy had one that should fit. So it went, chapel on the first day of school in September 1945, three hundred and forty nine boys in identical clerical gray suits, and one miserable wimp in ill-fitting dark blue serge.

But we get ahead of ourselves. Much to everyone's surprise, including my own, I did rather well on the exams;

and was awarded a scholarship that paid a respectable amount of my school fees. Although he never said anything about it at the time, my father actually set aside the money from the scholarship and gave it back to me after I left school. In matters such as these he never ceased to amaze me.

My first years at Blundell's were not happy ones. All the things that had saddened my life at my prep school came back in force: the compulsory "games" (sports), the homesickness and now the suit, a burden that must seem minuscule to normal readers but which to me was like a social millstone around my neck. To compound it all, there was sex: never easy when you're entering adolescence and for me, unfortunately both ignorant and pathetically innocent, unhappily difficult.

I suppose that in today's world it would be parents who provided the basic information, but not at Blundell's, and least of all where my family was concerned. Instead, all of us had to attend a one-hour lecture designed to bring us up to speed on the subject and warn us of its pitfalls. The lecture was delivered by the school doctor whose medical credentials, it was rumored, stemmed from a brief and unhappy career tending cavalry horses during the First World War. His advice came in three parts. The first dealt with the mechanics, and was accompanied by a colored diagram that had obviously seen much use. The problem was that this, like all such diagrams of the day, allowed the private plumbing to fade out into a kind of nether wasteland. There was a lot of talk about male and female seeds, but nothing related the magic of how they got together. An innocent like me, therefore, remained unenlightened with respect to arcane matters that the more knowledgeable discussed at great length. Nor was I better prepared to associate any of the words they used to the actions they purported to describe. The whole business remained a dark mystery. Others, who knew, or pretended to know, much more than I did, were not about to share the information. Knowledge was power, and those lacking power were doomed to be harassed by those who had it.

Further lectures dealt with what the good doctor referred to as personal hygiene, using a conveniently obscure Latin phrase: *mens sane in corpore sane* (a healthy mind in a healthy body) which, since he failed to define a healthy mind, failed lamentably to elaborate on his goal of a healthy body.

The final piece of advice was given in even more guarded terms, and meant absolutely nothing to most of the listeners who lacked any appropriate point of reference to understand its implications. Blundell's, it must be remembered was, like nearly all British public schools at that time, an all boy boarding institution where a large number of healthy young males, ages ranging from pre- to post- adolescence, were kept in monastic seclusion for some seventy percent of the year. Monastic, indeed, was the right word—to be seen talking to an unrelated, non-servant female was grounds for expulsion at the time.

Such conditions lead to the inevitable: relationships deemed "unhealthy" between older and younger boys. In fact, most of these were really quite innocent, the product of loneliness, lack of affection, whatever. Intense friendships between boys of disparate age became the subject of gossip and ridicule, and typically faded as fast as they began. Physical sex between young male couples was, I believe, extremely rare. However, the matter was of considerable concern to the school authorities not, it appeared, out of anxiety for the welfare of the boys, but for fear of scandal. The solution, simple as it seems, was even more dreaded than the problem. Legend has it that the head boy of the school approached the headmaster to ask for permission to arrange one or two dances a term with a local girls' school. He was angrily denied and, on asking why, was told "Better little boys than little babies!" (You can't make this stuff up!)

But to someone like me (and, I suspect, most of my contemporaries) who knew little enough about heterosex, the idea that there might be something going on between boys was unimaginable. Hence the good doctor's warning that we must not allow ourselves to form too close friendships with other boys passed over our heads. Indeed, so lonely was I during the first few months at Blundell's that a friend of any persuasion would have seemed a gift from heaven. But the real gift, that today sounds so elementary as to be laughable, would have been a vocabulary, a body of knowledge that would have enabled me to understand what was going on when the other boys were sniggering away over a joke or limerick that had totally passed me by.

Looking back, one might wonder what in all this made me so unhappy, and my recollections so unfavorable. Maybe we should return to the comments made earlier by the headmaster of my prep school, that I allowed things of little importance to occupy too much of my thinking. Possibly, but all those things of little importance added up at the time to what I perceived as a miserable existence. I was always homesick; I was perceived as "different" (never under-estimate the impact of the blue suit); and when it came to the big secrets of sex I was outside the tent trying to understand what was going on inside, rather than inside trying to keep the ignorant out. Although I was never physically bullied, I was often verbally harassed (or at least I thought I was – maybe I was just over-sensitive).

Like most British public schools, Blundell's encouraged the system of fagging. The prefects (seniors) were allowed to use the younger boys as glorified servants, cleaning out their studies, taking care of their clothes, polishing shoes and boots, and running errands. Each prefect was assigned a personal fag, (a name that implied none of the sexual orientation it would today). A prefect was also allowed to just yell "Fag!" at the top of his voice and the last of the boys so designated to come running up was assigned the chore. It wasn't a bad system and, unlike in the previous century as described in the novel *Tom Brown's Schooldays*, it was rarely abused. I spent a year fagging for a boy called Eades who treated me quite decently, and I hope I was equally good to my own fag when the time came for me to have one.

Blundell's was a strongly Episcopalian school. When I first went there the headmaster was the Reverend R. G. Roberts, a rather idiosyncratic clergyman who had entered into a passionate affair with the wife of one of the mathematics masters, a situation the student body was largely unaware of.

The good Reverend also harbored some significant doctrinal concerns that included strong feelings regarding the wooden cross that hung over the altar - why I don't know, religious doctrine has never been one of my strong points. I had been there a few months when a boy found him in the back recesses of the school chapel cutting up the cross with an axe. At this point the School's Board of Governors decided they had had enough, and the Reverend was put in a van and taken away to (I hope) some well-guarded spiritual retirement home. Our next headmaster was a plain Mister, and was indeed, just plain. His name was Carter and he continued in overall charge of my education in a rather nondescript way until I finished it in 1950. My brother, who spent more time under Carter's command than I did, thought he was slightly mad, but I suspect that was because at various times we must have felt that anyone responsible for our education had to be slightly mad.

When I was at Blundell's, being Episcopalian (Anglican) meant that a fair amount of attention was paid to Christian practices and teachings. It never seemed to me that we were force fed our religion: more so that by being British one almost automatically became a member of the Church of England unless our parents opted out of it. There were some Catholics (very rare) and the occasional Jew (mostly holdovers from the Kindertransport that had brought young Jewish children from Germany to Britain as refugees before the war). Most of us, therefore, attended morning prayers every day in the school chapel, evening prayers were said nightly in the individual boarding houses, formal Sunday morning services were held in the chapel, with the school choir and a student organist. The organist was brilliant: I think he eventually went to Oxford on an organ scholarship and from there on became quite famous: I can remember his name, although I haven't seen or heard him for over seventy years: Peter Hurford; he would play the introductory music and accompany our church services, and it was largely through him that I learned to appreciate some of the truly great works of English Church music.

While on this subject it's worth mentioning my family. My

mother and father both attended the Church of England services in Cornwood's small church, joined by me when I was home, and Tony when he was old enough. To be clear, I don't think this ever became a discussable issue: we went to church on Sundays, and everyone else we knew in the village went too. If I recall rightly, the locals went to a Non-Conformist village chapel: all drawn on distinctly class lines: they went to theirs, and we went to ours.

Later, when I joined the Navy, religious services were part of the daily routine; if you didn't want to go you had to say you were a Catholic, and you were then automatically excused. It never occurred to me to want to be a Catholic, I rather liked the predictability of the Church of England, so that's where I have stayed all my life; still today that increasingly rare specimen: a regular church-goer.

Boarding schools have much in common with prisons, including the drive for economy and security that causes them to be located in distant parts of the country. Blundell's wasn't too bad in this respect: Tiverton, the nearest town worthy of the name, was within walking distance, but access to its limited pleasures was restricted to three visits a term (semester). Much of our entertainment was thus made in-house, particularly music and theater. Music came to us via regular services in the school's chapel, classical concerts two or three times a term, and controlled use of our radios. I liked to listen to my radio during "prep," the time set aside for study during the evenings. Such was strictly forbidden, violations meaning loss of the radio. I managed to circumvent this restriction by wiring my radio with half a head-set that could be connected via a thin cable running down my sleeve. Anyone coming unexpectedly into my room would find me beavering away at my books with my head resting tiredly on my hand, in which the half head-set was buried. It was thus I discovered the American Armed Forces Network (AFN). This station, located in Germany and designed for the occupation troops there, played all the latest jazz and swing music from America, names such as Harry James, Benny Goodman, Duke Ellington, Louis Armstrong and Dizzie Gillespie. Tuning to AFN for the music also brought me the news, American, which appeared much more exciting than the rather bland material furnished by the BBC, although the latter was probably more accurate. Alert readers will note that I was already forming an attachment for things American: particularly music and literature. There would be more to come.

Blundell's was really an excellent school and I came away from it at age eighteen with about as fine an education as I think I could have asked for at the time. I was heavily into the sciences: math, physics, chemistry, biology, and less involved with the humanities, particularly foreign languages. However, with hindsight I think that is good. You can always catch up on the humanities by reading on your own, but science once missed is hard to provide. Languages, I am ashamed to say, while they continued an unpleasant burden while I was in school, never caused me much of a problem afterwards: everyone, it seems, wants to learn English; time that might have been misspent learning French irregular verbs could later be much better employed studying calculus or the Periodic Table.

I must also hasten to correct the impression I may have given regarding events that took place well over seventy years ago. The Blundell's of today is a very different place from the Blundell's of 1950, a belief supported by the fact that at the time of writing I have two great-nephews and a great-niece who have significantly benefitted from the education they received from what is now a very modern co-educational boarding school.

I was fifteen in 1947 when we had to take a nationwide exam called a School Certificate. It was quite tough and lasted two or three days. We would be tested in seven subjects and graded into four levels: Distinction, Credit, Pass and Fail. My school reports were beginning to fall into a predictable pattern: "could do better if he tried". In April my housemaster wrote to my parents: "It will be a pity if he fails his School Certificate this year for any lack of effort." Obviously, the powers-that-be were anticipating disaster, and preparing themselves and my parents for the worst. Before we went home for the summer my house master told me that he felt I was bound to fail all or most of these exams, my work that year had been so poor. And if I did perform as badly as he forecast, he would have to recommend that they take away my Scholarship. This very seldom happened and would have been quite a scandal. He wrote in much the same vein to my parents, and there was thus quite a lot of tension at home that summer.

I was at home during the summer holidays on the day the dreaded envelope with the results arrived. I took it up to my room to open it; I wanted some time to think, if things were as bad as everyone expected them to be. Three Distinctions, three Credits, and a Pass (French!). One of my Credits was in carpentry, of which more later. Overall, my results were among the best in the school, to everyone's surprise including my own. I had always been blessed with an unexpected ability to do well in exams, but this time only I knew how little work I had actually done, and how justified were my housemaster's gloomy expectations. When I went in to see him at the beginning of the next term he sighed and said, "What are we going to do with you?" But I noticed that punishment became less severe, however poorly I performed in class. Looking back on those miserable boarding school years, I must admit that much of the pain of that period was ameliorated from time to time by a considerable amount of good luck.

One afternoon that summer a visitor from America came to have tea with my mother. She was a warm and ebullient lady, but the main object of her attention was my brother Tony, whose long silky eyelashes she thought ab-so-lutely adorable. My friend Richard was staying with us at the time and, fed up with all this eyelash nonsense, we dragged Tony upstairs. (For more about Richard, constant and well-trusted friend from my early youth, see my book *A Boyhood in Wartime Britain*, available through Amazon.) While Richard held Tony down, I trimmed his eyelashes with a pair of nail scissors. Unfortunately, his kicking and screaming attracted parental attention, and we only managed to complete our work on one side. My mother was furious, claiming (probably rightly) that we might have blinded him, and (hopefully wrongly) that his eyelashes would never grow back again. However, for a year or two he did look a little lop-sided from the front.

More importantly, our guest brought me two presents from our American friends, both books, and both strongly influential. They were *Twenty Best Plays of the Modern American Theater* and John Gunther's *Inside USA*. The twenty best plays included such classics as Erskine Caldwell's *Tobacco Road,* Clare Booth Luce's *The Women*, Steinbeck's *Of Mice and Men*, and Lillian Hellman's *The Children's Hour*. The book opened two doors for me. First, the idea that a play could be read and enjoyed as a piece of writing, and second that an America existed which was harsher and less forgiving than the image conveyed during the war by the smartly dressed and ever generous GI's, and the exotic advertising in the *Saturday Evening Post*. These were mostly depression era plays, dating from a time when much of the United States was undergoing a collapse of national confidence and, in many areas, a unique deprivation. I kept this book by me for several years, reading and re-reading the plays.

John Gunther had written a number of "*Inside*" books: in-depth reporting on a country or area. *Inside USA* was his first full-length and detailed look at his own country. And a truly fascinating look it was, especially for someone who had never been there, but who had become insatiably curious about that far off land. Gunther dealt particularly with the governance of each state, asking the question, "Who runs it?" and then setting out to provide an answer. I was especially taken with some of the more colorful politicians. There was Jimmy Davis who literally sang himself into the Governor's mansion of Alabama with his own composition, the ubiquitous "You Are My Sunshine". But most striking of all was Huey Long of Louisiana, the powerful populist, Mussolini and Stalin combined, but who nevertheless built roads and public buildings, improved education, abolished the hated poll tax and improved the lot of the blacks.

Inside USA made me conscious of America's richness and

diversity. Written at the time that Washington was debating the provision of a $2 billion loan to Britain, it also made me aware for the first time that there was a solid body of opinion in that country which actually rather disliked mine, and particularly its Empire. Americans, wrote Gunther, weren't so much isolationist as anti-British (a somewhat startling observation for British people like me who had always assumed that everybody adored us). But overall, I loved the book, read all of its 967 pages, and became a boring walking encyclopedia of American trivia. Later, when I first visited the United States, I would astonish people by producing arcane pieces of information about their own country. Thank you, John Gunther.

The next two years dragged by with too little in the way of distraction from the rather dull business of being educated. I continued to be taught well in the sciences, though increasingly my real love was by now the humanities. I had an excellent English teacher, Mr. Burton, who nurtured an appreciation and understanding of Shakespeare and the Romantic poets, particularly Byron and Wordsworth. We had to learn by heart large chunks of their verse, a requirement I continue to appreciate when I find myself able from time to time to produce from memory an elegant slice of English poetry, to win an argument or, hopefully, impress a social gathering.

Blundell's had a small but quite eclectic library where I spent a lot of my free time. It was there and on my own that I discovered some of the great twentieth century writers. I devoured Aldous Huxley, best known for *Brave New World* but whose *Point Counter Point, Chrome Yellow* and *Eyeless in Gaza* I considered with the arrogance of youth to be finer works, maybe because they were longer or perhaps because they dealt with the immediate past rather than the far future. I wandered into Christopher Isherwood's verse plays: *The Ascent of F6* and *The Dog Beneath the Skin*. I also sampled T. S. Eliot, whose "The Hollow Men" would come in handy later. I was a quite sophisticated but very undisciplined reader.

My unexpected academic success earned me a truly

valuable reward: during Christmas holidays I was allowed to travel up to London by myself by train. I would stay with my maternal grandfather, a splendidly warm man who trusted me sufficiently to allow me to go out and around the city by myself. This privilege I took full advantage of by spending my limited pocket money on the theater. Even taking into account changes in the value of money since then, London theater in 1948 was remarkably cheap. For a couple of shillings (15 cents today) one could get into the upper balcony in most theaters, with a god's eye view of the stage. There, coming in from the raw cold of a January day, I discovered *Oklahoma!*

I was told that it had proved quite hard to stage *Oklahoma!* in London in the 1940's because the chorus was unable, after nearly a decade of short rations, to maintain the hard charging energy required by Agnes de Mille's dances. That may be so, but to me what I saw that day was unforgettable and, so I thought, unrepeatable. Wrong: the following day I saw *Annie Get Your Gun*. I thought I must have died and gone to heaven. Suddenly two love affairs ran in parallel: my slumbering affair with everything American, and my sudden discovery of what words and music and dancing and costume could do together on the stage. Already an admirer of America I had become a lifetime fan of that country's musical theater. I rushed out and bought the records, all of them. No LP's in those days, an original cast album would require some three or four breakable 78 rpm discs, each sheathed in its cardboard wrapper. These were brought home on the train with great care and played endlessly on my wind-up gramophone. Given any encouragement even today I can sing from memory large swatches of the music from these two shows.

I became very involved in the production side of school plays: the scenery rather than the acting. It was for a school production of Sheridan's play *School for Scandal* that I delivered what I believe was my finest set. One of the problems of our school plays was that we had no capacity to create flies, the things that go up into the ceiling when scenes are changed. Everything had to be moved on or off stage, which was cumbersome and meant that we normally focused on plays which could be done with a simple three-sided setting and a curtain which drew horizontally. As I read *School for Scandal* it seemed to me that this was a work which would benefit from a large number of scene changes, but which would suffer if such changes slowed down the pace. Looking at the high vaulted ceiling of Big School, I decided that with a bit of creativity we could have ourselves a real theater. So I got myself a long ladder and one quiet afternoon when no one was around I climbed up into the rafters. A quick look told me that a few well-placed pulleys should support several different pieces of scenery, which could be lowered into place behind flats which would slant in from either side of the stage; elementary today, but revolutionary in the Blundell's of the 1940's. Further, by blocking off the whole of the proscenium, and using a few more pulleys, we could have a curtain that went up and down instead of sideways. Mr. Clayton, our academic adviser, who being by profession a classicist fortunately knew nothing about the load bearing capacity of old buildings, was enthusiastic and gave me the go ahead. The effect was sensational; we finally had a serious stage. The action moved swiftly from scene to scene. The show was an enormous success. Suddenly, a career in the theater seemed quite a reasonable ambition.

It wasn't until they decided that Big School could do with a new coat of paint, thus requiring professionals to take a close look at the ceiling, that the head master was informed that "no one should ever 'ang anything from them there pulleys or the 'ole bloody ceiling'll come down." By that time I was about to leave the school, and was thus never taken to task for the fact that, had luck not been on my side, several hundred pounds of scenery and counterbalancing sash weights might well have brought the entire roof of Big School crashing about the ears of the worthies of nearby Tiverton.

After I left Blundell's, and while waiting for compulsory military service to catch up with me, I spent a few months teaching at a small Prep school near Pangbourne, which was within easy reach of London. While there I produced a version of *Cinderella* as a school play, taking upon myself to create the sets. I was painting away on the stage one afternoon when a twelve-year-old from Thailand came by, watched for a moment, and then asked if he could give a hand. I gave him a brush and, with a few deft strokes, he turned what had been a rather humdrum palace into a thing of magical beauty. Although talent without application won't get you very far, application on its own isn't much use either. The young Thai played Mozart to my Salieri, and I recognized then what I should have known all along: my design talents were not going to provide me with a living in the theater. That was the last time I shared the magic of the business side of the curtain. However, there was a continuing enchantment being out in front as a member of the audience, which remained a very important part of my life.

Blundell's had a contingent of the Army Cadet Force. Twice a week we dressed up in army uniforms, webbing belts and knapsacks cleaned with a rather messy khaki colored paste, brass fittings all polished, boots shining so you could see your face in them. We would march up and down, learn disassembling and assembling rifle and machine gun, and how to shoot them. We had a band and it was rather stirring to march along behind it. At first I hated it, but after a while I got to like it. I became a sergeant, which was the highest cadet rank, and became accustomed to shouting orders. We spent two summers at a camp on Salisbury Plain with regular army units. We would go on maneuvers and shoot blank ammunition and be supported by real tanks and real aircraft. It was all rather exciting and I think, without knowing it, I was being set up for a military career. Britain had a draft (National Service) then, and since its army was involved in numerous colonial wars, as well as holding the line against the Communist hordes in Europe, it looked highly likely that, after leaving school, I would have to spend two years in some kind of military activity.

Being an Army cadet also introduced me to shooting, and to my surprise I found I was quite a good marksman, becoming a member of the school shooting team. Clearly, and without knowing it, this was the sport I had been looking for ever since I first went away to school: it qualified as an acceptable substitute for the loathsome cricket and you could do it lying down. We shot .303 Lee Enfield rifles on 300-yard open-air army ranges, and .22 rifles on the school's indoor range. I was among the eight selected to represent the school at Bisley, where all the public schools competed for various trophies. This was considered quite an honor. Unfortunately, a couple of friends and I got access to some beer one night: we couldn't shoot very straight in the morning and ever after I was branded as having "let the side down." Letting the side down was always a rather heinous offense in Britain, arguably why so many young men died bravely in defense of rather uninviting pieces of Empire.

Chapter 2

LEARNING TO BE THE MASTER OF MY FATE – THE CAPTAIN OF MY SOUL

By the end of the third year at Blundell's my future was quite well marked out. I would do the required National Service, then go to Cambridge, the more technical of the two socially acceptable universities, and study engineering. No one, including me, ever questioned this and, since all my education after the age of thirteen had been focused in that direction, I saw few alternatives.

To go to Cambridge one had to be accepted by a particular college there, and such acceptance was predicated on a given course of study. There was no question of selecting a major down the road: admission and course of study were thus inseparable. Moreover, to go to either Oxford or Cambridge, one had to matriculate in Latin. Latin: the most hated of all the languages they had tried to teach me since the age of six. Latin: the course I had dropped with such relief when entering Blundell's. Latin: without which I could never go to university—it never occurred to me or to my parents that I might attend one of the less demanding "red brick" schools. It seems anachronistic today that a fellow (not me!) who might have the potential to be the world's leading nuclear physicist could be denied entrance to Cambridge unless he could successfully parse Caesar's Gallic Wars, but that's the way it was. Britain's technophobic educational establishment still saw its principal task as turning out young Christian gentlemen whose highest goal in life would be to govern the Empire and fight its wars.

It was decided that we should hire a tutor during the summer whose job it would be to cram enough Latin into me to enable me to pass the necessary entrance exam. The unlucky candidate was a Mr. Waddell, who duly arrived on our doorstep in July 1949. He was armed with the requisite textbooks and a manner servile enough to qualify him as a twentieth century Uriah Heep. Poor little man—we all took an instant dislike to him, much of which carried over to me: after all, I was the one who needed the Latin and thus I was the one who was cluttering up our lives with the wretched Waddell. It was, I recall, a fine summer and most afternoons provided an opportunity to go to the beach. The first time we took Mr. Waddell along he sat with his shoes and socks neatly placed beside him, his shirt sleeves rolled up and a handkerchief knotted at the corners over his sparse sandy hair, looking very uncomfortable and faintly ridiculous. He made us all rather uneasy, so the next time we suggested he might enjoy a walk on the moors. He went and enjoyed it. Each likely beach day after that we would say nothing about our plans during lunch, the silence becoming more and more pregnant, until at last Mr. Waddell would say, "I think I'll go for a walk on the moors," and off we would all rush to get our bathing suits and pile into the car. However, despite his unfortunate manner, Mr. Waddell must have been an outstanding teacher of Latin. I passed the exam and was accepted at St. John's College, Cambridge to read Natural Sciences in the fall of 1950. Everybody was quite pleased. As I look back, I realize my good fortune: I think both my brother and I benefitted from the fact that our family, certainly not wealthy in terms of outward appearances, was always able to provide financing from some place where our education was involved.

I had also done quite well in my Higher School Certificate, which was one of the determining factors for University acceptance, and it was decided that I should try for an open scholarship at St. John's. I went back to Blundell's in September and spent most of the fall cramming as much math, physics and chemistry into my head as possible and finally, in late November, traveled by train to Cambridge to sit for the exam.

I don't remember much about the written work, but I can recall vividly the day of the practical chemistry test, which took place in the legendary Cavendish Laboratory, where the great Rutherford had done whatever theoretical work was necessary to demonstrate that one could indeed split the atom. The exam was due to start at 1:30 in the afternoon, and by 1:15 the candidates were crowded into the lobby outside the lab. I stood there and listened to the conversation and looked around at the competition. I am sure they were all very worthy and would in due course make great contributions to British science or technology. But at the time none of them seemed to be people with whom I wanted to spend my working days, or leisure times, and what little of their conversation I could understand gave me no incentive to join in. It dawned on me that I was in the wrong place: I wasn't cut out to be a physicist, a chemist, or an engineer, and I wasn't going to give Cambridge the opportunity to come to the same conclusion.

By this time the door had opened, and everyone had taken his assigned place in the lab, each confronted with some unknown powder that had to be analyzed and identified. I opened the book and read the instructions, then closed the book and laid it carefully beside the mystery powder, and unobtrusively left the Cavendish Laboratory. There was a pub across the road, and I went inside for a quiet beer and then called my father collect.

My father and I had had our problems from time to time but in a crisis, he was always magnificent. I told him what I had done. There was a slight pause and then he remarked that, after all, the only reason they had assumed I would be an engineer was because I was good with Meccano (the British version of America's "Erector Set"). He told me to call him when I got back to school; he was never one for long telephone calls. His final words were: "Too bad we wasted all that time with Mr. Waddell."

CAVENDISH LABORATORY

"I opened the book and read the instructions, then closed the book and laid it carefully beside the mystery powder, and unobtrusively left the Cavendish Laboratory. There was a pub across the road and I went inside for a quiet beer and then called my father collect."

We agreed that I would see out the school year, add an additional subject to my Higher School Certificate, plus some other courses, and then leave. There was silence about my future, but I knew my father well enough not to assume that his reticence would be permanent.

That Christmas I went skiing in Switzerland with a group from Blundell's and broke my leg. A Swiss doctor wrapped it in plaster from hip to ankle, which meant that I could not return to school until March. In the meantime, I lay around at home reading, painting (I had taken up oils, but wasn't very talented.), and scratching the inside of my plaster cast with a long piece of wire. I still had the cast on when I got back to school; it limited my activity but had the enormous advantage of allowing me to beg off almost any activity which didn't enthuse me. I continued to read a lot, helped design and build the sets for *School for Scandal*, played my gramophone, and went to some classes. For the first time since the wonderful summer of 1940, I actually enjoyed school. (See my account in *A Boyhood in Wartime Britain* available from Amazon.)

It was late June 1950, that I came back to Francis House after morning school and, quickly scanned the newspaper headlines. Huge letters on the front page of the Daily Mail cried out that the North Koreans had brazenly attacked the South Koreans, and the United Nations (with urging from Washington) had decided to intervene to push them back. The United States was sending land, air and sea reinforcements, and the British government, pledging full aid to the United Nations, already had a battle-ready aircraft carrier steaming up from Hong Kong. Although there was a lot of extravagant talk about "World War III", it all seemed remote to me who, like most of my contemporaries, had difficulty locating Korea on the map and little knowledge or interest in its byzantine history. Yet, within three years that far-off and inhospitable country would play a brief but very significant part in my life.

For those not actually exposed to it, the Korean War continued as mostly background noise to other, often much bigger, events going on in the world. To summarize, the North Korean army ran rapidly over the largely unprepared United Nations forces, driving them back into a small enclave around Pusan, in the south of the peninsula. Then, in December 1950 United Nations commander U.S. General MacArthur, in a brilliant amphibious counter-attack, cut off most of the North Korean invaders, allowing the United Nations to proceed rapidly north towards the border with China, which they continued to threaten despite clear warnings from Beijing that such would not be tolerated. At the end of November, 1950 the Chinese People's Volunteer Army fell upon the United Nations' front line with great ferocity, forcing it back very close to the 38th Parallel where it had started in June. From that time on the war, although hard fought for much of the time, became largely a stalemate. For the next two and a half years, however, the North Koreans' role was minimal; the United Nations forces were fighting battle-hardened Chinese "volunteer" troops. And just to remind those with limited recall, the Korean War was fought between North Korea, supported by its Chinese allies, and South Korea, supported by a mixed bag of allies assembled by the United Nations. Many of us fighting for the United Nations believed in it as a force for good in the world.

Sitting at my desk at Blundell's, I was little involved in a war the other side of the globe, although friends unlucky enough to be drafted into it did write letters, the main content of which, I recall, concerned the intense cold of Korea in winter. My attention was focused on the English exam for the Higher School Certificate, which was the principal reason I had gone back to school, and which required, among other matters, an intimate knowledge of two or three "set books." In the summer of 1950 they included *Macbeth*, Pepys *Diary*, and Wordsworth's poetry. Macbeth I knew well already, as I did Wordsworth, a poet who, under Burton's enthusiastic tutelage, I had memorized in large chunks. The key to the exam in poetry was to illustrate one's arguments by throwing in some ten or twenty verbatim lines in quotation marks. The examiner would realize you had done more than just read the book and thus give you a good grade. The same was true with Shakespeare: Wordsworth and *Macbeth* I could ace blindfolded. Pepys, on the other hand, was another matter. Although I discovered later that he was in fact a delightfully randy little man who singlehandedly ran the Royal Navy by day, yet retained enough energy to bed any available woman by night; little of this came through in the heavily censored version of his Diary we were permitted to read. Besides, I had more interesting matters to attend to.

The moral fortress which had guarded young English eyes from depraved literature was beginning to crumble, and the year 1950 was noteworthy for the introduction, from America no less, of a shocking bodice ripper called *Forever Amber*. A subsequent reading of the genuinely pornographic *Adventures of Fanny Hill*, a steamy narrative of the life of an energetic harlot at the court of Charles II, indicated that *Forever Amber* contained little original thinking. Although readers today would not find much to shock a preschooler, to our sheltered minds the book was sheer dynamite. Amber rolled lustily from bed to bed and haystack to haystack and then back to bed again, although the writer employed the literary equivalent of a discreet camera fade just when things were about to go beyond the censor's most elastic interpretation of the obscenity laws. She also participated strenuously in the life of Restoration London, taking part in most of the pivotal events of Charles II's reign including the Plague and the Great Fire of London. It was a big book, and we were not supposed to be reading such trash, so my progress was slow. I found it easiest to read it during prep time, Amber underneath my desk, Pepys on top. The harlot received my undivided attention while the diarist got short shrift.

I went into the examination room and opened the book. Three essay questions: *Macbeth*—easy; Wordsworth—no sweat. Pepys—amazing: "Describe the Plague and the Great Fire, as seen through the eyes of Samuel Pepys." I may have been weak on Pepys, but after two weeks of prurient submersion in Amber's goings on I truly knew my Plague and Fire. The words rattled off my pen-- I was inspired; throwing in a few "And so to bed's, etc." I produced epic descriptions of these two events, accounts of which the great diarist himself would have been proud. Later, when I got the results, I wondered if I was the only boy in England to have been given a Distinction for writing about a book he had never read.

Actually, I give Pepys short shrift; he is a very funny writer with a most attractive lack of inhibition. I can recommend him, provided the edition in use is uncensored.

FOREVER AMBER

"The year 1950 was noteworthy for the introduction, from America no less, of a shocking bodice ripper called Forever Amber... *I may have been weak on Pepys, but after two weeks of prurient submersion in Amber's goings on I truly knew my Plague and Fire."*

So, in July 1950, I left Blundell's thankfully certain that my formal education was over. I felt that school had given me all it could; anything else would be a burden. More importantly, I wanted to earn my own living and be financially independent. Dependency on my father for money involved too frequent and rigorous investigation into my expenditures: what I deemed essential he felt frivolous, what I considered frugal he considered extravagant. The thought of three more years of being a fiscal supplicant made the already doubtful benefits of higher education appear impossibly confining. It obviously never occurred to my self-satisfied brain that a bit more well focused learning might possibly have served to reduce my continuing financial dependency.

Unfortunately, however, my life-changing decision to abandon the education my parents had been providing with, I am sure, considerable sacrifice, had been made with no prior planning or analysis. I had no immediate source of employment, and none in prospect. I really had no idea of what I wanted to do, and there had been no career guidance at Blundell's to steer me other than towards University. Also, National Service was waiting just around the corner. As the summer wore on my father's plaintive questioning of my intentions became more pressing and strident. "There must," he stated, "be something you want to do with your life." But alas there wasn't until, almost on a whim, I decided to join the Navy, and then there was. But, before considering my life as a sailor, it is worth taking a look at what was going on at my home, while I was spending all that time away at school.

A boarding student leads two totally separate lives. There is school, with all of its eccentric rules and customs, quaint characters and odd mannerisms, none remotely explainable to a person not intimately involved. Then there is home, for most the source of warmth, security, sanity, comfort and companionship of family. Every boarding school boy of my generation knew instinctively that nothing of his home life could safely be exposed at school without risk of this information being turned at some future time into a cruel verbal weapon.

Thus, between the ages of eight and eighteen I lived a schizophrenic life, the passing years marked by alternating periods of unhappy confinement and blissful liberty. But for the last half of this period my home life differed from that of most of my contemporaries in that it was largely structured around my father's newly chosen occupation. In 1945 (with no inputs from me), I became a farmer's son.

Chapter 3

LEARNING THAT I ABSOLUTELY NEVER WANTED TO BE A FARMER

I don't know what mutation in the Coles genes beckoned my father's generation into farming. Admittedly their great-grandfather had been a farmer in Devonshire, but hadn't John Coles, the family patriarch, walked all the way to London to get away from that cold, muddy, and unremunerative existence? And hadn't he succeeded to the extent that his descendants had access to education and connections sufficient to provide entrance to any of the worthwhile professions? Yet, one by one, they succumbed to the lure of the soil, a siren song that to any well-tuned ear must have sounded at best off-key and discordant. Eventually, my father and his three brothers were all engaged in farming; none of them (with the exception of one brother in New Zealand) doing it very successfully. And, to his credit, my brother Tony never was seduced by farming's temptation, escaping happily into his chosen life as a vintner, and a highly regarded one too.

Whatever the reason, one day in early 1945 my father set

out for Devonshire, in the West of England and, during the course of a brief visit, agreed to buy a farm. According to my mother he consulted no one, not even her. Certainly, nobody but he saw it before the deed was done largely, because had she seen it, there would have been no way he could have persuaded her that the farming life would be in any respect superior to her familiar suburban existence. However, I do remember that at the time she exuded considerable enthusiasm when talking to my brother and me about it, telling us all the great fun we would have with the crops and the animals.

The problem with farming is that it tends to bring out the romantic in people. Even today, when profitable farming is usually a large-scale business enterprise, politicians can successfully invoke the vision of the family farm, picturing the jovial farmer producing abundant and healthy nourishment from the rich earth while his rosy cheeked wife nurtures the chickens and churns the butter. Unfortunately, farming is one of the most truly cutthroat capitalistic businesses going. On the farm, capital, management and labor require daily decisions that, in the absence of government intervention, will determine the life or death of the concern on a year-by-year basis. The trouble is that so few novice farmers realize this and, unless they have bottomless pockets, they can run out of funds long before they have completed a tough education.

My father's mistake was providing too little capital and too much labor. At only 40 acres the farm was of insufficient size to support any serious kind of work force, so that my father spent much of his time doing farm laborer work. And since farm laborers in the late 1940's in England didn't earn very much, I doubt if any realistic accounting would have shown that all my father's carefully hoarded capital and back breaking work returned much more than a laborer's meager hire. But here, and possibly in other places in this book, I might appear as critical of him to readers who never knew him. Quite to the contrary: my brother and I both looked up to him with a large amount of awe; we certainly loved him, and as we look back realize that we benefitted enormously having him as a father. He didn't talk a lot, but when he did, he always made a lot of sense. He was always there when needed, and always came though magnificently in a crisis. He died peacefully at home aged 88, and later in this book I have included an extract from what I said at his funeral.

My first recollection of Little Stert (not actually little, just lower down the hill than its smaller neighbor Great Stert) was seeing my mother framed in an open door and behind her a glow of warm yellow light. As I stepped inside, I smelled for the first time that mixture of kerosene, wood smoke and damp walls which, even today and with my eyes blindfolded, would tell me I was in a Devonshire farmhouse.

This point requires a digression since that Christmas was the first and last time I would journey to or from school by car. From then on it was the train, and my recollection of the train journey is a major contributor to the schizophrenic divide between school and home. Going to school we would drive up to the Cornwood station to catch a train. As the time of departure approached my heart would sink lower and lower and, at least when I was young, the tears would come closer and closer to the surface. We would hear the steam locomotive huffing and puffing as it dragged its way up the foothills of Dartmoor. Finally, the train arrived, my school trunk would be stowed safely in the luggage van, and I would get one last goodbye from my parents. I would then hang out of the window as we waved to each other until I could no longer see them. Our station was pretty much at the high point of the line and, after a few miles of traversing the edges of the moors we would begin the long descent down to Newton Abbot, where there was a change of trains onto a faster one for Exeter. That part of the trip was a kind of transition, part home part school, but the full realization of what was happening would strike when I looked out of the window down the valley and saw my home, the last glimpse for twelve long weeks.

LITTLE STERT

"My first recollection of Little Stert (not actually Little, just lower down the hill than its smaller neighbor Great Stert) was seeing my mother framed in an open door and behind her a glow of warm yellow light. As I stepped inside, I smelled for the first time that mixture of kerosene, wood smoke and damp walls which, even today and with my eyes blindfolded, would tell me I was in a Devonshire farm house."

Coming back for the three seasonal holidays was a totally different experience. I was impatient to get home, and the train appeared to be deliberately going much slower than it had when it was taking me away. Also, there seemed much more time to look around and admire what was, after all, one of the great 19th century engineering feats. The Great Western Railway was largely the creation of Isambard Kingdom Brunel, a technical genius who was responsible for many of the structural marvels of the latter half of Queen Victoria's reign. Brunel's father had fled to America from the French revolution and ultimately became New York City's chief engineer. The son was one of the great builders of his age. He was a man of many parts: a builder of railroads, bridges, and ships. His ship designs included the paddle steamer *Great Western*, which was the first transatlantic passenger steamship in regular service.

In planning a railroad route to the southwestern part of the British Isles (known generally as the "West Country") Brunel had to contend with varied terrain that included unusually steep gradients and extremely deep valleys. The track he was responsible for laying became truly part of the West Country after Exeter. It ran south for a few miles along the River Exe estuary and one could see boats at anchor or, when the tide was out, lying on their sides in the mud. Then it turned west and wound its way along the coast in a most dramatic manner. Sometimes the train was only a few feet from the water's edge and on stormy days the windows would become flecked with sea salt. Occasionally it burrowed through small tunnels carved out of the red Devon sandstone. At one point it ran perfectly straight for several miles before crossing the Teign estuary at Teignmouth.

It was along that straight stretch of coast that Brunel had conducted one of his least successful but, in the long run, most prescient experiments. Rightly recognizing the inefficiency of converting steam pressure into forward motion through the medium of a reciprocating piston, he developed the idea of attaching the piston to the locomotive and the cylinder, in the form of a continuous tube, to the rail bed. The problem was how to permit the piston to move along the tube. Ingenious Brunel invented the slotted cylinder. Iron tubing several miles long was fabricated with an open slot on the top. This slot was closed by means of a leather flap, permitting the rod connecting the piston to the locomotive to slide along, opening the flap as it went and closing it behind. A steam engine at the end of the pipe created a vacuum in front of the piston, which was thus sucked along at what proved to be a breathtaking speed. It was indeed a much more efficient way of transmitting steam power. Sadly, however, there were hungry rats along the waterfront that saw the leather flaps as a rich contribution to their diet. Soon the slotted cylinder started to leak and the trains ground to a halt before reverting to a more conventional power source. Brunel's ideas never quite died, however and, in the 1950's, were resurrected by British engineers concerned at the problem of how to move ever heavier airplanes off the decks of aircraft carriers. The solution was the steam catapult, now the generally accepted way of launching shipborne airplanes that, in simplest terms, consists of a long slotted cylinder, a piston which can be attached to the airplane via the slot, and an ample supply of high pressure steam. But we are ahead of ourselves; the steam catapult had yet to be invented when I was at Blundell's, and it was the thought of the happy looks on the faces of the hungry rats, bellies now well filled by old Brunel's leather cylinder closures, that intrigued me at the time.

The great engineer has a much-deserved statue on London's embankment, which I make a point of visiting every now and then. I think I must have had him in mind when I earlier decided I wanted to be an engineer. I wanted steam and oily pistons, huge cantilevered bridges, great ships and bigger buildings. All of this, unfortunately, appeared to have little connection at the time with the Cambridge Natural Science Tripos.

With the market town of Newton Abbot behind it, the train (heading west on its return journey) began the long climb up onto Dartmoor. Express trains going all the way to Plymouth and beyond would add an additional engine for this stretch and continue quite smartly up the steep gradients. My local train, however, had to make do with only one locomotive that, although adequate on the level, made heavy weather of the ascent and indeed at times appeared almost literally to run out of steam. However, eventually it would make it up to the top where the track leveled out and one could see out of the window the outskirts of Ivybridge.

ISAMBARD KINGDOM BRUNEL

"The Great Western Railway was largely the creation of Isambard Kingdom Brunel, a technical genius who was responsible for many of the structural marvels of the latter half of Queen Victoria's reign. The great engineer has a much-deserved statue on London's embankment, and I make a point of honoring him with a visit every now and then."

Cornwood was "near Ivybridge" in its mailing address, and this was our closest town of any size. After Ivybridge the next landmark on the way home was our own viaduct. The River Yealm ran by the farm, and Cornwood station was up a steep hill from our house, which meant that there was probably about a 150 ft. difference between the railroad grade and the level of the river where it was crossed. Here Brunel had constructed a remarkably beautiful viaduct, consisting of six very tall arches, all built of brick, connecting at the top with a roadway just broad enough for two railroad tracks. As we looked up the valley from our house, we could see it connecting the two sides in as unaffected a manner as any work of nature would have done. Should planners today propose such a thing it would be shouted down by protectors of the environment, but it had been there nearly a century when I first saw it, it was still there when I crossed it fifty years later, and will probably be there a century on. Any talk of moving it would probably be resisted by the same conservationists who would have fought its erection.

CORNWOOD VIADUCT

"Brunel had constructed a remarkably beautiful viaduct, consisting of very tall arches, all built of brick, connecting at the top with a roadway just broad enough for two railroad tracks."

We could see the viaduct from our house, which meant that I could see the house from the train. The wheel noises changed, indicating that we were now relying on Isambard's workmanship to keep us safe as we crossed high above the River Yealm. That was the point when, disregarding stern notices from British Rail that it was dangerous to lean out, I would lower the window and, oblivious of soot, steam and flying cinders, peer eagerly down the valley seeking the first glimpse of our house. Then, almost immediately, the train would slow and pull into Cornwood station where my mother or father would be waiting. My school trunk would be lifted out by the guard, who would wait a few moments and then wave his green flag, signaling the locomotive to pull out. We would lift the trunk into the car and drive happily down the hill to Little Stert. A journey that had taken a few seconds in one direction had taken what seemed several hours in the other, but hours spent many times more happily in anticipation of a few weeks of freedom.

Little Stert could, in fact, have been a quite delightful house and, indeed, subsequent owners made it so. Unfortunately, nothing had been done to it since the 1930's and even then it had lacked some very basic amenities. Absent, for example, were gas and electricity, and any form of central heating. Sanitation by septic tank was barely adequate, and our water came from the river by means of an ingenious hydraulic pump. We weren't supposed to drink it but we often did. Some years later an earnest young woman from the Ministry of Agriculture came to examine our dairy facilities. "Oh dear," she said, "I hope you don't let your cows drink this water!" Our official drinking water came from a hand pump outside the front door which we were always assured was the purest, freshest, coolest, etc. water one would ever find. Since the well it drew from was some twenty feet from the barnyard where many generations of cows had dropped their dung, I doubt these claims would have stood up well to objective scrutiny. Nevertheless, none of us came down with any dread disease while we lived there, which probably says more about the resilience of the human body than the cleanliness of the water.

Lack of electricity meant that we relied on kerosene lamps for illumination. These took two forms: hurricane lamps that, burning a wick inside a glass dome, could be carried around and taken outside, and "Aladdins." The Aladdin was a remarkable affair: a kerosene flame was used to heat an incandescent mantle, a fine gauze like net which at high temperature would give out a wonderfully warm and bright light. Splendid to read by, it was an Aladdin which had provided the luminous glow which backlit my mother when I first arrived home. The odor of burning kerosene provided one component of the not unpleasant smell that so firmly characterized houses like ours. Unfortunately, the Aladdin was very susceptible to drafts, and Little Stert was a truly drafty house. At the slightest hint of a breeze the delicately adjusted kerosene flame would flare up, covering mantle and glass chimney with soot. All in all, lack of electric light was one of several major drawbacks to our new life-style.

Eventually my mother rebelled. It was her second winter without electricity and my father was away in Switzerland leaving her and the farm hand to take care of things. An ex-serviceman came to the door selling a line of second-hand generators: "ex-Army, but thoroughly reconditioned." It only put out 24 volts, but that, in her mind, was infinitely better than nothing. My father was predictably angry when he came home, but soon recognized that the little engine did indeed make everything much easier. It had to be started by hand and each evening, as it got darker and darker, my mother would insist that it was time to start up the engine and my father would reply that there was still plenty of light. Finally, when we could barely see each other across the room, he would reluctantly go out to the shed which housed the machine and crank it up, producing enough current to illuminate a few strategically placed reading lamps and some overhead bulbs in the bathrooms and lavatories. Too many on at the same time and everything would flicker and grow dim. At eleven o'clock my father would go to bed, his last action of the evening being to turn off the fuel cock to the generator. After a few minutes the engine would slowly die, the lights get dimmer and dimmer, until anyone still up would be left in near darkness, mitigated only by the glow from the dying fire. When Joan (who later became my wife) first came to stay she thought it a terribly romantic gesture on his part. I hadn't the heart to tell her that he had been doing it nightly for the past eight years.

Lack of household gas meant that we had initially to rely on a coal-burning fire for cooking and water heating. My mother told me later that the day she moved in the previous owners' daily maid had told her that she was quitting but would stay around long enough to show her how things worked. One of the key pieces of knowledge was how to light the ancient cast iron cooking stove. A bundle of dry sticks, known in those less culturally sensitive times as a faggot, was placed in the top of the stove and, when lit, filled the kitchen with smoke and flames.

When these had died down, coke (a coal byproduct, not an illegal stimulant) was placed on top and, after a while, the whole thing settled down to a nice steady roar and a heat that, while satisfying in winter, was somewhat enervating in the summer. The arrangement also heated the water system. However, it required constant feeding with coke and thus could not be kept burning at night. The whole process, which had looked so simple at the expert hands of Ruby, the maid, completely frustrated my mother when she tried it on her own. Near tears she went up to the village and begged Ruby to come back for another demonstration. She did and, taking pity on my mother, agreed to stay and remained with us for some fifteen years, becoming a vital and much-loved part of the family. The stove, however, was less long-lived. As a condition for remaining on the farm my mother insisted on a replacement that, after some back and forth between my parents, was installed about a year later. An ingenious heat storage cooker of Swedish design it provided 24-hour a day heat and hot water, was always ready when we needed it, and only required lighting a couple of times a year after its insides had been cleaned. It was a great advance, although I think Ruby rather missed the power that its predecessor had given her.

The main part of the house was constructed of local granite. Thick walls had, over the centuries absorbed enough moisture so that damp was a continual problem, frustrating any attempts to decorate the inside of the house other than by using paint. In addition, generations of footsteps had so worn away the doorsteps that there was a gap of some inches between the sill and the bottom of the door. Since there were several entries to the house, cold weather resulted in gale-like drafts whistling through every downstairs room. These were offset to some extent by the living room fireplace which was, literally, big enough to roast an ox. Loaded up with massive logs, the fire gave out a splendid heat that warmed at least a third of the living room and, on good days, penetrated to some of the upstairs. On cold days we thus concentrated ourselves around the fire, our fronts heated to a nice golden crisp while our backs, exposed to the bitter drafts of winter, remained icily cold. Joan later commented that such was a characteristic of English country houses: she had never been so hot and so cold at the same time.

Since there was no central heating, those parts of the house that were not located strategically close to the main fireplace became cold during the winter and stayed that way until spring. Bedrooms caught some of the heat escaping up the main chimney, warmth that could be supplemented by kerosene space heaters. But the extremities of the house remained below freezing for much of the winter and, not unexpectedly, it was along those extremities that crucial water pipes ran. Frozen pipes were the bane of my mother's existence, and the fact that the pipes up in the attic typically froze in February when my father was away skiing added more fuel to the smoldering fires of her marital resentments.

Plymouth, our nearest town of any size, was a natural harbor that had been enlarged in Victorian times by the addition of a lengthy breakwater. The port had historically acted as Britain's first line of defense against predators advancing up the English Channel. Sir Francis Drake had leisurely finished his game of bowls on Plymouth Hoe before setting out to defeat the Spanish Armada, thus giving rise to twin legends of British sang-froid and naval invincibility. In later years Devonport dockyard had become a major facility for the Royal Navy, providing a significant source of employment, a thriving demand for all the entertainments sailors look for when ashore and, in 1940 and 1941, a tempting target for German airmen.

In 1945 the memories of the bombing were still fresh in people's minds, and the city's scars showed how devastatingly it had been attacked. Night after night the bombers came over until many inhabitants preferred to leave the city and sleep in the hedgerows rather than face the cruel punishment they would get at home. Plymouth's city center was a heap of rubble when we first saw it. Indeed, in 1945, so bad was the destruction that the town received priority in reconstruction funds and materials, with the result that it raised, quite rapidly and phoenix like from the ashes. Unfortunately, however, it thus suffered from the worst banality of post-war British architecture, supplied we must suspect, by practitioners seeking approval from Socialist masters when it came time to receive allocations of scarce building materials.

Cornwood was some fifteen miles north east of Plymouth. To the north lay Dartmoor, a forbiddingly beautiful area of wild moorland that covered most of central Devon, nurturing little but rock, heather, and wild ponies. To the south lay the English Channel that we could, if we wished, reach on our bicycles. To the west was Cornwall; the intervening area marked by the brilliant white tailings from the china clay pits that, along with agriculture, provided most of the local non-farming employment.

Mention Dartmoor to the British and those unfamiliar with its natural beauties will almost certainly associate it with its prison. Originally built during the Napoleonic wars to accommodate captured French soldiers and sailors, it has since become one of the country's principal maximum-security jails. A grim granite pile more often than not shrouded in fog, it provides important employment for much of the surrounding area and occasional bursts of fear for its neighbors. Despite its much-vaunted security there would from time to time be escapes. Roadblocks were immediately thrown up across the principal breakout routes, so the fellow on the run would take to the moors. If he survived the treacherous bogs, and was able to elude the bloodhounds devotedly following his scent, his first need was to get out of his prison clothing. Thus, anyone living on the edge of Dartmoor would be warned that a convict was on the loose and likely to be looking for something to wear.

Whether it was just my mother's imagination or some statistical aberration I don't know, but she became convinced that the breakout rate went up alarmingly the moment my father left on his annual ski vacation. With Tony and me away at school she would be alone in the house. Every door was bolted, every tempting article of male clothing hidden away, and she would retreat to bed with a small bore shot gun conveniently within reach. If a hardened criminal had made his way in, I suspect her reaction would have been ambivalent: shoot him dead or make him a cup of tea and be glad for the company.

One side of our forty acres was bordered by the River Yealm, an attractive but unimportant stream that rose on the south slopes of Dartmoor and ran down to the sea where its estuary hosted a pretty little town called Newton Ferrers. Next to the river we had a two or three acre orchard which grew cider apples, an area behind the house known as the "mooey" (Devon for mow-hay, whatever that might mean), and two main fields: the Ram field, because that was where our Hydram water pump was located, and Long Meadow, which happened to be long and narrow. On the other side was the road up to Cornwood Station and the village. Across this road lay a stretch of woodland and two more fields.

The plan was to conduct mixed farming. We grew wheat on some of the fields for sale to the local miller who would turn it into flour, and grazed cows in the other meadows. Up in the mooey we kept pigs and chickens. The cows were dual purpose: the breeding cows produced calves and then gave milk which we either made into cream or butter or sold to the government's Milk Marketing Board; the male cows were emasculated, thus becoming steers, and were fattened for meat. Together with the pigs, which were kept for bacon, the steers were eventually sent off to market at nearby Newton

Abbot to be sold and subsequently slaughtered.

To take care of all this my father had inherited when he bought the farm a rather mean-spirited old man called Bright who lived, together with an equally mean-spirited Mrs. Bright, in a hovel the other side of the woods. I say hovel with some sense of residual shame, since it was a tied cottage, which meant it belonged to the farm and came with the job. It should have been condemned years before, but housing was short after the war and I suppose it was better than nothing. As I look back I realize that the Bright's living quarters were sufficiently sub-standard to fully justify their apparent meanness of spirit.

I'm not sure what my father knew about farming when he arrived, but whatever he learned subsequently came from the odd book and listening to Bright, the farmhand. The problem was that Bright, who came from Cornwall, had an accent so thick that none of us could understand more than a fraction of what he said. However, between them, and with considerable help from my mother, they worked it out so that the cows got milked, the pigs and chickens fed, and the wheat planted and harvested. My father's role in all of this was much more laborer than manager/capitalist, with the inevitable result that he seemed to work harder and harder for less and less. But, on the other hand, I presumed he preferred his life as a farmer more than he had enjoyed working as a stockbroker, although I could never understand why–certainly he made more money stockbroking!

I didn't know much about the economics of all this at the time, other than the fact that we always seemed to be short of money. Funds for improving the house or providing amenities for my mother were never available. However, my brother and I did go to fairly expensive private schools (albeit, not always with the right clothes) and my father still made his annual pilgrimage to the Swiss ski slopes.

Since I was at boarding school for much of the year, I was not given a regular set of chores to do around the farm. There were, however, seasonal activities that we shared, and which were quite enjoyable. Best of all, because I loved machinery, was driving the tractor.

In the winter we ploughed. My father was proud of his straight furrows and seldom allowed anyone else to do this. But sometimes, when he had other things to do and the ruler straight lines were already well established, he would turn it over to me. The ploughed fields would lie untouched during the winter while the frost helped break up the soil. Then, in the spring, we would harrow, drawing a heavy instrument with lots of sharp spikes in it across the fields so that the soil was well broken up ready for seeding. I was allowed to do much of the harrowing. Seeding, I recall in those early days, was done by hand, my father and Bright walking back and forth across the fields with buckets of seed that they threw across the soil very much as they might have done in biblical days.

Then came the harvest. The reaper, a machine pretty much the same as the one invented by Cyrus McCormick in the nineteenth century, would be pulled through the wheat fields by Polly the carthorse, cutting the ripened stalks, bundling them up into sheaves, tying them around the middle—all automatically—and then throwing them (now called stooks) out onto the ground.

Finally came the threshing. A contract threshing machine would arrive one day and set up business in the mooey. It was a vast and cacophonous contraption whose complex machinery was driven by a huge belt from a pulley on the side of our tractor. The stooks would be gathered on a horse-drawn cart that drew up alongside the machine. Men with pitch forks would toss the sheaves up to the men on top of the thresher who would feed the wheat stalks down into its bowels. Straw, used for bedding cattle would come out one way, chaff, a fine dusty waste product another, while kernels of wheat would pour in a heavy golden stream into sacks. On a good day it was glorious work, and very thirst making.

The summer of 1947 was an unusually sunny one and the harvest went as it should but, because of the unpredictability of English weather, seldom did. My father, as was customary, had set up a barrel of cider in the shade beside the threshing machine to quench the workers' thirst. Richard and I were given the job of filling jugs and keeping the men on top of the machine supplied with liquids. It is worth noting that cider, in Devonshire, is a powerful brew, quite unlike the apple juice that currently sells under the same title. "Hard" cider has an alcoholic content far in excess of that of beer, and a tendency to creep up behind one with unexpected violence. The men were used to this stuff and were sweating enough that it did them little harm. Richard and I, on the other hand, were innocent and relatively sweat free. Although no one noticed, frequent sampling had by the end of the afternoon produced two very intoxicated fifteen-year-olds. The first time my father observed anything wrong was after the threshing was over when he looked out of the house to see me at the wheel of a five foot wide farm truck, driving it full tilt at a four foot wide gate while my friend Richard stood beckoning me on, saying "Come on, there's plenty of room." My father was very nice about the consequent damage to the truck. Fortunately, neither Richard nor I was injured; he made us lie down in the ice-cold river to sober up. (Richard was my long-time friend who had spent most of the war years with my family, and occasionally thereafter.)

The pigs were my father's pride and joy. He was determined to raise the best pigs in Devon, and in many years he actually did, gaining a number of prizes and considerable celebrity in the process. A headline in our local paper (undated) read "Cornwood Producer Wins First Prize in Bacon Contest," going on to say that Mr. D. H. Coles of Cornwood had been awarded 85 points out of 100 for his Landrace pigs. I had never seen him so proud.

Feeding the pigs was a classical public/private enterprise. The City of Plymouth had established a central steam heated facility where all the salvageable food scraps were sent to be cooked down into an odiously smelling thick soup called swill. Once a week my father would drive our truck into Plymouth to pick up his share of this, poured into big buckets and brought home to where the hungry consumers waited in noisy anticipation.

Then one day my father announced that the Ministry of Agriculture had suggested strengthening the nutritional value of the swill by adding to it a new kind of dark green cabbage we had never seen before. The pigs seemed to like it and, although it was cheap, there was never a suggestion that it was a food appropriate for humans. Its name was Kale. As I write this today, I marvel at the marketing genius who managed to convince several generations of young people that Kale might possibly be good for them, and the vast number of fashionable restaurants that immediately leapfrogged to the top of the Michelin leagues by the addition of modest amounts of Kale to their salads.

The farm's truck had formerly belonged to the Royal Air Force where it had been rudely treated by a number of ill-trained wartime drivers. My father had bought it for a song at a surplus equipment auction and had got what he paid for. The suspension was shot, and the engine was on its last legs. The back was enclosed in a canvas cover that still bore faint signs of camouflage paint. However, it took us on farm related chores without complaint for several years. I learned to drive in that truck and, when it finally died and had to be towed away, it still bore on either side the honorable scars of when I tried to take it through a four-foot-wide gate at harvest time.

Little need be said about the chickens: they laid eggs and when past egg producing prime were ready for the pot. They made a lot of noise at times, but otherwise left us alone, and we them. Others, however, were less charitable: chickens had food and food attracted rats, and rats liked eggs. The mooey behind the house was rat heaven. The upstairs bathroom looked out over the mooey and my father kept a 12-gauge shotgun near the toilet. He liked to retire there for some serious contemplation after breakfast, and every now and then we would hear a deafening report from upstairs. When I first heard it I thought a bomb had gone off. “Don't worry dear,” my mother said, “it's just your father shooting rats out of the lavatory window.”

It was the cows, however, that really set the tone of Little Stert. First because my father liked to give them names; he named the pigs too, but innocuously after British warships. But the cows were different: these he called after relatives, mostly on my mother's side. Sure, Aunt Margaret might be amused to see a bullock called Andrew, after her nephew, energetically mounting a heifer called Girlie after her sister-in-law, but amusement turned to some chagrin when she asked the name of the pendulously uddered cow the other side of the meadow and, after a slight pause, was told it was Margaret. After a while the game caught on with the rest of the family who in general were not amused. Relatives would sit tensely over their afternoon tea as my father called the cows in for milking, rather like concentration camp inmates dreading to hear their names called out at roll-call.

Although British farming has produced numerous different breeds of cow, in our part of the country the cow of choice was the South Devon. Its coat a reddish brown, rather like the local soil, the South Devon produced the richest milk of all, from which came that most succulent of products, Devonshire Cream. It is worth dwelling on the process that resulted in that mouth-watering delicacy, since in my judgment it was one of the few things that made the whole farming bit worthwhile.

The milk would come out of the cow into large pails. There was no nonsense about pasteurizing it or homogenizing it: if we wanted to drink it, we did, right out of the bucket, and if a little bit of dung got in during the process it didn't seem to do us much harm. From the cowshed it went into the dairy, a cool room at the back of the house, where it was poured into large flat pans. Left there for about twenty-four hours, the thick cream would rise to the top, so dense that you could scoop it out with your fingers.

Next the pan containing the milk, but with most of the cream now risen to the top, was placed on top of another pan in which water was boiling. This process, scalding the cream, resulted in more rising to the top and, together with the stuff there already, formed a lush yellow crust. When allowed to cool this was the famous Devonshire Cream, thick enough to spread with a knife. We would have it at teatime, with strawberry jam on scones or, sometimes, flat pancakes that Ruby would make, a local version of blinis called floddies.

But the Devonshire Cream was only a halfway step. Next came the butter, created by a process I will always recall as near miraculous. A large slab of the cream was placed in a wooden tub some eighteen inches in diameter. As taught by Ruby, my mother would place her hand palm down on top of the thick yellow mass and, pressing down, rotate it slowly in a clockwise direction. The cream would flatten out under her hand and, as she moved it round and round, sometimes for as long as twenty minutes or more, she could feel it getting harder and chunkier. Then, suddenly the miracle would occur: the cream would separate into a hard golden butter, and a mixture of skim milk, butter particles and residual cream that was called butter-milk but bore no resemblance to the commercial product of the same name.

Mixing in a little salt, my mother would squeeze and stroke the butter with two wooden paddles until all the buttermilk was forced out of it. Remaining was a pat of the most perfect butter, butter with such little similarity to its store bought cousin that it would be hard to believe they both warranted the same name. Sometimes we used paddles with special carvings on them so that the butter came out with emblems on top: acorns, thistles, roses etc. But the stuff itself was so delectable that it needed no visual embellishment: taste and texture were enough.

Although milk was the raw material of both cream and butter, I was clever enough to realize that the cows would get milked no matter whether I was involved or not. But the next stages in the process were a different matter, stages that might, through human neglect or carelessness, be omitted or mishandled. I thus took care to learn the art of butter making, and was often to be found, up to my elbows in cream, my hand slowly rotating in the butter tub. Always clockwise, however; the other direction, known locally as "widershins," would never produce the right results: I tried it a couple of times out of perversity and ended up with a mess of something which was no longer cream, but would never be butter. No one could explain this phenomenon, which I placed in the same category as bathtub water running out one way in the northern hemisphere and the reverse when south of the equator.

We have already noted the local cider, a heady brew that was made out of small sharp apples that were squeezed into pulp in a huge press, the liquid then separated and allowed to ferment, and finally sold in oaken kegs. Bottled cider was for sissies: the serious stuff was sold on draft in rough or sweet forms. It was the rough that could really do the damage. Our apple crop was sold to the cider press at Lee Mill just up the street, and part of the purchase price was a barrel that we kept in the cool dairy for our own purposes. The Lee Mill cider press was wooden and some twelve feet in diameter; the top was forced down onto the apples by means of a monstrous threaded shaft made out of oak that was turned by a capstan big enough to haul the anchor of a man-of-war. Tradition called for a dead rat to be dropped into the liquid just before it was left to ferment. What it was supposed to do to the cider I don't know, but so far as I can tell it did us little harm.

Food rationing remained a pervasive part of life in post-war Britain and farmers, who were surrounded by hard to get meat on the hoof, were an obvious source of corruption. The authorities adopted a stick and carrot approach to the problem. The stick was an army of inspectors whose job it was to track the fate of all large livestock (i.e., pigs, sheep and cows) from birth to the slaughterhouse. Woe betide any farmer whose tally of pigs failed to match the head count recorded by the man from the ministry. (The splendid movie *A Private Function*, starring the incomparable Maggie Smith, records all this foolishness with humor and accuracy.) On the carrot side was a system whereby each farmer was allowed to kill two of each kind of animal for his own use. The problem, back in those days of little or no domestic refrigeration, was how to preserve the stuff.

We didn't do much slaughtering for our own use, but I happened to be at home when we put away a pig that was supposed to provide us with an abundant supply of pork products, but which unfortunately produced only a fiasco. The pig, a large animal whose name I forget (it was probably something like Indomitable or Royal Sovereign, reflecting my father's habit of naming his pigs after British warships), was dragged squealing into the barnyard. A noose was slipped around its two hind legs and it was rapidly hauled up by a pulley hung in the door of the hayloft. The noise was unbearable but subsided rapidly to a frenzied wheezing and then silence as the butcher hired for the occasion drew a razor sharp knife across the wretched animal's throat. A torrent of blood poured out into a series of buckets. Eventually the flood turned into a trickle and we could turn our attention to the insides. A quick slit up the belly, and a mound of intestines and other vital organs slithered down into a big tub, to be saved for making sausage skin later. Finally, the now eviscerated porker was laid on its side on a bench so that the butcher could slice it neatly into hams, hocks, loins, ribs, chops and chitterlings and all the other pieces of a pig that make for excellent eating.

Some of the valued pork we ate while it was still fresh; some was given away to friends and neighbors but by law none could be sold. Thus the major portion of the meat had to be preserved and, lacking a freezer, it had to be done the hard way: salted and smoked. After soaking for several days in saltwater brine, the various cuts of meat were suspended over a smoky fire in our vast living room fireplace that, for several days, reverted to its historic use. Finally, deemed to be properly preserved, it was all hung up on hooks in our dairy, which soon came to resemble a butcher's shop.

It must have been a few weeks after we had killed the pig, while we were having lunch that my mother said, "That's funny, I thought I heard rain. Outside was bright sunshine, but, sure enough, as we too listened, we could hear what sounded like light rainfall. To solve the problem, we left the dining room and tried to track down the noise. Eventually we established it was coming from the dairy. As was only too evident, the sound of falling rain was in fact the noise made by hundreds of maggots which, overindulged on their meal of poorly cured ham, had succumbed to their own weight and fallen plumply onto the dairy counter, where they lay quietly wriggling. The remains of our fine pig were rapidly taken off and buried, the maggots hurriedly swept outside, and our future efforts to live off the land confined to cows and their cream and chickens and their eggs.

The River Yealm, which ran through our farm, was a source of much pleasure. Despite the urgings of the young lady from the Ministry that we not allow our cows to drink the water, it was in fact a very clear stream. At the bottom of the Ram field was a deep pool that we would use for swimming during the summer. The water was breathtakingly cold, but there was a clear twenty feet or so of swimmable water and a bank high enough to be able to dive from. Sometimes the water ran low, but we could always keep enough depth to swim by building a dam out of rocks across the downstream end as it flowed through our property.

Lurking in the depths of the pool were some quite large trout. My mother had bought a fly rod and she and my brother would spend happy hours flicking carefully hand-tied flies out over the ripples that were supposed to betray a fish lying below. They didn't catch that many, but those they did tasted delicious. We owned both sides of the river, and across it lay a strip of brambles and gorse about ten yards wide that led up to the property line. My mother decided to clear this and, pretty much on her own, subdued the inhospitable vegetation and produced a miniature park with grass, trees and, in the spring, daffodils.

Clearly there was a need to be able to get across the river dry-shod, and I, the budding engineer, was ordered to build a bridge. The next time my father went into Plymouth I went along with him, returning with an expensive load of construction materials. The bridge I built was grandiose in the extreme, rivaling its Brooklyn cousin in concept and complexity. Trees from our wood were the main raw material. Two poles either end were supported by a spider's web of guy wires and in turn bore the two cables that stretched across the river and supported the main platform of the bridge. This consisted of two stout tree trunks running longitudinally, while a number of thinner poles ran crossways and provided the walkway. When completed it looked sturdy and functional; although it lacked the beauty of Roebling's great design, it gave an appearance of sound engineering principles applied in a relatively low-cost manner.

THE RIVER YEALM

"At the bottom of the Ram field was a deep pool that we would use for swimming during the summer. The water was breathtakingly cold, but there was a clear twenty feet or so of swimmable water and a bank high enough to dive from."

Closer inspection revealed some potential weaknesses: although it did what was intended—allow people to cross the river—those who ventured on it did note a slightly ominous sway. I told them not to worry; after all, wasn't that why troops always broke step when crossing a suspension bridge? Then it started to rain. It rained heavily for several days, and each day when I went down to inspect my bridge the water was nearer to the river banks, and thus closer to running over my construction. Finally, it happened: I came down one morning to find nothing left of my beautiful bridge but a few pieces of wood and a tangle of wire.

My father said nothing at the time, but the next time a bridge was under discussion he gave the task to my brother. Tony went into the wood and cut down a couple of trees. He dragged them down to the river and laid them across, with a rope handrail to steady users. It worked fine and, so far as I can recall, was still there several years later when we sold the place.

The Yealm estuary was our main contact with the wider English Channel. There we could, literally, go down to the sea in boats. My mother had acquired a small sailing dinghy which we would sail or, if the tide was adverse, motor using an elderly outboard engine. Where the estuary met the open sea there was a small beach guarded from the waves by a large rock. This was "our" beach and "our" rock, where we would spend many happy afternoons swimming and sitting in the sun. Memory plays tricks: the English summer is normally predictably wet. However, my recollection of summers at Little Stert is an endless parade of sunny days and peaceful afternoons with my mother, father, Tony, and assorted cousins, when we would squeeze into our battered farm truck and go down to the sea.

Chapter 4

LEARNING TO LOVE THE SEA AND BOATS

Summer at Little Stert was one of the few bright spots in a period of my mother's life she later recalled mostly with distaste. Cousins and friends would come and stay and the benefits of a farming life would, for a short while, appear to outweigh the drawbacks. Fresh air and fresh food, a river to swim and fish, woods to explore; even the farm work itself appeared less arduous when shared with visitors. Moreover, it was during the summer that one of the key advantages of having a farmer father became apparent. On a hot day he would arrange to get necessary chores finished in the morning. Often at lunch he would turn round in his chair and look out at the sky appraisingly. We would eagerly wait his judgment, "Well, it looks like a nice afternoon over the coast, let's go down to the beach." The beach was a lovely stretch of golden sand on the English Channel, some twenty miles from our house.

The sea and boats were always important parts of our lives. Although before the war we lived well inland, the family made an annual summer pilgrimage to visit my mother's parents in the Isle of Wight. As we drove to the shore, there was always a competition to determine who would catch sight of the sea first. There would be a magic moment as we came over the South Downs to Portsmouth when, between the hills, one could just make out the straight gray line, which was the horizon over the English Channel. Only then had our holiday really begun.

At Portsmouth we would take a ferryboat to the Isle of Wight, which would steam slowly down Portsmouth Harbor. My mother, who had been a Navy buff from childhood, would point out the various warships: battleships, cruisers and destroyers. Occasionally she would show me one she had been on board with Navy friends. I think she often wished she had married into the Navy; her best friend had married a Naval officer, and she had once spent a holiday with them in Malta, where his ship was based, and had obviously taken a liking to the lifestyle.

As soon as we were out of the harbor I would go below to watch the engines. The ferries were paddle steamers, driven by very large reciprocating steam engines. The crank shaft was connected directly to the paddles, and one could stand on a grating and watch the huge piston rod moving slowly in and out below. The noise was impressive and the atmosphere hot and humid. Wisps of warm vapors would drift out of the cylinder, and the whole thing would smell deliciously of hot oil and steam, an aroma that would accompany me for much of the next two decades. Hanging over the main bearing which connected the piston rod with the crank shaft was a cup, suspended from which was what looked like a piece of the engineer's underwear. Oil from the cup dripped down the piece of fabric and splashed on the bearing as it went around. Every now and then the engineer would come out on the grating and pour oil from a can into the cup. One day, noticing that I seemed to be a fixture in his engine room, he asked me if I would like to pour the oil. I must have been around six at the time, so I had scant understanding of the real meaning of the phrase "died and gone to heaven," but clearly that little piece of oil-soaked rag had brought me a glimpse of paradise.

PADDLE FERRY *RYDE* CROSSING TO THE ISLE OF WIGHT

"The ferries were paddle steamers, driven by very large reciprocating steam engines. The crank shaft was connected directly to the paddles, and one could stand on a grating and watch the huge piston rod moving slowly in and out below. The noise was impressive and the atmosphere hot and humid. Wisps of warm vapors would drift out of the cylinder, and the whole thing would smell deliciously of hot oil and steam, a smell that would accompany me for much of the next two decades..."

A few years before the war we were very adventurous, and we flew to the Isle of Wight. The plane was a single-engine machine that appeared to have a lot of important looking mechanical parts bouncing dangerously around out in front. The pilot was out in the open but the four of us—my father and mother, Nanny and me, plus Jane the dog—were in a tiny cabin in the back (Tony was as yet unborn). I remember little of the flight except that Jane was sick into my father's bowler hat. I would like to say that the experience left me with an enduring determination to become a pilot, but it didn't.

My mother would tell me a lot about ships and the navy and had some splendid photos in her album of battleships and cruisers. However, it never dawned on me that I would ever get involved in such things. Still, we did always remain very conscious of the sea as an important part of our lives. When we moved to Devonshire my mother bought a small gaff rigged dinghy in which she taught me to sail. We kept it on the River Yealm estuary, and I think that during her time in the West Country she was probably happiest when sailing that little boat.

When I was fifteen the school Chaplain at Blundell's arranged to take a group of us on the Norfolk Broads during the Easter holidays. The Broads are a remarkable stretch of lakes and canals in the east of England that have always provided wonderful recreational sailing. As one of the principal locales for *Swallows and Amazons*, the riveting series for young readers, the Broads were also familiar to me from earlier reading. Large flat-bottomed sailing boats were chartered, and I made considerable progress in boat handling during my week there.

Peter Gillingham was a former naval chaplain and a wonderfully patient sailing instructor. Our chartered boat came with a small dinghy that we could take out on our own and, since the Broads are all enclosed, there was little that could go wrong. Gillingham was a very open minded man. At night we would tie up alongside a canal bank in some village and make our supper. Then, evading his unwatchful eye, we would slip across to the nearest pub and drink beer supplied by a tolerant innkeeper unfazed by the fact that we all looked and acted our ages, which were well under the level that even the most benevolent barman would find acceptable.

Apart from our little dinghy at home, this was the last sailing I did before I joined the Navy. When I decided to make a career at sea, I faced a lot of unknowns. But one thing was certain: anything that involved the sea and boats was going to be all right. Maybe, as in so many matters, I had been unduly influenced by poetry learned at school; in this case John Masefield's "Sea Fever", a "must learn" for most British boys of my vintage:

I must go down to the seas again, to the lonely sea and the sky,

And all I ask is a tall ship and a star to steer her by,

And the wheel's kick and the wind's song and the white sail's shaking,

And a gray mist on the sea's face, and a gray dawn breaking.

I must go down to the seas again, for the call of the running tide

Is a wild call and a clear call that may not be denied;

And all I ask is a windy day with the white clouds flying,

And the flung spray and the blown spume, and the sea-gulls crying.

I must go down to the seas again, to the vagrant gypsy life,

To the gull's way and the whale's way, where the wind's like a whetted knife;

And all I ask is a merry yarn from a laughing fellow-rover,

And quiet sleep and a sweet dream when the long trick's over.

Unlike me, my good friend Richard had always wanted to join the Navy. The only socially acceptable way for a young person to do so at that time was through the Royal Naval College at Dartmouth, which had two forms of admission: cadet entry at age thirteen, or “special entry” at age eighteen for young men who had completed High School. Richard was heading for the special entry as an engineering officer but was having great difficulty with the exams. It wasn’t that he was dim, quite the contrary. However, like many people, he handled tests badly, echoing Winston Churchill’s petulant complaint that they always seemed to want to find out the things he didn’t know, rather than the things he did.

He was staying with us during the summer of 1950 when he got his second or third rejection letter. He read it and then tossed it over to me, angrily exclaiming that not only were they rejecting him, they were insulting him too. The letter said that he would not be accepted as an engineer (the rejection), but that the Navy was actively recruiting pilots on short service commissions and would he be interested (the insult!)? I read the letter and thought it rather engaging: I had left Blundell’s that July with no real aim in life except a determination not to spend any more time in school, my father was pressing me to do something, and didn’t seem too particular regarding what, yet here I was at age 18 severely unqualified to do anything that might actually produce some income. National Service (the draft) was just over the horizon requiring a minimum of two years of military service, and I knew I didn’t relish the idea of being a soldier. The Navy wanted me for eight years but during that time would teach me to fly, send me to sea to glamorous foreign places, give me fifteen hundred pounds when I got out and, as an aviator, I would have the added reward of extra “flying” pay. I had never considered becoming a pilot, but the more I thought about it the more I recalled the pleasure I had derived when, as a small boy, I had spent hours making and flying model airplanes. I realized that launching rubber powered model airplanes was a far cry from flying real aircraft off the decks of aircraft carriers, but the fifteen hundred pounds seemed like a lot of money at the time. I borrowed the form Richard had received in the mail, filled it in and settled back to wait. (I should add here that Richard did finally make it into the Navy, became a well-regarded Engineer and then, later, started his own related business and did very well in life.)

The wait was a long one. First there were a lot more forms to fill in; then a multiple-choice exam; then a visit to the headquarters of naval aviation at Lee-on-Solent, near Portsmouth, where we had a physical exam and were tested for leadership capabilities. None of these gave me any particular trouble. In fact, the leadership tests were quite enjoyable. They took place in a big gymnasium, where we were divided into groups and we were given two or three large pieces of timber and some rope and told we had to get our team of six across an imaginary river. The idea was to see who took charge and who meekly followed. Being naturally rather bossy, I suppose I must have taken charge at some point: my membership in the Blundell's Army Cadet Force finally played a useful role in my life.

A final stage was an interview at the navy base with several imposing Captains. All naval bases were commissioned as ships, and this one was HMS *Daedalus*. During my interview they asked me whether I knew where the name of the place came from. I explained that Daedalus and Icarus were, according to Greek mythology, the first men to fly. They had built wings out of bird feathers held together by wax in order to escape from imprisonment in Crete. Daedalus had warned his son Icarus not to fly too close to the sun in case it melted the wax. On the way the father flew close to the sea but the son soared too high, his wings melted, and he fell to his death in the waves. This is a familiar story to anyone who has browsed the classics, but one of the captains there said he'd been asking that question in interviews for over two years and I was the first person to get the answer right. Given my contempt for latin, I would classify this as lucky rather than smart.

They told me I had scored the highest on record in the exams. I thought it needless to mention that, during the war, my father had been administering similar tests to officer candidates. He used to bring the tests home and we would do them together for amusement (there was little else to do during the blackout); in fact, I could probably I do them in my sleep. However, my overall impression was that they were quite anxious to find prospective naval pilots, and indeed, may have had difficulty recruiting for an occupation that, at the time, had a somewhat doubtful life expectancy. Most pilots at that time preferred to take off and land from stable asphalt runways rather than from quite small vessels that tended to roll in bad weather. That, and the fact that Britain's economy was finally beginning to recover from the previous war, and indeed was showing signs of vigor from the armaments build-up required for the Korean action, may have caused recruiting standards to become somewhat elastic.

The final hurdle was a flying aptitude test. All candidates spent a day at a Royal Air Force (RAF) base in Kent. There we not only went through additional medical tests but had to perform all sorts of physical and mental tricks, to see if we would be able to fly. What I didn't realize until afterwards was that the tests weren't simply to pass or fail as a pilot, they were also looking for observers, people who would sit in the back of the plane and navigate while the pilot flew. Maybe this had been explained, and I just hadn't read the fine print. I had always assumed that if I did it at all I would be the driver, never a passenger. Fortunately, it worked out that way: I would become a pilot. Readers will learn later why I retain a high regard for the "passenger".

Alert readers will have noticed that this is the second time in this narrative that I have made a significant, life changing decision without spending a lot of time thinking about it or, more importantly, without having an exact understanding of the commitment I was making. Indeed, since no one had thought to remind me that there was a war going on the other side of the world, in which the Royal Navy's Fleet Air Arm was actively involved, one may conclude that whatever faculty I had for critical thinking was asleep at that time.

Chapter 5

BEFORE BECOMING A NAVAL PILOT:
LEARNING TO BE A NAVAL OFFICER

In January 1951 I finally received a notice from the navy telling me I was to start my service as an aviation cadet, and to report on board the training carrier HMS *Indefatigable* in Weymouth Harbor on the last day of the month. My parents, who by now seemed to be remarkably resigned to my choice of occupations, had taken a long-planned vacation in the Canary Islands, so I was alone in the house. Fortunately, they had left Bright behind to take care of the animals; it did cross my mind that "I'm sorry I'm late, but I had to stay behind to feed the pigs." might have been a poor introduction to the Royal Navy.

I spent the night before I left Little Stert realizing the enormity of what I had done. Voluntarily I had signed my life away for eight years, to enter a profession about which I knew very little, and which required skills I was by no means sure I possessed. However, when I first set foot on the huge warship that was to be my home for the next six months there was one familiar thing to greet me. She carried with her that heady aroma of steam, oil, and salt air that had characterized the Portsmouth-Ryde ferries. I knew I belonged.

There were some twenty aviation cadets in our course, and another twenty who had already been there for three months. The goal was to turn us into naval officers in six short months, after which, so the thinking went, the seamen would lose us to the airmen. Clearly, time was of the essence because on Day One we were given our uniforms and on Day Two the ship sailed, in company with HMS *Vanguard*, Britain's latest (and last) battleship, destination Gibraltar. We had to cross the Bay of Biscay, one of the world's roughest patches of water in January, one the worst months to be on it. Our duties included scrubbing the decks, for which they gave us two buckets: one to hold the scrubbing water, and the other to vomit into. I thought I was going to die, but within a day I notched up two achievements: I stopped vomiting, and I became an outstanding deck scrubber.

I remember standing on the after end of the flight deck and looking back at *Vanguard*, some half mile astern in our wake and marveling at the waves which broke right over her tallest mast, as she dipped and rolled in the immense seas. If this was going to be my life for the next eight years, I could have chosen a lot worse.

Indefatigable was one of the *Implacable* class of aircraft carriers, ordered in 1938 as part of Britain's pre-war rearmament program. After completion in 1944, she saw action in European waters, particularly several attacks by her air groups against the German battleship *Tirpitz*.

Following *Tirpitz*' final destruction in early 1945, many of the British naval vessels that had been pursuing her (including *Indefatigable*) were transferred to the newly formed British Pacific Fleet, where they joined the United States Navy in support of Allied forces invading Okinawa, and finally in a series of raids against the Japanese home islands.

During her time off Okinawa, *Indefatigable* was attacked by a Japanese suicide bomber that struck the corner where the vessel's island (main superstructure) met her armored flight deck. There were considerable casualties among crew members near the scene. But the damage to the ship was negligible and caused only minor interruption to her combat capability.

For much of the remainder of the Pacific war, and the later Korean conflict there was considerable debate between the British and American navies regarding the utility of the Royal Navy's armored flight decks. On board *Indefatigable* in 1951 we new Aviation Cadets were thrust into one side of that discussion when we were shown with great pride how little damage the armored deck had suffered from the Kamikaze attack, and told how rapidly our vessel had been able to resume normal operations after the damage. Implied here was how much more rugged were the British ships, compared with American carriers, given the latter's much lighter flight decks.

Only later were we exposed to the other side of the argument when we learned that Britain's large ("fleet") carriers could only carry much smaller complements of aircraft than their American equivalents and (only discovered long after they had been built) would take much longer to convert to the angled deck that would prove essential for the operation of jet aircraft.

Our business on board *Indefatigable* had little to do with aviation, and much to do with military drills and seamanship. After a brief visit to Gibraltar, our ship returned to Portland harbor, an artificial structure built during the 19th Century. One side of it was Portland Bill, a peninsula sticking out into the English Channel, the other side seawalls built out of huge rocks. The nearest town was Weymouth. While anchored in the harbor we learned a lot of things relating to ships and the sea and being a naval officer, all in a remarkably short period of time: drilling on the flight deck, launching and recovering boats, signal flags and Morse code. We found our way around the huge vessel, which was a marvel in itself, and stood harbor watches. However, my happiest time was sailing, which we were encouraged to do at every opportunity when the ship was in port. We were taught in naval cutters or whalers, rather heavy boats designed for the open sea, but once it became apparent that some of us already knew our way around small boats, we were allowed to use the ship's dinghies. I used to sail with Jerry Caird, descendent of a long line of much decorated Marines who, I am sure, were horrified that he had joined the Navy and, what was worse, as a flier. He was an expert sailor and a crafty racer. I crewed for him in a series of races in Portland Harbor, many of which we won. I was saddened a year or so later when Jerry flew into a mountain in Scotland and was killed.

The very Naval name of the Captain of *Indefatigable* was St. Vincent Sherbrook (his name recognized a significant British naval victory during the Napoleonic wars, his parents thus demonstrating astonishing foresight). He had earned his Victoria Cross (Britain's highest award for gallantry) in 1942 when a destroyer flotilla under his command was attacked north of the Arctic Circle by a superior German force. He held the enemy off for several hours, allowing a convoy of essential weaponry to continue its voyage to Russia. He was severely wounded in the process, losing an eye and part of his face. By 1951, it seemed, his job was largely inspirational: we saw little of him other than at Sunday inspections, when we had to make the difficult decision: did we look at him manfully in the rather ghastly place where his eye and face used to be, or tactfully turn away. The enlisted Petty officer who largely ruled over us outside the classroom bluntly instructed us: "And when the Captain looks at you, look at 'im right back, but in 'is good eye, not in 'is 'orrible 'ole."

There was at the time a theory that only two kinds of young men took readily to military service: those who had been to boarding schools, and those who had served time in reform school. Both were used to being away from home, harsh and unpredictable discipline, spartan living conditions, and poor food. I suppose it would be unfair of me to focus on these shortcomings; in practice I found my absence from home much more bearable in the Navy than I had at Blundell's, and the food wasn't all that bad. Possibly there had been some accrued benefits from my ten years in boarding school.

Spartan living conditions, on the other hand, did take a toll. I believe that the Royal Navy, like other advanced navies, had decided soon after the end of World War II that for many reasons hammocks no longer provided the optimum sleeping arrangements for enlisted sailors, and that they would sleep better, and get up healthier, if they rested in bunks. However, like most organizations priding themselves on the length and toughness of their history, the Navy felt that newly enlisted cadets should taste some of the discomforts their forbearers had become used to. Hence, when we joined *Indefatigable* we were each provided with a hammock and its associated skimpy bedding.

Few if any of us had slept in hammocks before on a regular basis – some more privileged members of our group had, during their summers, slept warm afternoons away in a simple affair made of netting, slung between two trees, but I don't think anyone had come across this demanding, bulky beast that at its best looked like an overgrown breakfast sausage, and at its worst could, without any encouragement, throw you out of a sound sleep onto a hard steel floor.

The hammocks were kept stacked in a corner of our mess deck and, in the brief period between our final evening class of the day, and loud cries of "lights out" from our petty officer, had to be slung between two metal bars that stretched the width of our sleeping quarters. Everything had to be "ship-shape" and we had limited time to get everything done and looking smart and tidy before our desperately hoped for sleep took over. (We were always tired.)

Getting into the hammock was a struggle: there was nothing rigid to hold onto; the bed itself was a narrow canvas tube, suspended at each end by a mess of cordage; and the whole thing threatened to roll over on top of you if you got it slightly out of balance – and there was a five foot drop between bed and deck.

Sleep came rapidly, with dawn just behind it. Our Petty Officer was merciless – he woke us at 4:30 AM and we had some twenty minutes to get up and stow our hammocks before we were on the flight deck doing calisthenics, followed by sitting down to breakfast, when the day began. When the Petty Officers slept we never found out. Stowing the hammocks was an art, and I don't think I ever discovered the secret. The ideal always looked full and plump; mine always looked like it had fallen off the back of a fast moving truck.

As we got towards the end of our *Indefatigable* time, I don't think any of our fellow cadets had proved unable to handle the demands of our first six months in the Navy; we had all begun to feel an integral part of the Service. We were allowed to stand watches, although under close supervision, and we felt we knew enough about sea-going vessels to call ourselves Naval Officers, but only the least modest among us would have considered themselves aviators. Those of us over twenty-one were promoted to Sub-Lieutenants (USN = Ensigns) while the rest of us became Midshipmen (referred to as "The lowest form of animal life in the Navy", though what that had to say about us before the promotion, I don't know).

Chapter 6

LEARNING TO BE A NAVAL AVIATOR

Leaving *Indefatigable* meant leaving the sea for a while, it being deemed safer and more economical to have trainee pilots start their learning process on dry land. I rode my motorcycle up to the naval air station at Donibristle in Scotland just across the Firth of Forth from Edinburgh and on arrival was amazed at the improvement in our living conditions. We were now proper officers with our own "gunroom" mess and stewards to take care of us. Donibristle gave us three months of pre-flight training, both schoolwork, (maths, physics) etc, and more practical things relating to airplanes and flying. These included taking engines apart and putting them together again, learning radio procedures, shooting at clay pigeons (to get us used to aiming at moving targets) and, occasionally, actually going up in the air.

One very important thing we had to learn about airplanes was how to get out of them if things went wrong. To do this they had taken the cockpit part of a Seafire, (a Spitfire naval variant), and placed it sixteen feet above the floor of one of the hangars. The aviator-to-be was strapped into his parachute harness, which was in turn attached to two strong pieces of elastic. On the command "jump" the pilot was supposed to go head first over the side, straight down towards the floor, and hopefully the elastic would arrest him before his head actually struck concrete. (Experienced bungee jumpers would probably have far more faith in the strength of the rubber than we did.) Our instructor asked for someone to volunteer. No one did, and it soon became apparent that he had a mutiny on his hands. "Alright," he said, "we'll have to send for the officer." As if on cue, the officer appeared. She was a good-looking young woman, about five foot two with long blonde hair done up in a neat bun and looking very attractive in a snug fitting flight suit, officer's rank insignia prominently displayed. Not saying a word, she strapped herself into the harness, climbed up into the cockpit, shouted "jump," and went head first over the side. With what appeared to be one sinuous movement she turned herself upright again, unsnapped the parachute harness, turned and pointed to the first in line. "You," she said, "up you get." And off we went to the slaughter, one by one, shame-faced, but without a murmur. No one died.

Our female parachute instructor was not an anomaly; we were now on a naval air station, and much of the staff consisted of Wrens. The Women's Royal Naval Service (WRNS or Wrens) was unique among women's military services in that they were not subject to normal military discipline. Quite how that worked I never found out, but the net result was that enlisted Wrens were allowed to date officers, and vice versa, and many did. A further result was that the Wrens attracted a remarkably fine group of young women. Considering that it was the early 1950's, it was surprising to learn the range of functions performed by Wrens on naval air stations, from mechanics and armorers to meteorology and air traffic control. No one appeared unduly bothered that they performed, mostly with above average competence, tasks for which their civilian sisters later would find entry difficult until well into the 1970's. There were not a lot of them, and the Fleet Air Arm (the aviation side of the Royal Navy) was a close-knit community, so it wasn't surprising that one gradually accumulated a network of good women friends—and sometimes more than friends—around the various naval airfields, particularly since these were often located in very isolated places.

WREN AIRCRAFT MECHANICS

"Considering that it was the early 1950's, it was surprising to learn the range of functions performed by Wrens on naval air stations, from mechanics and armorers to meteorology and air traffic control. No one appeared unduly bothered that they performed, mostly with above average competence, tasks for which their civilian sisters later would find entry difficult until well into the 1970's."

At Donibristle I fell dramatically in love (for the first time, but certainly not the last) with a Wren called Judy who had short dark hair and a lovely smile. We were members of the Merlin Players, the station drama society, and had been cast together in a play called "See How They Run," in which I played a parson and, with all modesty, was rather a hit. Judy and I went out a lot and one thing led to another until, naive fool that I was, I decided it was time to have her meet my family. We arranged to go down to London together and I booked sleeping car berths on the night train. My mother would meet us in London. A day or two before the trip we decided that it was all rather premature, so I had a spare sleeping car berth and asked Peter Heatherington if he'd like to use it. Unfortunately, I hadn't focused on how British Railways ran their sleeping cars in those days: there were compartments for men and separate ones for women. Peter, who would never be mistaken for a woman, turned up with his ticket and was made to spend the whole night standing in the corridor since all the men's berths were taken. Worse was to come: I'd forgotten to tell my mother about the change of plans. For the rest of her (long) life she would talk about the acute panic she felt when she first saw me coming down the platform of Euston Station with the person I had assured her was the love of my life - tall, rather poorly complexioned, and unmistakably male.

Joining our course at this stage was Brian Jones, who had served in Royal Navy minesweepers during the last year of the war and was thus deemed not to need the first stage of naval training. He was older than the rest of us but fitted in very well. He and I became extremely good friends, sharing a passion for film and theater. He also introduced me to Scott's Bar in Edinburgh and helped me develop a taste for the local whiskies. I was an usher at his wedding some three years later and after that our assignments kept us apart until I was very saddened to learn that during night exercises in the South China sea, his airplane had disappeared over the bow of his ship. His body was never found, and he left behind his wife and two children. Of all my Fleet Air Arm friends who lost their lives in flying accidents, he was the one I missed the most.

Three months went by fast: more exams, some leave, and then we were off to learn to fly. What is surprising is the fact that, from the time we had been given aptitude tests a year earlier, no one had made any attempt to see if we would indeed be able to fly an airplane. An enormous investment of time and effort had gone into our education, much of which would be wasted if we couldn't actually get the thing off the ground and bring it back again in one piece. Some of us, it turned out, couldn't.

At this time the navy operated under an arrangement insisted on by the always cost conscious British Government whereby its pilots received basic flying training from the Royal Air Force. A few of the instructors were naval pilots, but the curriculum, on the ground and in the air, was all RAF, as were most of the instructors, including mine. All of our flight training would be concentrated at RAF Syerston, a large airfield pretty much in the middle of England (which, speaking mathematically, means about as far away from the sea as we could possibly be).

PERCIVAL PRENTICE

"Our first training airplane was an evil looking monstrosity called a Prentice, manufactured by the Percival Aircraft Company."

Our first training airplane was an evil looking monstrosity called a Prentice, manufactured by the Percival Aircraft Company. The Prentice was the first British trainer to seat instructor and student side by side so that each could each see what the other was doing (as opposed to the more traditional one behind the other). Unfortunately, early models had a nasty habit of slipping sideways out of turns, to counteract which the designers had turned up the ends of the wings, giving them a rather bizarre appearance. An RAF contemporary memorably commented that he never determined whether it really was meant to fly or was just someone's idea of a joke.

My instructor was a Flight Lieutenant Whitely, who surprised me on November 20, 1951 by sending me solo, after only seven and a half hours of dual instruction. The navy required us to keep a diary, and mine for that period tells a bit about what I was thinking, despite the rather inflated language:

> November 3, 1951, my first flight. "Flying—for nine months most of us have been waiting for this: nine months that for many have seemed a pointless waste of time, and now here we are, in the air, and a voice says 'You have control.' How easy it seems—you push the stick forward and she dives, back and she climbs, sideways with stick and rudder and she turns. All the time though there is an instructor ready to take over should anything go amiss. How lonely it would be without him, and how easily could all those false ideas of simplicity be shattered . . ."
>
> November 11, 1951. "I wondered, when I first went up with my instructor, why he asked me if I had ever flown above clouds before. I told him I had, but it was only the other day, when there was nothing above us but the sun, and nothing below but a vast snow field of cloud, that I realized why he asked the question. No one could ever concentrate on the job in hand while confronted with that dazzling whiteness below him. I could never tire of it, those mountains and plains, cliffs and corridors, all looking so solid but in reality, only vapor . . ."
>
> November 26, 1951. "Last Tuesday I went solo for the first time. The empty place at my side wasn't really

very perturbing, but then I only did one circuit of the field before doing my first solo landing."

We learned to navigate, to do basic aerobatics, to control the airplane relying solely on instruments (there was no lack of real cloud to practice in during England's long winter) and to fly at night. We suffered accidents, some fatal, lost companions who couldn't handle the airplane.

This point in my narrative seems to demand a short digression, mainly because so much of my life at the time in question was absorbed in flying, so much of flying involves technical terms, and readers unfamiliar with these terms certainly deserve some explanations. Not so much "how to fly," but rather to lay to rest the obvious question: "just what is he talking about?"

Although this book is mostly about learning, it is also focused heavily on naval flying. There will therefore be considerable discussion about learning when the eventual goal is to fly military missions from ships.

There were four key elements in training that took those of us who had just learned how to fly the airplane on their own (soloed), to broader skills that would prove essential in combat: navigation, instrument flying, aerobatics and (peculiar to the Navy and taught a fairly long time after the other three had been thoroughly digested) landing on an aircraft carrier ("deck landings").

Navigation requires little explanation at this point: the fledgling pilot had to be able to find his way from (A) to (B) without getting embarrassingly lost, if necessary making use of a few elementary radio aids.

Instrument flight means that in bad weather, with low visibility, the pilot controls the airplane solely by means of the various dials in front of him in the cockpit. Our inexperience was recognized: bad weather flying required an instructor's authorization and, more often than not, instrument training was conducted in good visibility with the student's vision artificially restricted. A properly trained instrument pilot should be able to complete his planned flight regardless of visibility and arrive at his destination without difficulty.

Aerobatics are not an essential part of learning to fly, indeed, many pilots can go their entire flying career without ever having deliberately turned an airplane upside down while in flight. However, it is a significant part of a military pilot's training, unless he intends to confine his future flying to transport operations. Aerobatic skills also enhance the abilities needed to attack or avoid an enemy. In addition, the non-commercial civilian pilot, if properly trained and equipped, will find that aerobatics vastly enhance the enjoyment of flight.

In the early stages of training we were taught basic aerobatic maneuvers such as loops, and rolls and how we could recover from the resultant stall or spin if we made a mistake. During a loop, the pilot maneuvers the airplane so that it describes a vertical circle in the air. In most training aircraft pilot and plane become weightless (negative "G" at the top of the loop). Ideally the maneuver will be completed with the airplane at the same height, and heading in the same direction, as when it was initiated.

Two simple rolls were part of our starter menu: an aileron roll and a barrel roll. The intention of the aileron roll is to maintain a constant height while rotating the airplane around an axis identical to the original heading. Actually, it is not as easy as all that, unless one is flying a jet fighter; slower airplanes require a lot of work with the rudder to maintain level flight. A barrel roll is just that; the pilot flies the airplane so that it transcribes an imaginary line around the outside of an imaginary barrel pointed in the desired direction of flight. The aileron roll involves weightlessness (negative "G") at some parts of it; the barrel roll is normally completed with positive "G" throughout.

A stall occurs when the flow of air over the wing provides insufficient lift to maintain stable flight, the nose drops and, unless proper corrective action is taken, the airplane will continue its downward progress or, more likely find itself with one wing developing more lift than the other, resulting in a spin. The spin, although easy to recover from when the pilot is well trained, frequently proved a bit unnerving to us beginners, who would often thus avoid incurring them (which is sensible), or avoid practicing recovery from them, which is stupid. A good aerobatic display will offer many variants of these maneuvers, but generally the most significant parts of a trainee pilot's aerobatic menu will involve some mixture of loops and rolls.

We were continually drilled in these basic airmanship skills, but best of all was the occasional opportunity to low fly close to the ground legally. Probably the biggest cause of flying discipline problems was the urgent desire of young men in powerful machines to increase the sensation of speed by flying as close to the ground as possible. This of course greatly annoyed the local farmers and, so they claimed, caused cows to deliver sour milk, and sheep not to deliver at all. But there were certain places where, at certain times, you could do this with little restriction. Low flying exercises were a cherished part of the curriculum, and anyone who has not experienced the thrill of flying up a valley fifty or less feet off the ground will never know what he (or she) has missed.

Later in my career, after I became a flying instructor, I had to demonstrate stalls and spins to a young Iranian pilot trainee (at a time when we were quite friendly with Iran). As we cut the motor and started to pull the nose above the horizon to initiate the stall, he let go of the stick and started to either weep or pray: "No, No, not the stalling, not the stalling." Washington was trying to sell the Shah high priced F-14's at the time. I always hoped my student was not part of the prospective customer base.

John Matthews, a fellow student who later went on to be a university professor, was a valued friend. At the time I had intellectual pretensions that appeared way out of place in the Navy, let alone the RAF, and only he seemed to share them. During especially dull lectures we would start softly chanting from T.S. Eliot's "The Hollow Men": "We are the hollow men, we are the stuffed men, leaning together, head piece filled with straw." No one seemed quite to know what to make of it; why they didn't throw us out, I don't for the life of me know.

LINK TRAINER – EARLY FLIGHT SIMULATOR

"On rainy days we would learn how to fly on instruments in a Link Trainer, an airplane simulator for practicing maneuvers that were then tracked on a plotting board for the instructor to review. They were very expensive, and really quite realistic."

On rainy days we would learn how to fly on instruments in a Link Trainer, an airplane simulator for practicing maneuvers that were then tracked on a plotting board for the instructor to review. They were very expensive, and really quite realistic. John Matthews put one into a spin one day, and it performed a very authentic crash. It sat there wobbling on its mounting, looking exceedingly sad, until Matthews opened the cockpit door, stepped out, turned to the instructor and said, "one of our Links is missing," and then walked out of the door without looking back. I was quite impressed - it was the kind of thing I wish I had said.

Syerston was a major RAF flight school, and the naval contingent was small in relation to the whole. We were trained mostly by RAF pilots and alongside those who would become RAF pilots. There was a considerable amount of rivalry, and some tension. We knew that we were a cut above, more carefully selected, more rigorously trained–destined to land our airplanes on a ship, for goodness sake. They, on the other hand, knew that they would probably go on to fly jet fighters or bombers, while the Royal Navy at the time was only just beginning to discover jet propulsion.

We were encouraged to compete at everything and at all levels. Someone had the bright idea of a boxing tournament, and in a moment of acute stupidity I volunteered to be the naval champion and was allowed to be because no one else was foolish enough to raise his hand. At my prep school we had been forced to take boxing that, like all other compulsory athletics, I had hated with a passion, and this time with reason. You could get hurt. I remembered Sergeant Crutchley, our physical training instructor, making us face sideways to our opponent and jab with the left hand, while covering the face with the right. I also remembered the numbing pain when someone had slipped through my guard and landed a hard one on my nose. Why I embarked on this recklessness I have no idea, but I will admit that it fitted nicely with my predilection for ill-considered decision-making!

We got into the ring, all very professional: I had two seconds who came amply supplied with beer as the most reliable reviver, but which the referee wouldn't let them use. I wore black silk shorts and a singlet with navy colors. They put on my gloves and I went into the middle of the ring to shake hands with my opponent.

It was just like the books I had read at my prep school. He was bigger than me, but he was very flabby, and his skin was rather blotchy. I remember thinking that he was probably rich and a bully. Actually, as I found out afterwards, he was as poor as any of us and really quite gentle. But by then it was too late.

The bell rang and I came out in my well-remembered

position, sideways with the left arm out. And, lo and behold, the other fellow was facing me, both hands up, and a large gap through to his face. I jabbed, hard, and caught him square on the nose. Blood began to flow. I jabbed again—more blood. Now I knew how a victorious gladiator in the Roman Coliseum must feel, I wanted more blood. And then more blood, I was actually thirsty! About two and a half minutes into the fight, my opponent's face a crimson mess; the referee stopped the fight, held up my hand, and declared me the winner. I have never boxed since, knowing full well that my luck is finite. They gave me a medal to prove my valor. Occasionally someone would ask me how I won it. "Turn left and jab!" was the tried and true formula. I only used it one time, but it certainly worked.

Brian Jones and I shared a passion for American musical theater. I was also enjoying a platonic relationship with a girl called Valerie who, while extraordinarily beautiful, handled herself, at least with me, in a rather glacial manner. However, she was flattering to be around and liked going to the theater. Brian and I would leave after flying stopped for the weekend, drive down to London, and do a theater/dinner/night-club routine on Friday and Saturday nights. We would stay at the RNVR Club which, while located in the middle of Mayfair, still provided a bunk bed in a dormitory for the equivalent of $1.50. London had started to look up by 1952; the previous year the Conservatives had succeeded the Socialists and immediately lifted some of Stafford Cripps' austere egalitarian shackles. There was a season of debutante dances and all the orchestras were playing the latest show tunes from New York. I joined a rather upscale "members only" nightclub called the Carousel on Piccadilly that closed around 5 am. One could stay all night for the price of a jug of Pimms, dancing to music from *South Pacific, The King and I, Call Me Madam* and, of course, *Carousel.* Then it was daylight outside, and we would come out from below street level, tired and bleary-eyed and, innocent age that it was, we put our dates into taxis, and went home to our separate beds.

In January 1952 we completed our initial training in the

Prentice and graduated to the Harvard–known in America as the T6. This was a real airplane: a big Pratt & Whitney 550 horsepower radial engine with lots of noise, terrific performance, and an undercarriage that retracted so that if you forgot to put it down you did a lot of serious damage. With a wingspan of over 40 ft., and standing high off the ground, it was built like a tank and appeared awesome when we first approached it. It was, however, a dream to fly. Brian Jones and I shared a new instructor, a very amiable Flight Lieutenant Fuller. He was an extremely good teacher and we both got on well with him personally, which was unusual in the instructor/pupil relationship in those days. We were saddened to hear that he had been killed in a flying accident a few months after we graduated.

HARVARD – KNOWN IN AMERICA AS T6

"This was a real airplane: a big Pratt & Whitney 550 horsepower radial engine with lots of noise, terrific performance, and an undercarriage that retracted so that if you forgot to put it down you did a lot of serious damage."

There was also persistent attention to instrument flying, taught very realistically by having the plane's cockpit enclosed in yellow tinted glass: the instructor could still see outside, but the student, wearing blue tinted goggles, had no outside reference at all. He was forced to rely solely on his instruments or lose control of the aircraft unless the instructor was paying attention. In mid-June I took and passed my instrument test, next to going solo probably the most important hurdle, since many of those who couldn't make the grade failed on account of poor instrument work. This was one area where England's wretched climate was a blessing. The Royal Navy, with an eye to speeding up the supply of pilots, was sending some of its candidates over to America to be trained. Most of their flying took place in Texas or Florida, and many of them came back to England never having seen a real cloud. In addition, I was surprised to discover when I returned as a private pilot in America that they relied on a vision-blanking eyeshade to simulate lack of visibility–helpful, but less demanding than our tinted cockpits. Some rather nasty accidents caused by lack of experience in seriously bad visibility, resulted in all American trained pilots returning to the United Kingdom having to take a special course, tactfully referred to as an "instrument refresher."

Soon we started formation flying, learning to fly really close to another airplane, without actually hitting it, and to trust the lead pilot to maneuver so that all you had to do was focus on him. Our skills in this area were put to the test as we approached the end of the course and were sent for two weeks to the naval air station at Arbroath on the east coast of Scotland. The idea was to get us used to flying with the navy again, but since we were now virtually certain of getting our wings, the whole exercise was treated with a considerable degree of levity. The weather was perfect, we got to fly over the sea for the first time, had an aerobatic competition, and flew home in formation feeling very full of ourselves.

By the end of my time at Syerston I had decided to become a "strike" pilot, specializing in bombing or torpedo strikes, with an emphasis on sinking an enemy's ships, or destroying his property, rather than a fighter pilot, whose job is to destroy the other side's airplanes. This decision was a combination of several factors, not the least of which was my recognition that I still got somewhat queasy after a lot of aerobatics and seemed to lack the spatial perception that is vital for a good fighter pilot. Also, I had been seduced by the Wyvern, then the navy's hot new prop-jet attack plane. It later proved so deadly to its pilots that it had to be withdrawn from service, but at the time seemed to embody the kind of flying I most enjoyed. However, I later regretted this decision when I was given a chance to fly a Meteor, the RAF's first operational jet fighter.

> Diary entry for: July 9, 1952. ". . . An RAF instructor took me up in a Meteor Mk.7. This was my first flight in a jet, and one of the most exciting flying experiences I have ever had. I was given control at the end of the runway and took off. The acceleration was terrific, and as soon as we were off the instructor took over and did a hectic ten minutes low flying to get the fuel load down to a level safe enough for aerobatics. Then we climbed up and I took over for some loops and rolls. The effortless smoothness was amazing. In an eight-point roll the nose did not drop at all and there was none of the shuddering and groaning associated with aerobatics in a Harvard. . . It was a half hour that really made me regret not choosing to be a fighter pilot."

I could never figure out why, but I never felt any of the queasiness doing aerobatics in a jet that I did when trying the same maneuvers in a propeller driven plane. Later I would become part of a Vampire (jet) formation aerobatic team. We performed at some local air shows and spectators appeared to think we were quite good at it.

METEOR – RAF'S FIRST JET FIGHTER

"An RAF instructor took me up in a Meteor Mk.7. This was my first flight in a jet, and one of the most exciting flying experiences I have ever had. I was given control at the end of the runway and took off. The acceleration was terrific..."

On July 25, 1952 I passed out of Syerston with a total of 120 hours flying in my log book, an instrument ticket, and a report which said I was a high average pilot who was keen on flying and should do well, that I had plenty of "guts" (whatever that meant—probably referred to my prowess in the boxing ring) and that I was an excellent leader in the making. How they got these ideas I don't know, but if they were happy, I certainly was.

Over the course of my life since learning to fly at Syerston, I have had plenty of other occasions requiring a formal course of instruction, and as time has passed, I have come to realize how truly excellent were the teaching abilities of my RN and RAF instructors. Flying in the armed services can be difficult and dangerous, but if the subject is well taught the chances of survival increase dramatically. And, as we will see later, the tough disciplines of the RAF's Central Flying School made sure that the subject was well taught.

My parents came to the parade where we were given our wings, and then we drove home for two weeks leave. I was a real pilot! Among those who didn't make it to the wings parade was Peter Heatherington, who was flunked out for some reason—I think it was "lack of officer like qualities" which, put in plain English, meant a prejudice against unwarranted discipline and a rather intolerant attitude towards those who liked to impose it. As if determined to prove that the navy didn't know what it was doing, Peter turned around and joined the air force where he was a star in one of their top squadrons and much later ended up as a trainee flying-instructor on the same course as me. To my surprise I bumped into him some thirty years later when I was crossing the Atlantic on my way to Dublin. Peter was a captain in an Aer Lingus 747, and I was one of his passengers, on my way to do some banking business for his employer.

I don't think I ever found out how my parents really felt about my flying, they never had much to say (at least to me directly) about my chosen occupation. I think my father was pleased that I was doing well at it, especially in the light of my school years' questionable performance, but I think he would have been happier if I had followed a path more in line with the careers of sons of some of his stockbroker friends. My mother, on the other hand, like most similarly situated mothers, lived in constant fear that I would forget to do something important while flying and end up party to an expensive accident. After all, the Wright Brothers only took to the air for the first time around the year she was born; it is logical to believe that she probably still retained doubts as to whether this newfangled nonsense would actually work. However, she never hesitated to indicate how proud she was that I was serving in her beloved Navy.

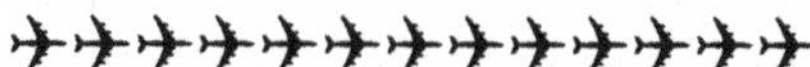

For historical and strategic reasons, the Royal Navy always had a strong presence in Scotland. During both World Wars the main fleet had spent many months swinging at buoys in Rosyth or Scapa Flow in order to bottle the Germans up in the North Sea. There were several naval air stations there, the largest of which was Lossiemouth, where we were sent for the first of two Operational Flying Schools. Fighter and strike pilots were still kept together, although for the first time we flew different airplanes.

> From my journal:
>
> August 23, 1952, at Lossiemouth. "I must admit I am beginning slightly to regret the definite way in which I stated my preference for the strike role. The sight of all these Seafires being thrown about the skies, and the derogatory manner in which their pilots refer to us as "bomber boys" gave me an urge to fly the fighter aircraft."

The Seafire was a naval derivation of the Spitfire, the plane that had outfought the Germans during the Battle of Britain. We will meet it again, but at this stage in training, my aircraft was the Firefly. Since this wonderful airplane was to become my principal occupation over the next fifteen months, it is worth saying a little about it.

For various political reasons the Royal Navy had always

got the short end of the stick when it came to allocating resources between the Fleet Air Arm and the Royal Air Force. Indeed, so poorly equipped was the navy in comparison with the Americans, Germans or Japanese that, by 1942, the decision had been made to turn to the United States for help; by the end of the war America was supplying the major portion of Britain's need for naval aircraft. What British-made airplanes were employed, principally the Seafires, were air force cast-offs that generally failed to perform as well as American products. The Fairey Aviation Company was virtually the only British manufacturer prepared to focus on naval requirements and, by 1943 had produced a carrier airplane that did the job it was designed for, plus a lot of others. It continued to do so for a number of years.

At the time I was introduced to it, the Firefly was the Royal Navy's primary anti-submarine plane, equipped with sonar buoys that could be dropped into the water so that the observer could listen for enemy under watercraft. It also carried a weapons load sufficient to sink any hostile submarines it managed to find, or do damage to other hostile targets. Its Rolls Royce Griffon engine put out 2,200 horsepower. Like all naval airplanes, its wings folded (to facilitate storage) and it had a hook in the tail. It was overall a useful versatile airplane and as a result was one of the two types of attack planes chosen by the Navy for use in Korea.

Given all this there should be no reason to doubt that I had a love affair with this well-tried, multi-purpose airplane. There was, however, one snag, its name. I must admit to being somewhat sensitive to names: I think they should provide some idea of the identity of the person or object being spoken of, and, if possible, give the observer some concept of its major characteristics. Unless somewhat peculiar one would not, for example, call one's pet ant "Jumbo."

The United States Navy seems to understand this; their warplanes have red-blooded names like "Corsair," "Avenger," or "Hellcat", mostly preceded when needed by the name of the manufacturer: Grumman or Lockheed, not bad names to go into combat with. But the Royal Navy, at least in this instance, failed dismally. If my grandchildren ask me what I flew during the Korean War, all I can muster is a rather embarrassing "Fairey Firefly." Not exactly a battle cry!

FIREFLY WITH TAILHOOK DOWN

"If my grandchildren ask me what I flew during the Korean War, all I can muster is a rather embarrassing 'Fairey Firefly'. Not exactly a battle cry!"

The purpose of the three months at Lossiemouth was first to familiarize us with this operational airplane, and second to teach us tactical maneuvers in the air. In addition, we were now back at a Navy base, where the standard landing pattern conformed to that used for carrier landings, so we flew the landing circuit at 400 feet instead of the normal 1,000 feet. Approaches were made at what appeared to be treetop level, with a lot of power on and the great long engine cocked well up in the air, so that the pilot could only see the runway by leaning out over the side.

Lossiemouth was located on the south shore of the Moray Firth, the long inlet that leads up to Inverness, where the Highlands really begin. About ten miles west of us was Findhorn, a little village with a very hospitable yacht club. Officers from Lossiemouth were honorary members, and soon several of us were dinghy racing regularly on Saturdays and Sundays and getting to know the locals in the bar afterwards. Doubting whether my little MG would make it all the way up to Scotland I had shipped my Royal Enfield motorbike (prudently kept as fall-back transportation) there by train. I thus had wheels, of a kind.

One notable member of the yacht club was Mary Hansel, whose family owned a distillery. Their regular Scotch, which was made quite close by, was the familiar brown stuff in the triangular bottle. However, Mary had her own supply of a special malt that was more the color of gin. It came by the case, which she kept behind the bar at the club and managed to consume at the rate of about one (case) a week.

Another member was a Major Beattie, retired from the Argyll and Sutherland Highlanders. The Highland Division, of which the Argylls were a part, was one of the fiercest bodies of men in the British Army. They would go into battle preceded by bagpipers. If that didn't scare the enemy to death, the Colonel, at the head of his troops usually armed with nothing more powerful than a walking stick, was supposed to do the job. If all else failed the regiment, massive men in kilts who favored bayonets over bullets, would usually prevail. The Beattie family had always been very big in the Argylls, and the Major's son was now following in the footsteps of three or four earlier generations. The Major lived in a small cottage in the village, quietly drinking away his pension.

I hadn't been sailing at Findhorn for very long when the Major's daughter arrived on the scene. She was a comely, well-built girl who could probably have made mincemeat of me if she had wished to. Fortunately, she didn't, and we soon struck up a pleasantly warm weekend relationship. We would sail in the afternoon, then kill several hours and large quantities of good whisky in the bar. If her father could make it home unaided, she would cook us dinner. He would then retire to bed with dignity while I would proceed to lay siege to his daughter's well-defended virtue. We did really enjoy each other's company and kept in touch for several years after I had left Lossiemouth.

One of my problems at this time, which took me several years to deal with, was the unshakable conviction that large quantities of alcohol made me a better driver, while in fact quite the opposite was true. It wasn't just me; Tom Wolfe in his great book *The Right Stuff* defines the "holy coordinates of a naval pilot's life. . . Flying and Drinking and Drinking and Driving." Towards the end of September this aberration nearly finished my flying career.

John Matthews was dating Helen Anderson, a very attractive Wren. He had also acquired a 1922 Lagonda, a marvelous old car with wooden spoked wheels and a fussy engine that required hand cranking to get it started. Helen had a midnight curfew on Saturdays, and around 11 p.m. John told me he was much too drunk to drive and that I would have to take Helen home. I said I was too drunk to drive too, but that since I was spending the night at the Fairie's it didn't matter. John said that I couldn't be spending the night at the Fairie's, and nor could I be too drunk to drive, since I was taking Helen home. He also argued that my motorcycle was much easier to drive than his Lagonda, except for the starting off bit, which he would help me with. This logic seemed irrefutable at the time, though in the cold light of the next day it did appear to have some weaknesses.

We got Helen onto the back of my bike, and John held it steady while I got it started and then gave us a shove to get it going. We sped off up the road, doing quite well considering, until we came to a rather alarming bend. Try as I might, I could not persuade the motorcycle to go in the same direction as the road, and we hit the bank with a tremendous thud. Helen went into the bank and I sailed over it, catching the barbed wire full in my mouth. Fortunately, we hadn't gone very far and rescuers from Findhorn came running, taxis were sent for, and we were both soon safely in the naval hospital at

Lossiemouth. I had knocked two front teeth quite far back and cut my mouth open, requiring a fair number of stitches and leaving a scar that thankfully faded with age. The naval doctor, ascertaining that I had a considerable amount of anesthetic on board already, felt more would do harm, so stitched me up as I was. Helen had burst a blood vessel in her eye, but thankfully ended up with nothing more than a terrible shiner. Her mother, who must have been an extraordinarily understanding woman, kept on calling Helen to find out if I was all right. We spent time in the sickbay but, evidence of the tolerance of the time, nothing else bad happened to us.

I had to face charges in court in Elgin, which a local lawyer managed to get reduced to careless driving. We went out together to view the dangerous bend that had proved my downfall. It was hard to find. I guess a surveyor with a theodolite might have proved a curve, but to the naked eye it looked straight as an arrow. The motorcycle never really recovered from its impact with the bank and had to be written off. I lost my license for a month, but made Matthews pay the price by becoming my chauffeur.

When we arrived at Lossiemouth we found that our numbers had been increased by the addition of several pilots who had flown with the Royal Navy during World War II, gone back into civilian life, and then been recruited as part of the Korean War build up. Referred to as "retreads" they obviously had no need for the earlier basic flying but had been given a brief refresher before joining us at the Operational Flying School. Four out of the six were from New Zealand, reflecting the disproportionate number of wartime Fleet Air Arm pilots from that splendid country. They were refreshingly casual about the naval side of things, obviously in it first for the flying, then for the money, and very much last for the geopolitics. They provided a significant leavening of humor for our course.

Britain in 1952, although no longer governed by socialists, was still suffering from a residue of wartime austerity, even though we had by then been technically at peace for six years. One evidence of this was the fact that meat, much of which had to be imported, was still rationed (readers with sharp memories may recall the difficulty we had several years earlier turning one of our own home grown pigs into edible pork). In fact, as part of the belt tightening resulting from the new and unexpected Korean War, the meat ration had been reduced to about four ounces (yes, one quarter pounder!) a week. Our New Zealanders, coming from a country where meat, or at least sheep meat, was cheap and plentiful, considered this an intolerable deprivation. They would disappear up isolated glens and persuade sheep farmers to sell them large pieces of mutton for considerable sums of money. Our rooms were heated by coal stoves – and given enough coal, the flat top would glow red-hot. A slab of raw mutton placed on top would cook reasonably well, and could then be torn apart by bare hands and eaten. Often coming back from the pub late at night we would smell the delicious fragrance of roasting meat and, knowing the New Zealanders were at work, drop casually into their rooms in anticipation of being handed a sizzling chop or two.

Most of our flying at Lossiemouth took place at Milltown, a satellite field a few miles down the road. A bus picked us up outside the mess after breakfast and brought us back at the end of the day. Brian Jones would drive over in his car, and those of us who dearly needed a few minutes extra sleep would load into it and chase the bus at lethal speed along the lanes, arriving with a few seconds to spare.

Some wealthy Scottish landowner had a house just off the end of one of the Milltown runways and, at the time Princess Margaret, the Queen's then unmarried younger sister, was an item with the laird's son. The Princess liked to sleep late so whenever she was in residence we had to adjust our training in order to avoid flying noisily over the house. The Royals impacted us in another way: the Princess was a passionate devotee of Scottish country dancing and was liable to call up the Lossiemouth wardroom (officers' mess) on any evening and demand that some male dancing partners be sent over. Thus, to avoid any possible embarrassment, we all had to learn to do eightsome reels and other horrible Scottish inventions. A local dancing master was brought in weekly and we would swirl round and round to the ghastly music that only bagpipes can produce. I never managed to catch on and was always in the wrong place at the wrong time, going in the wrong direction. Thankfully Her Royal Highness never sent for me in person (not surprising, she almost certainly had no knowledge that I even existed), since I understand she was intolerant of many things, including inelegance on the dance floor. One wretched young officer attending one of her parties announced at about one o'clock that he must get to bed because he had to fly quite early in the morning. The princess gave him a withering look and told him crisply that no one was permitted to leave the room until she chose to retire.

Most of our instructors had seen combat in either World War II or Korea, some of them both. We learned tactical combat maneuvers, involving loose formations of four aircraft in two pairs. These formations were quite different from the so-called "Vic" of three, used in the Battle of Britain a decade or so earlier, and owed much to the United States Navy's "Thatch" weave, developed for warfare against the Japanese Navy in World War II. We learned how to maneuver such a four-airplane group while maintaining a good lookout all around, and the vital importance of each number two covering his leader's tail. The leader of the four would be an instructor – ours was a Korean War veteran – and his directions carried the authenticity of recent experience.

The scenery in the north of Scotland is particularly beautiful: mostly open heather, broken by majestic mountains (the Cairngorms) and stunning lakes (Loch Lomond) and from the air we could see far off the Islands of Skye and the Orkneys. Back in the 1950's there was very little civilian competition for airspace, and we could fly pretty much where we wanted. Also there was minimal restriction on low flying, so a lot of our trips were carried out just above the ground, or the waves. Occasionally we would break off into pairs and practice shooting each other down. Our planes had a quite sophisticated gyroscopic gun sight and we would approach head on, reversing course in a turn designed to keep the center pip of the sight on the opponent's cockpit. Often these interceptions started off at quite a distance, the attacker being controlled by radar until he had the "enemy" in sight.

PRINCESS MARGARET 1950

"...the Princess was a passionate devotee of Scottish country dancing and was liable to call up the Lossiemouth wardroom on any evening and demand that some male dancing partners be sent over. Thus, to avoid any possible embarrassment, we all had to learn to do eightsome reels and other horrible Scottish inventions."

It was at Lossiemouth that I took the opportunity to fly a Seafire, the naval version of the Spitfire. I had watched the forerunners of these incredible airplanes defeat the Luftwaffe in the summer of 1940. Now, twelve years later, I was given some cursory ground instruction and then allowed to take the beautiful little machine away on my own. There was no dual-control variant available for flight training: you just read an instruction book, strapped yourself in, started the motor (another Rolls Royce Griffon), and away you went. Small, incredibly maneuverable, fast and really quite easy to fly, my main memory of this grand experience was the sensation of wearing the plane rather than just sitting in it. It was like a good suit; it seemed to be part of one's body rather than an appendage.

I became very fond of Scotland and consequently truly enjoyed Lossiemouth (my relationship with Miss Beattie certainly helped). It was a good learning experience, on the ground and in the air. I added another seventy-five hours to my logbook and my final report said that I needed experience to temper my enthusiasm.

After graduation from the first operational flying school we were separated into two groups. The fighter pilots stayed at Lossiemouth and learned more advanced fighter combat tactics. The strike pilots were sent to Eglinton in Northern Ireland for an anti-submarine course, a ground attack course and, most importantly the final and most demanding rite of naval aviator passage: carrier landing qualification.

I loved Scotland in the fall; the autumn weather seemed invariably fine, the air clear, the water sparkling, the people friendly. Northern Ireland, on the other hand, was miserable. It had not yet become the terribly unsettled place it turned into a few decades later, but the root causes of part-buried problems were not hard to see: there were essentially two classes, Protestant and Catholics, and the Protestants had the power, the money, and the best jobs.

We arrived at Eglinton in late November. Our rooms leaked and were three hundred yards across a field from the nearest bathroom. It rained continuously. Indeed, so hard that we were there three weeks before we could fly, thus spending a lot of time in the classroom. After a while, however, the weather cleared and we took to the air, working with submarines, learning how to bomb moving targets, and understanding the intricacies of sonar work. A lot of the air work was done at night.

SEAFIRE

"It was at Lossiemouth that I took the opportunity to fly a Seafire.... I had watched the forerunners of these incredible airplanes defeat the Luftwaffe in the summer of 1940. .... Small, incredibly maneuverable, fast and really quite easy to fly, my main memory of this grand experience was the sensation of wearing the plane rather than just sitting in it. It was like a good suit; it seemed to be part of one's body rather than an appendage."

Soon we were introduced to the techniques that would ultimately, we hoped, enable us to land safely on the deck of a carrier. We had two "batsmen" assigned to our course, Landing Signals Officers whose job it was to advise us what we should be doing in order to touch down at the right place and thus catch one of the arrester wires running at right angles across the flight deck. Their principal means of communication were two bats, about the size of small tennis racquets, each made of brightly colored fluorescent material, one held in each hand. The learning process consisted of a number of Airfield Dummy Deck Landings ("ADDL's")—141 to be precise in my case, which was about normal, designed so that when we finally got out to the ship, we would do exactly what was required, accurately but instinctively.

BATSMAN GIVING LANDING SIGNALS

"We had two "batsmen" assigned to our course, Landing Signals Officers whose job it was to advise us how to touch down at the right place and thus catch one of the arrester wires running at right angles across the flight deck. Their principal means of communication were two bats, about the size of small tennis racquets, each made of brightly colored fluorescent material, one held in each hand".

I worked most with "Junior" Turnbull, a Lieutenant who claimed in his introductory talk that, by the time he was finished with us, he would know us better than our own mothers did. I think he was right. He explained the signals: leaning one way or the other to indicate that we should tighten or untighten the turn; arms above the head indicating too high; arms held down meant too low; arms waving in front indicated too slow; while one arm chopping down his side told us we were too fast. All of these were advisory, although ignoring them meant real trouble. The only truly mandatory signals were the "cut", a chop of the paddles across the body signaling the pilot to fully close the throttle, and the "wave off", a frantic waving of the paddles above his head, telling the pilot to go round and try again. Ignoring a cut or a wave off could result in a real mess, as we shall see shortly.

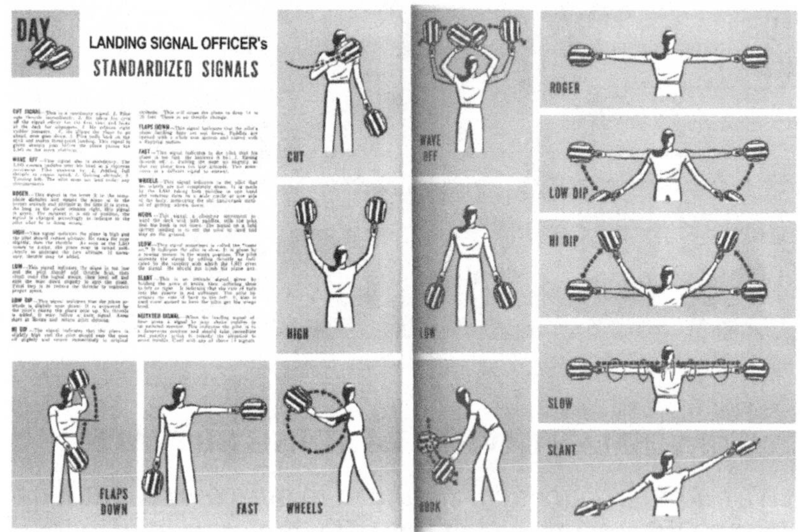

LANDING SIGNALS (1952 VINTAGE)

"The only truly mandatory signals were the "cut", a chop of the paddles across the body signaling the pilot to fully close the throttle, and the "wave off", a frantic waving of the paddles above his head. Ignoring a cut or a wave off could result in a real mess, as we shall see shortly. All of these signals were given with a pair of brightly colored fluorescent paddles."

Junior in fact had two tasks: to teach us these signals, and especially to wean the "retreads" off the old British ones used in the prior war which were, in some important respects quite the opposite to the American ones. For them, paddles held high meant go higher, while held low meant go lower.

Confusion could lead to serious trouble and, as with so many things in those days, as the North Atlantic Treaty Organization slowly creaked into life, it was the powerful Americans who chose the way things should be while we dutifully followed,

The batsmen had Wren assistants who would take notes about each pilot's approach, to be discussed during late afternoon debriefing. Junior used his own shorthand: "TIBMN" meant Thumb in Bum, Mind in Neutral, and was deemed severe criticism. His note about retreads who could not understand the new technique is unprintable here and made the Wrens blush.

For our ADDL's practice we would fly over to Limavady, a satellite airfield, two to a plane. There would normally be three or four airplanes in the landing pattern, one up wind, a couple downwind, and one on finals. Pilots not flying would hang around and watch. The pattern was flown at 150 ft. and reasonably tight in; the final approach speed was, I recall, about 90 knots, which did not leave a lot of margin above a stall. We were warned quite strongly about the dreaded "torque stall," the main danger during a wave off. With the airplane flying at a speed close to that below which it would stall and fall out of the sky, the sudden application of all the 2,200 horsepower the Rolls Royce Griffon engine was capable of producing, could have the rather unnerving effect of making the aircraft spin around its huge four bladed propeller, rolling over on its back before crashing into the ground. Since recovery from this situation was virtually unknown, we were advised not to try it. The best way to avoid it was to be gentle with the throttle.

Social life at Eglinton was a bit less lively than at Lossiemouth. Londonderry was a dank and ill-equipped little city whose streets seemed permanently coated with a thin sheen of wet mud. The people all looked downtrodden, and probably were, and smelt strongly of damp unwashed clothing. What entertainment we could discover there took place mostly in the bar of the Eglinton Wardroom.

There was, however, one unique institution, a pub called Joe Knox's that had existed long before the airfield. Someone with imagination had run the airfield boundary right through the middle of the bar, so that you could enter the front door from outside the field, and then go out of the back door and be right on the base. What this meant for security I don't know, but it provided a welcome port of call on Saturdays when flying was over and everyone gathered for an afternoon of recreational drinking.

Another advantage of Eglinton was its closeness to the Irish Republic, whose bars, unlike those in (British) Northern Ireland, were allowed to stay open on Sundays. The wardroom bar normally operated from noon until two p.m. on Sundays, and then closed again until six. At closing time someone would arrange a fleet of taxis and we would pile into them with a crowd of Wrens and set off across the border to little towns with names like Muff or Buncrana, where there were splendidly hospitable Irish pubs that welcomed our custom all afternoon, offering cozy peat burning fires and large quantities of inexpensive Bushmills whiskey.

By the time we went on Christmas leave I had some 120 hours in Fireflies, and thought I was pretty good. No one had told me to the contrary: life might have been better if they had. After two weeks in London and at home I met up with various friends at Liverpool Station for the long train ride up to Heysham, where we would catch the boat across the Irish Channel for Belfast. There was a lot of beer drunk on the train, and more on the boat; none of us had cabins and what little sleep we got was sitting up in the noisy smoke-filled saloon. There was only a chance for a quick nap as the train from Belfast to Londonderry lazed its way across the moist Ulster countryside, and then we were at Londonderry.

Back at Eglinton there was a call to test fly the airplanes, which had not been used for over two weeks. I volunteered.

(Big mistake: experienced members of the armed services, regardless of nationality, know that the most important rule is "never volunteer".) We have already learned something about this particular weakness of mine. I got into my flight kit and took off for a half hour flying around the local area. I decided to try my hand at the ADDL pattern, did a couple of uneventful circuits at Limavady, and then headed for home. The pattern at Eglinton was normal until the final approach, where I allowed the airspeed to get dangerously low. A slight shaking of the stick indicated the onset of a stall; without thinking I jammed open the throttle; the engine responded immediately and powerfully, as did the airplane, which reared up in the air and then over on its back in the first half turn of a spin. Within seconds I was pointing straight down at the ground, some 400 ft. below me and coming up fast; there was no room for any of the recovery procedures I had so painstakingly learned. I knew I was dead. There was no alternative, and it was all rather undramatic, no quick passage of my life in front of my eyes, not even a feeling of regret. Just dead.

Many years later I read a remarkable book by the medical doctor Sherwin Nuland: *How We Die*. Most significantly in the present context, Nuland believes that, contrary to popular opinion, when we know we are about to die our life's story does not flash in front of our eyes. Rather, when death appears inevitable, the dying person is surrounded by a great calmness, which was my precise experience on January 8, 1953 – except that I did not die. But this event has remained engraved in my memory ever since, a really significant moment in my life.

Amazingly, the approach to the active runway at Eglinton lay over soft ground, made even more so by the recent heavy rain. The Firefly landed in the bog and buried its nose up to some three or four feet. One wing broke off, as did the tail. The cockpit was untouched, and I realized that I was sitting there, alive, conscious only of a slight hissing noise. I loosened my safety harness, fortunately tight, and slipped out of the cockpit. The canopy was normally kept open for actual or practice deck landings. Miraculously, there was no fire, a big relief since I was sitting on top of some 120 gallons of high-octane gasoline.

The crowd of people who had come running from the airfield could not believe that anyone could have lived through the crash. I was whisked off to the sickbay where the only thing wrong was a bruise on my forehead where it had struck the gun sight and a place on my leg where I had lost all sensation. I could still stick a pin in it without any feeling thirty years later. My pulse was 140 and took some 2 days to come down to its normal level.

Along with other lessons learned that day was the fact that although being lucky is important, it is also smart to have a helping hand from a higher power: a brief "thank you" to God at the right time wouldn't come amiss in a pilot's self-preservation kit.

Junior Turnbull visited me in the sickbay. He said it appeared there would be no disciplinary action. He pointed out, however, that my wheels were up and that, had I landed in that condition, I might have been in serious trouble! My navy issue watch came off in the crash and disappeared. No one seemed too worried about the total loss of one of Her Majesty's valuable airplanes, but the supply people were still bothering me about the watch over a year later.

The official endorsement in my logbook for that day reads: "January 8, 1953: After a detail of general flying practice on return from leave, pilot allowed aircraft to stall on approach and spin into soft ground —pilot error." I am told I am probably one of the few people ever to have spun an airplane that close to the ground and lived to talk about it. I think it was the phrase "on return from leave," with all the related connotations of a liquid passage across the Irish Sea, which saved the day for me. I was still technically a student, and someone should have noticed that I was wearing the journey rather badly. I flew again five days later, with no ill effects.

It was a gray rainy day with a slight chop on a leaden Irish sea when I first caught sight of HMS *Triumph*, the carrier used at the time for deck landing training. She had just emerged from a light shower and her empty deck was glistening wet. She looked very, very small. But Junior had done his job well: I landed on safely and spent the next five days enjoying the hospitality of the ship and completing the required number of deck landings, in my case twenty-one. It was at this point, carrier qualification completed, that I officially became a naval aviator.

Actually, in my opinion the hardest part was the business we hadn't practiced (and for obvious reasons couldn't), taking off. For most of our take-offs we didn't use the catapult. We were parked at the after end of the flight deck with brakes firmly on. A man with a green flag pointed it at the next pilot in line, waved it around indicating to him to gun the engine until it was producing as much power as the brakes could hold. When the flag was dropped he released the brakes, opened the throttle up full, and the aircraft accelerated down the deck. The plane had a strong tendency to swing to the right due to the rotation of the propeller. This had to be carefully corrected as the carrier's superstructure loomed very close to the starboard wing tip. The end of the deck came up fast, there was usually a little sink over the round down, the sea looked awfully close, and then you were airborne. Since this was before the age of rescue helicopters, a "plane guard" destroyer was stationed neatly in front of the carrier for take offs, and astern of it for landings. Fortunately, I never had to be picked up, but later I did see it done for somebody else and they were reassuringly good at it.

Most of the time on *Triumph* we would come straight round again to land back on. After a good approach the hook should catch the third or fourth of six wires. The plane decelerated very rapidly, causing the tail to rise into the air, and I recall a lot of rather expensive noise of scraping metal as the hook caught. For the first few times it was a somewhat mind-numbing experience, best described as a controlled crash. All the time one was conscious of the two high wire barriers, in front of the plane, seemingly only a few feet away. When the plane was safely down, the barrier was lowered and the plane could taxi forward out of the way. If your hook failed to catch any of the nine arrester wires, there was no choice: you crashed into the barrier which would normally mean that the airplane ended up with its propeller all bent, its nose resting rather humbly on the deck, and its tail up in the air. There was a gun sponson just aft of the island superstructure called the "goofers" where off-duty sailors would gather to watch the fun.

MICHAEL LANDING ON HMS *TRIUMPH*

SEEN THROUGH CRASH BARRIER WIRES

"All the time one was conscious of the two high wire barriers, in front of the plane, seemingly only a few feet away. When the plane was safely down, the barrier was lowered, and the plane could taxi forward out of the way."

RESULT OF CRASHING INTO THE BARRIER

"If your hook failed to catch any of the nine arrester wires, there was no choice: you crashed into the barrier... the airplane ended up with its propeller all bent, its nose resting rather humbly on the deck, and its tail up in the air."

After a couple of days of normal take-offs and landings we were introduced to the catapult (booster), which was a moderately hair-raising adventure. The plane was held back by a "weak link" piece of steel. A bridle attached to the landing gear was connected to the catapult. The engine was revved up to full throttle, the pilot signaled his readiness to the catapult officer who, when all was clear, dropped his flag. The hydraulic catapult surged forward, taking the plane with it, and breaking the weak link. The bridle would drop away as the airplane became airborne. (Hopefully. If anything went wrong with the engine on take-off there was no opportunity to rethink things.)

ROCKET-ASSISTED TAKE OFF (RATO)

"...the most sphincter-tightening and mind-boggling experience of all was rocket-assisted takeoff (RATO) – not for its physical demands (for in that respect nothing could beat the catapult) but because it all seemed so unscientific and unmilitary."

Lastly the most sphincter-tightening and mind-boggling experience of all was rocket-assisted takeoff (RATO) – not for its physical demands (for in that respect nothing could beat the catapult) but because it all seemed so unscientific and unmilitary. To assist takeoff in low wind conditions or when the airplane was heavily loaded and the catapult was unavailable, a bundle of rockets would be strapped onto either side of the fuselage. The take-off would be made normally from the flight deck, except that when the plane went past a marker flag the pilot would press a button. The results were startling. With luck, all the rockets would go off at the same time and the plane would leap into the air, trailing smoke and bits of firework debris. Without luck, only one side would ignite and the plane, unless very skillfully flown, would skid over the side into the water. There will be more about this later.

Learning how to land on the deck of an aircraft carrier is a demanding activity that requires an excellent teacher. Luck was with us during our training and all our time in *Triumph*. Our instructors were wonderful, nothing went wrong and no one got hurt.

But a couple of our group didn't satisfy Junior's exacting standards and had to be sent ashore for further practice. Sadly, one of them was my friend Brian Jones, who spent three months at the school where they trained batsmen, flying round and round the pattern helping them learn their signals and hopefully improving his own landing technique. Based at Abbotsinch, this unit was always referred to as the Clockwork Mice. "He's spending some time with the Mice" was a rather curious phrase unless you knew that it meant the person concerned had been deemed in need of some deck landing practice. Although we saw each other from time to time, Brian and I never served together again until we both went to the Central Flying School to become instructors.

Back at Eglinton I learned that I was designated to join one of the squadrons due to go to Korea. This was very much what I wanted; I certainly was not interested in spending the next few years flying around the ocean dropping sonar buoys and the Wyvern of my dreams, having accumulated a lot of developmental problems, appeared to remain a long way from realization. Like most young pilots contemplating their first combat missions, my principal concern was that the war not be over before I got there. However, I did have one more thing to do before I was considered fit to keep the world free from communism: the Ground Attack Course.

This involved almost too much pure enjoyment for it to be deemed a serious part of our flying training. Two of us were assigned to it when I did it. We each had an airplane, and mine was maintained by two good-looking Wrens. We were given a large quantity of ammunition, rockets and bombs, and a firing range on the coast to shoot it all at. Two, sometimes three times a day, we loaded up with ordnance and sashayed off to do our worst with it. The standard maneuver was a rocket or bomb attack from a sixty-degree dive. We flew the plane at about six thousand feet until the target was under the wing, and then heaved it up and over so that the nose appeared to be pointing vertically downwards. Indeed, the trick was to be sure to get the dive steep enough. You placed the center pip of the gyro gun-sight on the target and held it there until about a thousand feet above the ground when you released the bombs or fired the rockets, and then pulled up in a climb that would drain all the blood from the brain. The range officer called out the hits and misses—over or under, left or right–after a while we became fairly competent.

But the most pleasurable part of all this was strafing. The Firefly had four twenty-millimeter cannons that fired together when you pushed the button, making a most satisfactory noise and creating a lot of dust and debris on the ground. The recoil from all four guns was amazing; indeed, we were told that a trick to use if ever we had to make a forced landing at sea ("ditch") was to fire the guns just before hitting the water in order to slow the airplane down. We must have pumped out thousands of rounds of ammunition with joyous abandon, returning only to have our faithful Wrens reload with more. Winter was coming to an end, spring was in the air, and we were being paid and otherwise encouraged to spend time wastefully with noisy and expensive toys.

One day, with nothing better to do, I climbed to about 15,000 feet and flew out over the Irish Sea towards Scotland. Although it was a beautiful day, there were some enormous cumulus clouds building to the northeast. I found myself flying down valleys and over mountainsides, all consisting of no more than the water vapor of the clouds, but still appearing very solid. The sensation of speed was incredible and the challenge of fitting the plane down through a narrow corridor between the white walls of a deep valley was truly exhilarating. It was one of those days when, if you didn't already love flying, you would have to become infatuated. The kind of day I would feel the urge to thank my friend Richard for casually tossing me the letter that had initially headed me in this direction. Royal Canadian Air Force pilot/poet John Magee wrote "High Flight" in 1941, just before he was killed in action. He said it all better than I can:

Oh! I have slipped the surly bonds of earth
And danced the skies on laughter-silvered wings;
Sunward I've climbed, and joined the tumbling mirth
Of sun-split clouds—and done a hundred things
You have not dreamed of—wheeled and soared and swung
High in the sunlit silence. Hov'ring there,
I've chased the shouting wind along, and flung
My eager craft through footless halls of air.
Up, up the long, delirious, burning blue
I've topped the wind-swept heights with easy grace
Where never lark, or even eagle flew—
And, while with silent lifting mind I've trod
The high untrespassed sanctity of space,
Put out my hand and touched the face of God.

In early February I was on leave to await posting to my first operational squadron. It was a tense period, since I knew I would soon be going off to war, but wasn't sure when. Nor did I know what to expect when I got there. I couldn't go away or get involved in any long-range project since I was really only at home on a day-to-day basis. I know it tried my parents too, since they couldn't be sure when or whether they would see me again.

Chapter 7

LEARNING DURING A SMALL WAR, WITH REAL BOMBS AND REAL BULLETS

Finally, in late March I got news that, while a relief, was not altogether encouraging. The Korean War had broken out about a year before I joined the Navy. A number of members of the United Nations, led by the United States, had come to the rescue of South Korea (under attack from communist North Korea). Britain's main contribution was naval aviation and several army divisions. The Royal Navy, and its next of kin, the Royal Australian Navy, provided two aircraft carriers which together with a United States Navy carrier, rotated duties off the west coast of Korea. The Royal Navy's Fleet Air Arm had stepped up recruiting and training in response to this new requirement, and my service was part of that response.

HMS *Ocean* was one of the Royal Navy carriers involved. She carried some thirty-four aircraft: 807 Squadron of Sea Fury fighter/bombers, and 810 Squadron of Fairey Fireflies. During a practice sortie the last Firefly pilot to land on had tried to go round after being given the cut, an unforgivable sin. His plane had jumped over both barriers and landed in the deck park which at the time was full of airplanes, newly refueled and thus highly explosive. There had been massive destruction of aircraft and several deaths, including two or three aircrew. I was to go to Malta and join 810 Squadron as a replacement. A week later I was a passenger on a naval charter flight to the Mediterranean, ready for the big adventure.

Malta was heat and sunshine and the most improbable combination of odors and noises and mahogany-faced Mediterranean people. Perhaps at the time the most Catholic country in the world, naval people summed up its ambience as "smells, bells and babies." Hal Far was a Royal Navy air station on Malta, created to provide support for Britain's Mediterranean Fleet.

WARDROOM MESS HALL AT HALFAR

"Built in classical British colonial style with long shady verandas, its rooms cooled by the massive stone blocks typical of Maltese construction"

I checked into the wardroom at Hal Far, a dusty place bathed in blinding sunlight, but one I will always remember with affection. Built in classical British colonial style with long shady verandas, its rooms cooled by the massive stone blocks typical of Maltese construction, it was at the time a crossroads of Empire, a watering spot for naval flyers going to or coming from England or the Far East. 810 Squadron's offices, also carefully constructed of local stone, were located on the edge of the field and it was there I met 810's Squadron Commander "Pants" Bloomer and the Squadron's other pilots and observers.

810 SQUADRON

Michael, first row, second from left; Bloomer, center, second row.

Naturally, the Squadron, although in a state of some shock over the recent debacle, was anxious to be on its way to the Far East. Fresh faces like mine were welcome and the Squadron was ready to put us to work. First, not having flown for some time, I had to demonstrate my deck landing skills. A couple of days of ADDLs (simulated deck landings) were considered enough by Johnnie Mortimer, one of *Ocean's* two batsmen, and I was cleared to do some real carrier landings. *Ocean* was in harbor having some defect corrected, but *Indomitable*, a much larger fleet carrier, was available off Malta, and I was told to go out and do a few landings on her. Out at sea she looked huge after *Triumph*. Maybe too huge.

I came into the landing pattern and did the normal turn in opposite the island. All went well until I got the "cut," when everything suddenly went wrong. Much too far to port, my hook caught the wire way well over to the side of the flight deck so that I landed on one of the ship's gun turrets mounted with their tops flush with the deck. Johnny Mortimer, seeing several tons of Firefly about to decapitate him, vaulted head first into a net placed under his platform for just that purpose. The plane's left wheel ended up in the catwalk, and the whole episode came to a rather undignified and lopsided finale. Sheepish but unhurt, I climbed out of the cockpit. The rescue team, seeing that there would be no fire to test their skills, put away their axes and asbestos suits, while the watchers in the "goofers," disappointed, went about their business. My friend Richard, who unknown to me at the time, had just joined *Indomitable* as part of the engineering crew, had come to see what all the noise was about. He looked at me disparagingly and said, "Oh, it's you Coles. I might have known it." and went on about his business.

Probably the most embarrassing thing about the whole episode was a widely distributed signal, which announced that Sub-Lieutenant Coles had crashed on *Indomitable* causing substantial damage to the arrester gear, meaning that the ship would be out of action for some weeks. Next most embarrassing was meeting Bloomer for only the second time and having to explain why I had badly bent one of his airplanes and its attendant ship. Clearly, he was getting somewhat tired of deck crashes and did not wholly welcome a new pilot of such doubtful competence.

MICHAEL'S FIRST (AND ONLY) DECK LANDING CRASH

"The plane's left wheel ended up in the catwalk, and the whole episode came to a rather undignified and lopsided finale. Sheepish but unhurt, I climbed out of the cockpit.... My friend Richard, who unknown to me at the time, had just joined Indomitable *as part of her engineering crew, had come to see what all the noise was about. He looked at me disparagingly and said, "Oh, it's you Coles. I might have known it." and went on about his business."*

A few days later, after another spell of ADDLs at Hal Far, I flew out to *Ocean* and completed four satisfactory deck landings. It was good of the Queen to trust me with more of her equipment, and I was happy her confidence had not been misplaced. Later we flew back out to the ship, which then set sail for the Far East. I was still a little shaky, but no one was making "leave him behind" noises. We flew every day as we made our way across the Mediterranean, a day of rest as we passed through the Suez Canal, and then more flying in the Red Sea, where I celebrated my 21st birthday. Most of the time we exercised various combat maneuvers in flights of four or as a squadron of twelve, each plane with a full bomb or rocket load. We would finish with target practice, using our ordnance against a raft towed behind the ship. Spotters on board would judge how well we were aiming, and after a while we all became quite proficient at using our weapons.

Lt. Cdr. Bloomer, known to all as "Pants," was still somewhat cool, worried that I might do some devastating damage to ship or airplane or even a member of his squadron. However, one day in the Indian Ocean he called me over and said that he thought things were going much better and that from now on he wanted me to fly as his wingman–the person responsible for minding his tail while he concentrated on the job in hand. This was considered quite prestigious, and I wondered what I had done to deserve it. Only several months later did I find out that with the mail brought on board at Suez was the transcript of the various reports accumulated during my flying training. The final assessment read: "Provided this officer is handled intelligently, he will become a good officer and an outstanding aviator." Pants had obviously decided to protect his investment and handle me intelligently, whatever that meant. Regardless of the reason, things did start to go a lot better. I became a consistent and reliable deck lander and completed over 150 more during my time in the navy without laying a scratch on ship, plane, or self. Whether I ever became an outstanding aviator I can leave to the judgment of those of my grandchildren who were bold enough to fly with me as passengers in my own airplane many years later.

As we moved from the Red Sea into the Indian Ocean the weather grew hotter and hotter. Flying conditions were excellent: visibility almost always unlimited and the few clouds in the sky were small fluffy and friendly. Below decks, however, things were a lot less pleasant. HMS *Ocean* had been designed for the closing effort in the Pacific War and was thus intended for use in the tropics. This meant that certain working compartments and living spaces were air-conditioned. Nine of us Sub-Lieutenants lived in a sort of dormitory known as the Casbah, located right under the flight deck just aft of the catapult. It was notionally air-conditioned and the designers, presumably hoping to trap all the hard-earned cool air, had hermetically sealed it. Unfortunately, air-conditioning was a relatively new idea to British shipbuilders, and ours didn't work all that well, and paradoxically, though understandably, worked less well as the climate grew hotter. So those of us assigned to the Casbah found ourselves immediately under a steel deck, which in turn was exposed to a tropical sun, without benefit of any natural ventilation, and blessed at short and unpredictable intervals by a thin trickle of partially cooled air. Most of us gave up and chose to sleep on deck, using portable camp beds that the ship kindly provided. For those hardy souls who stuck to the Casbah's sweaty humidity, sleep beyond 5:00 a.m. was impossible since that was typically the time of the first aircraft launch. The roar of the catapult was ear-splitting on deck and appeared to be amplified within the close confines of our quarters.

HMS *OCEAN* 1952

"Nine of us Sub-Lieutenants lived in a sort of dormitory known as the Casbah, located right under the flight deck just aft of the catapult...The roar of the catapult was ear-splitting on deck and appeared to be amplified within the close confines of our quarters."

Singapore, our first real taste of civilization since Malta, was still very much a British colony where all the trappings of Empire, although slightly tarnished, remained superficially in place. As visiting officers, we were made honorary members of the Tanglin Club, a truly luxurious oasis right in the middle of the city. We floated languorously in the pool while a white-coated Chinese servant brought cold gin and tonics; England and its residual socialist austerity seemed a long way away.

There was a war going on in Malaya (post-colonial: Malaysia). British troops, to some extent supported by the indigenous Malays, were trying to put down a communist-inspired insurrection that mostly involved the local Chinese. The war was far from being won, and there were large parts of Singapore deemed too dangerous and declared out of bounds to British troops and sailors at night. After a rather decorous welcoming cocktail party, half a dozen of us decided to seek out some nightlife. One thing led to another until, sometime after midnight, we were in a taxi heading off to what the driver assured us was a splendid place with very clean girls. Cleanliness is, of course, subjective, and I was among those sober enough to determine that none of the ladies measured up to our ideas of wholesomeness. Four of our group went upstairs, while Reg Simmonds, TJ Penfold and I sat on the steps outside to await their pleasure. Suddenly, with a loud blaring of sirens several Land Rovers containing a large contingent of Singapore's Red Caps (Military Police) came roaring up. Found in a strictly forbidden area, in imminent danger of kidnapping or worse by the communists, and despite protestations that we were new to the place, we were placed under arrest. As we drove off, each securely held between a couple of large Red Caps, we looked back and saw the prospective fornicators, arms around their chosen girls, waving at us from the balcony. Someone from the navy came down to get us out, and we spent the rest of our time in Singapore confined to our ship. The libertines returned the following morning, unchastened and unpunished. Such are the wages of virtue.

From Singapore we entered the South China Sea. British carriers in the neighborhood of Malaya were encouraged to bomb, and otherwise menace, carefully selected targets, presumably with the intention of frightening the communist insurrectionists. Early one morning a flight of *Ocean*'s Sea Fury squadron took off to attack a "known Chicom assembly area." Unfortunately, someone had goofed and they did a considerable amount of damage to some important person's tin mine and a neighboring "safe" village. *Ocean* was told not to mount any more attacks, and rather crossly, to go away and not come back again. This was considered a quite inauspicious entry into combat operations.

My first sight of Hong Kong was a rather dramatic one. As part of a flag-showing exercise, *Ocean* had been told to launch her aircraft while some sixty miles southeast of the island in order to simulate an attack on the harbor. Unfortunately, the cloud base was under a thousand feet, which made any real test of the harbor defenses impossible. Nevertheless, Pants decided that we would show that we had arrived. I was flying on his wing and, after he brought us into close formation, could do little but watch my leader and try to keep precisely in position. Out of the corner of my eye, however, I could see that we were right down on the water flying into a dark tunnel with what appeared to be mountainous islands on either side, sea below and clouds right above. Things flashed by: masts, buildings, junks, and then, for a brief second, the houses of the Hong Kong wealthy stretching up into the clouds on the Peak. It must have been only a few minutes before we were out over the open sea again, but it seemed an awfully long time while we were doing it. When we got back to *Ocean*, Pants assured us that he knew Hong Kong harbor like the back of his hand, but it would have been comforting if he had told us so beforehand.

We anchored for a couple of days in the harbor that we had seen so briefly that morning. Amazingly for those of us who hadn't been there before, the ship was suddenly invaded by a swarm of young Chinese girls wielding paint chipping hammers and paintbrushes. "Jenny's Side Party" was a Hong

Kong institution; money from the ship's welfare fund was expended to save the sailors the grief of painting ship in the tropics. Jenny and her girls would have the largest ship rust-free and painted spick and span in an incredibly short time. Jenny served the Royal Navy faithfully from 1928 until the British left Hong Kong in 1997. I read that she died in 2009, aged 92.

JENNY'S SIDE PARTY SCRUBBING HMS *OCEAN*

"the ship was suddenly invaded by a swarm of young Chinese girls wielding paint chipping hammers and paintbrushes. 'Jenny's Side Party' was a Hong Kong institution"

The Korean War was the first attempt by a multi-national alliance using the authority of the United Nations to counter an act of aggression by one country using massive force to invade the territory of another. United Nations resolutions had been approved by most member nations, resolutions that the Russians, due to a fortuitous error on the part of Moscow, had not been able to veto. Command of the United Nations forces fighting in Korea was assumed naturally by the Americans who (apart from the often-ignored South Koreans) were making the largest troop contribution to the Allied effort.

Royal Navy ships operating off Korea were normally based at one of the two main Japanese naval ports: Sasebo or Kure. *Ocean* steamed into Sasebo harbor shortly after dawn on Sunday, May 17, 1953. An hour later HMS *Glory*, the other British carrier alternating with *Ocean* on the west coast of Korea, arrived to be relieved. We spent two days in port taking aircraft and other equipment from *Glory*, while our air crew were briefed on escape and evasion techniques.

The briefing was all rather surreal. We were given a kit that contained a revolver and a walkie-talkie radio, both deemed useful if we were shot down, together with survival rations. In addition, there were gold sovereigns for bribery purposes, a map of Korea printed on a silk scarf, and a piece of cloth called a pointy-talkie which had useful phrases in English with their Korean translation. You were supposed to attract the attention of some passing North Korean and point to the right phrase. Realizing that you were telling him that you were a British pilot and that if you were taken safely to the front lines, he would be well-rewarded, he would supposedly break into a broad grin and set off at a fast clip southwards, with you firmly in tow. Once I saw what we had been doing to their country, I strongly suspected that any North Korean coming across me and my pointy-talkie would promptly string me up on the nearest tree. But maybe not: the final piece of equipment was a rather gruesome "fighting knife," and we were shown how to use it. I somewhat doubted that I would actually bring myself to eviscerate my captor, and even a gung-ho lecture on fighting spirit from a gunnery officer failed to convince me that this piece of steel, plus all the other paraphernalia, would save me from a long march to the North should the occasion ever arise.

One other memorable piece of advice: if you were shot down and managed to bail out, was to be sure to avoid the Turkish lines. The Turks were our allies, very much so in those days, important to the NATO alliance, and now making a significant contribution in Korea, but they had a rather odd attitude to a pilot who abandoned his airplane, regardless of cause. An aircraft was very clearly an object of enormous value, whereas a mere mortal was easily expendable. So, if they saw a pilot leave his cockpit, and the airplane then crashed, they would assume it was all the pilot's fault: he had lost this valuable machine, and should thus be executed forthwith. It wasn't suggested that the North Koreans would be more merciful, but the implication was there.

Japan was a different kind of Orient, and Sasebo, now a vast American naval base erected upon the remnants of the docks where the World War II super-battleships *Yamato* and *Musashi* had been built, was a different kind of Japan. Wooden houses, mostly bars and "nightclubs" lined muddy streets odorous with the smell of human excrement, the ubiquitous fertilizer, and the poorly combusted gasoline, powering the equally ubiquitous two stroke tri-shaws. The U.S. Navy Officers' Club offered a sanitized Madam Butterfly version of Japan where kimono clad hostesses offered cheap drinks and harmless indigenous pastimes to polite uniformed officers. The streets outside provided more down to earth recreation. With the wisdom of youth we did our drinking on our ship or in the officers' club, then turned for baser pleasures to the local economy. But much of this was in the future. On our first visit we loaded stores, attended lectures, and spent what little time was left over, sightseeing and bargain hunting.

Ocean left Sasebo early on May 21st, 1953, our first day heading for the war zone. During the day we checked our airplanes and equipment, then in the evening assembled for a briefing, which proved interminable. Although we spent much of the time looking at target photos, there appeared to be equal or even more attention to all the precautions needed to prevent our being shot down by our Allies. American gunners engaged in Korea, it seemed, even at this late stage in the war, feared another Pearl Harbor and were wont to shoot first and ask questions later if confronted with a strange airplane. The Firefly was deemed a strange airplane.

My diary noted that our first sight of Korea was uninspiring: a lot of barren coastline completely shrouded in mist, with sudden jagged rocks jutting out of the water combined to give an effect rather like the lonelier parts of Scotland in winter. In the evening the mist gave way to rain. I wouldn't have been surprised if, after all the long preparation, we did not fly the next day. But I didn't recall any nervousness. Nor do I think anyone lost any sleep at the prospect that soon we would have guns popping off in our direction with hostile intent.

In fact, the next day *Ocean* and her escorts, American and British, found themselves in dense fog. Flying was postponed and, despite various false alarms during the day, never took place. There was a gale warning for our area and orders were given for the aircraft on deck to be firmly lashed down. We spent most of our first afternoon at war trying to maintain our balance in a rolling wardroom while we watched a movie.

My diary entry for that night might have applied with equal relevance to a later war, in Vietnam:

> "One thing stands out, and that is the seeming unimportance of whether or not we actually do strike at the target assigned to us when we are not actually trying to win a war but only to maintain it...it matters very little whether the strike is successful—all that counts is whether it is completed. It is a question of vital statistics rather than victory."

I wrote this a long time before I'd ever heard of Robert MacNamara, U.S Secretary of Defense during the Vietnam War, but he would have been in full agreement with those ill-defined war aims.

The following morning, we were awakened at three-thirty

a.m. to find a clear starry sky and weather over the land ideal for the task ahead. Our target was a village reported to be sheltering 250 enemy troops, a suspiciously precise number. After breakfast and a final briefing, we launched into the darkness, starting at exactly five o'clock. One of the problems of a dawn attack from the west coast of Korea was that the flight to the target was always directly into the sun. Keeping station on Pants, who was doing an energetic weave, plus maintaining a good look out for enemy fighters, whose actual appearance, I must stress, would have been an enormous surprise to all concerned, plus looking for the target, all kept me pretty occupied. Leading us around to the south of the target, Pants took us right over Haeju, an area we had been warned was heavily defended by flak, but the NKA's must have been still asleep or short of ammunition since no one fired at us. Very little was moving on the ground, which appeared exceedingly desolate. "Weaving" in this context was our main defense against enemy ground fire: alternately stamping heavily on the rudder pedals caused the airplane to follow an erratic course that made it much more difficult to hit than if it was just flying in a straight line.

I could not see any target until I was following Pants down in a sixty-degree rocket attack, when I realized that our "village" was actually a collection of rather shabby huts. I got a largish building in my sights, fired my rockets at 1,500 feet, and pulled up sharply to the right, weaving enthusiastically as I did. I think I hit the target, and someone told me I had started a small fire, but I couldn't see much myself. We got back to the ship at six-thirty and landed on right away. One of my rockets, which had failed to fire, came off when I caught the arrester wire and slithered down the deck to be caught in a small nylon barrier erected forward of the main barriers for just that purpose. Our second breakfast was a convivial affair; after all, we had fired shots in anger at an enemy on his own turf and were thus warriors of a sort. Only on further reflection did I realize there was a remote possibility that I had for the first time taken a human life.

Later that morning we did a reconnaissance mission to

photograph the railroad running between Omjon and Haeju. This was thirty-mile stretch of what must have been one of the most heavily bombed railroads in the world.

MAP OF THE KOREAN PENINSULA

"Pants took us right over Haeju, an area we had been warned was heavily defended by flak, but the NKA's must have been still asleep or short of ammunition since no one fired at us."

From my diary:

"I could not see one single stretch of railway that could possibly be used by the enemy for his own ends: it was pitted and destroyed by bombs throughout its entire length. The bombs had been dropped accurately in the middle of the track, at every bridge and crossing place, and often in between. Only one bridge did I see still standing, and the line was broken either side of it."

After finishing the photography, we set off back to the ship.

"The country might be dead if it was not for the fact that we receive reliable information from partisans that troops have replaced the civilian population in all the villages."

BOSUN'S CHAIR JACKSTAY

"The trip back in the bosun's chair [after a liquid lunch] was often quite hazardous."

When we got back, some American officers from the USS *Thompson*, one of our escorts, came over by jackstay transfer to have lunch. This was always a popular jaunt for our allies who, unlike us, had a "dry" ship. The trip back in the bosun's chair was often quite hazardous.

The following day was Sunday and we had a late start scheduled: six-fifteen for an eight o'clock take off, but I got up earlier to go to Holy Communion, more I think for the drama than the religion. There was something rather striking about taking the Host in our little chapel just off the flight deck, while carrying knives, revolvers and war paraphernalia, before clambering into our airplanes to go off and kill people. On the other hand, allowing myself a modest search for support, I silently recalled General Jacob Astley's famously brief prayer before the Battle of Edgehill (1642): "Lord, thou knowest how busy I must be this day. If I forget you, do not thou forget me."

CHAPEL ON *OCEAN*

"There was something rather striking about taking the Host in our little chapel just off the flight deck, while carrying knives, revolvers and war paraphernalia, before clambering into our airplanes to go off and kill people."

Our primary target was covered in cloud, so we went off looking for a "target of opportunity." We didn't have to look long since Pants had already picked out some sluice gates. I think he had been reading *The Dam Busters* (a World War II history) and wanted to see a huge wall of water come rushing down on the wretched Koreans living below. If we had indeed hit it the results might have been quite impressive, but, in fact, we all missed. However, a lot of flak and small men in uniform rushing around and diving into slit trenches indicated that we had found something of military significance. When we got back, my airplane caused quite a bit of excitement when the mechanics found a large piece of shrapnel buried in the radiator, causing a slow leak. It was the first such damage sustained by any of our aircraft and thus provided me with a few fleeting moments of shipboard fame. In fact, if it had dropped out of the radiator it would have caused a seriously big leak and my engine would have seized up and I would have crashed, resulting in a more lasting, but less desirable, celebrity. Writing much later, an American author commented that a lucky hit on its liquid-cooled engine could rapidly convert a Firefly into a glider.

Our Supply Officer, who doubled as assistant Intelligence Officer, kept his own diary, a section of which was later included in an official anthology. He wrote, "Not a lucky morning for the Fireflies, who went off to beat up a village reported by intelligence as full of communist troops and came back well peppered. I am most thankful that they all got back—one with a hole in the engine, another with a hole half an inch from the fuel feed, another with holes in the rear cockpit, wings and tail. I gather "Pants" Bloomer, the Firefly C.O., shot off his rockets and then took the Flight in for a second strafing run, when they got almost as good as they gave." Making a second pass at a target was generally frowned upon, since all the advantages of surprise would have been lost.

On the second mission of the day two of us were photographing more railroad and when we were finished, we had some time to spare before we were due back on the ship. We cruised along the Ochon River, looking for something to shoot at. We shot up four ox-carts and a motorcyclist from about two hundred feet. The last ox-cart (all carts and their wretched oxen were considered military targets since they were the main form of ammunition transport for the Chinese People's Volunteer Army (PVA)) loosed its ox as we attacked, and I chased the terrified beast all over the adjacent paddy fields until finally, chewed up by twenty millimeter shells, it became hamburger. I felt rather sorry for both beast and owner, but secretly quite proud of my marksmanship. It was, after all, a rapidly moving target!

FIREFLY CARRYING SIXTY-POUND ROCKETS AWAITING PRE-DAWN TAKE-OFF

"We flew for four days, typically two, or occasionally three, sorties each day, from dawn until dusk. We carried out photographic reconnaissance, bomb and rocket attacks on troop concentrations and supply dumps, and occasional close air support of ground troops"

The patrol continued on a fairly predictable pattern. We flew for four days, typically two, or occasionally three, sorties each day, from dawn until dusk. We carried out photographic reconnaissance, bomb and rocket attacks on troop concentrations and supply dumps, and occasional close air support of ground troops or friendly partisans. The fifth day we would take easy during replenishment at sea: oilers and supply ships would come alongside and send over fuel oil and Avgas by pipeline and ammunition and food by jackstay. It was all quite efficiently done. Then we would have four more days of flying. The night before replenishment, knowing there was to be no dawn take-off, was serious party night. Fog was endemic and frequently caused flying to be canceled or postponed. Flak was the main concern: of enemy fighters we saw little, and then mostly contrails, which we knew weren't F86's because we were told so. Every now and then we started a major fire or set off a big explosion, which was encouraging since otherwise we might have suspected that we were making a rather minimal impact on the course of the war. My biggest problem was a persistent cramp in the buttocks caused by sitting four or five hours a day in a small cockpit on top of a rather hard dinghy pack.

My diary describes an early morning flight:

> "May 30, 1953, 0330. It is still quite dark when we get up, rather cold and I put on an extra sweater, fumble my way along the dimly lit passage and call the boss who is already awake. Breakfast is fried eggs and bacon and coffee–it always is! We make our way forward to the briefing room and prepare our maps and kneepads. Hear the weather, a lot of technical jargon that leaves us with the impression that we will be able to see the target quite clearly. A few words from the boss and we go up onto the flight deck. It is still quite dark and the aircraft are indistinct looming shapes on which one can dimly see the mechanics who have been up since 0400 unlashing and getting them ready. I say good morning to Elkin (my mechanic) who is in a foul mood. He straps me in and hands me

my kneepad and maps. Already I can feel the cramp in my left hip. I settle down and check the rocket selector and gyro gun sight. The boss comes by with some last minute instructions, and then comes back again to change them. As they plug in my rocket leads I hang my arms over the side of the cockpit to be sure I don't accidentally touch the trigger. A voice over the deck-hailer: 'Stand by to start engines.' There is a blue helmeted man lying by each chock now, everyone else stands at a respectful distance away. I prime the engine, fuel and ground switches on. 'Stand clear of propellers.' I prime the intake manifold, switch on the mags, hand on the primer, one on the starter, wait for the klaxon. It comes and, simultaneously, all the engines burst into life, roar for a moment, then settle down. Navigation lights come on one by one, and all down the deck are tongues of fire from the exhaust manifolds. I settle down to cockpit checks, and respond as the boss call us off on the radio.

It is now quite light and I can see the marshaller in his yellow cap–he has discarded his luminous wands. Brakes on, chocks away, and he brings me forward down the deck behind the boss. Past the island another man takes over and so on until we reach the diagonal white line leading to the catapult. Now I have a tail wheel arm on and a man behind me is guiding my right wheel down the line. We reach the block and turn onto the catapult, coming up against the chocks with a bump. A man is holding up a board: 'Check tail-wheel locked, flaps to take-off.' Brakes off, and he is waving a green flag at me. Fuel pump on, open the throttle, seventeen pounds of manifold pressure, 2,750 RPM. Raise the left hand, head firmly back on the headrest. There is a sensation of enormous force, but one remains conscious of the controls, if nothing else. Airborne: brakes on, up undercarriage, up flaps, close hood, off goggles (my preference, but against the rules). I follow the boss and we join up on the turn, setting course for the coast.

The weather is perfect and soon we can see land. It is like a colored picture out of a geography textbook. The sea is very blue, and white sand frames the light green of the paddy fields ahead. The roads are rutted by the parallel tracks worn over the years by ox-carts. Here and there are villages, small single-story houses built around a courtyard. The mountains rise abruptly out of the plains, dark green covered by purple heather, brown where the rock shows through. Miles of trenches line the mountaintops.

Soon we reach the target, which is easy to identify. I go into my dive, the target is just over the bottom diamond on the gun sight, speed is building up rapidly, a thirty-degree dive from 5,000 to 1,600 feet. The change of trim is quite pronounced. At 1,600 feet I press the trigger. The rockets go off with a whoosh, leaving a trail of smoke. I pull up steeply, off to the left, and briefly black out. My rockets appear to have slightly over-shot. I join up with the boss, and we circle around. I can see a flash of small arms fire on the ridge to the north of the target: It is coming from some sort of bunker. I go into a dive and continue firing my cannon as far down as I dare. I don't know whether I hit him, but hope so since my plane gives a nasty lurch: maybe he's hit me. But pressures and temperatures remain all right, no sign of damage.

We reform and return to the ship, coming into the squadron circuit on the port side. We go into echelon right formation and fly down the starboard side of the ship. One by one they break away at twelve-second intervals, until I am left alone. One, two, three...eleven, twelve. Flaps down to take off, turn, lose some height, speed 150 knots, wheels down as I go down wind opposite to the ship's course. Speed 120, flaps full down, prop fully fine, three green lights tell me wheels down and locked. Opposite the island start the turn, fairly steep, then ease it off, 95 knots at

> the ninety-degree position. Bats picks me up with a roger and keeps it there until the cut. The noise of the engine dies away, the nose drops. Back with the stick, then the sudden deceleration that means I have caught an arrester wire. The hook men undo the wire and I taxi forward at full speed over the barriers, which snap up as soon as I am through to allow the leader of the next flight on. Wings folded, brakes on, switches off. Home.

Occasionally I would get a bad attack of morality about the war that, at the time in question, was being prolonged mainly over the question of prisoner repatriation. Were the villages we strafed with such abandon really military targets, or possibly some wretched peasants who happened to live on the wrong side of the thirty-eighth parallel?

> "Supposing," I asked my diary, "the Stuka pilots in 1940 had been told that enemy troops were hiding in refugee columns. They would, and did, attack them with as little compunction as we attack these villages. Think of the number of civilians we must be killing over the question of POW's. How much better to let the POW's go back to China, force them if necessary, than continue the needless waste of life now going on."

Any student of the Korean War has to become deeply immersed in the question of prisoner exchange: we wanted ours back, and the Chinese wanted theirs back, but while nearly all of ours wanted to come home, a lot of the Chinese preferred to stay with us. Forced repatriation was unacceptable to the United Nations, whose collective national memories presumably included Russian prisoners of the Germans, forcibly sent home at the end of World War II, many of whom committed suicide rather than face the KGB and the Gulags. So, the war went on, and I am sure a lot of innocent civilians were killed over this intractable question.

MICHAEL IN FIREFLY OVER NORTH KOREA

"Now I knew for certain I had killed not one but several, and unlike most air attacks, had seen them fall. I noted in my diary 'Quite a successful do'."

On the final day of the patrol we were sent off to attack a radar station. No one could find it, but we did spot a well-camouflaged gun emplacement. Pants attacked it from 5,000 feet and, as he went in, I saw a lot of khaki clad men come running out of a nearby house in a very military, five yard interval per man, column. I went into strafe them as they dived for a slit trench. Several did not make it and lay still on the pathway. Now I knew for certain I had killed not one but several, and unlike most air attacks, had seen them fall. I noted in my diary "Quite a successful do."

At this point a not unreasonable question might be: "Why were we there?" Essentially our role was to support the United Nations Ground Forces. It was the absence of such air support for the Chinese People's Volunteer Army, Chinese Premier Chou En-lai admitted to Stalin in 1953, which pushed Chinese casualties to a level that even they found unacceptable. But once the war had become largely stalemated our role had become mostly interdiction. We were there to prevent the Communists from moving men and supplies up to their front, by destroying road and rail transport, and by seeking out hidden groups of their troops who, now that the UN had almost total control of the sky, would move by night and rest up wherever they could find cover during the day.

Our main area of operation was the west coast of North Korea, and one of my principal memories from flying over it was how beautiful and unspoiled were the mountains, their foothills sloping down to the unpolluted ocean (very different from my first fog shrouded glimpse of the country). There was virtually no development, and although having no aspirations to go into that line of business myself, it did from time to time cross my mind what a great opportunity existed for an enterprising hotel operator to use his skills there. I still think of it sixty-five years later, marveling at the opportunity Korea would offer to a larcenous hotelier/politician seeking to make money for himself by using national diplomacy to grease the discussions.

Our specific task was to provide close air support to the British Commonwealth Division. The Division's left flank had formerly adjoined a sector held by the U. S. Marines, and there was some disappointment on the British Commonwealth part when they learned the Marines were to be relieved by an American infantry division. But there was considerable relief when the British found that the Americans' right-hand brigade was a Turkish unit. As one history of the conflict put it, the Turks, like the Marines, would still be there as the sun came up, no matter how hard-fought the night.

It never occurred to me at the time to question why we were on the West Coast, and the Americans (mostly) on the East Coast. Many years later I was told that it was simple: there was a possibility that one of our ships or aircraft might wander off course and end up in Chinese waters, to be impounded there, with lots of related problems before we could get it released. The British, who had Diplomatic relations with China at the time, were considered better positioned to deal with such a problem, as opposed to the United States for whom Communist China (and its hundreds of millions of people) for practical purposes had no official existence. I fortunately never had to find out whether that theory worked in practice.

After each patrol *Ocean* would return to Sasebo to take on stores, fuel etc. and to allow the aircrew some time for what was euphemistically known as rest and recreation (R&R). Our first night in port I went ashore with Reg Simmonds, an observer with whom I would fly for several years (including two carrier deployments) and who became one of my closest friends. We finally ended up in a bar called the Kozy Korner where we ran into two American naval officers. One of them, John, appeared to have some kind of financial interest in the place. The other was Fritz Finger, a splendidly non-conformist fellow with whom I would enjoy a warm friendship for many years following our respective Naval service.

The Kozy Korner was owned by a former Japanese admiral and his wife. They had three beautiful daughters: "Diane," who played the piano and "Rosemary" and "Mary," who sang. The mother was pretty good-looking too. Fritz, Reg and I spent many a wonderfully wasted evening at the Kozy Korner and other similar bars, drinking and philosophizing with the degree of earnestness that seems appropriate only to very young men.

The following day Queen Elizabeth II was crowned in Westminster Abbey and the British in Sasebo took the event extremely seriously. Since it was raining we had our coronation parade in the hangar so we had to get up early and make it spotlessly clean, and me with a raging hangover. Then, dressed all in white, we lined up for inspection by a slew of braided admirals and such. The band played a number of appropriate anthems and there was a lot of to-ing and fro-ing but I was in the back row and couldn't see much and besides, my feet hurt. Twenty-one guns were fired off without a hitch and we sang "God Save the Queen" lustily and for the first time. Then the admiral announced that we would "splice the mainbrace", meaning that all the sailors would get an extra tot of rum and the officers, who normally did not get a rum ration, would get a tot as well, to drink Her Majesty's health. Clearly this was the most popular thing he had to say all day. The cheers that greeted his announcement appeared a lot more spontaneous than those which honored Her Majesty, but of course, back then, she was new to the job.

KOZY KORNER, 1953

"Fritz, Reg and I spent many a wonderfully wasted evening at the Kozy Korner and other similar bars, drinking and philosophizing with the degree of earnestness that seems appropriate only to very young men."

We had planned to celebrate the coronation with a fly-past over the Commonwealth Division in the front lines in Korea. Twelve Sea Furies were lined up on deck and two tugs were used to point *Ocean* into what was an almost non-existent wind. Then they launched them using RATOG (Rocket Assisted Take Off Gear), which, so far as we knew, was the first time this had ever been attempted in harbor with little or no wind. Word had spread around the assembled allied fleet that the crazy Limeys were going to try this, and every ship was crowded with eager bystanders hoping to see something spectacular in the way of airplane crashes. They were to be disappointed, but only just. Whoever had calculated the take-off distance and firing point had cut his reckoning pretty close.

The first plane went off with the roar of engine and rockets, hidden in a cloud of smoke and debris. It reached the end of the deck and sank gracefully out of sight. For an interminable time, nothing more could be seen, although the sound of a mightily straining Bristol Centaurus airplane engine could be heard reverberating off the surrounding hills. The Sea Fury was stuck in ground effect, kept in the air by the pressure between wings and sea surface. As soon as the pilot tried to climb, he lost ground effect and sank back down. Eventually he gained enough airspeed and staggered into the air. Much the same happened to number two. After that, the take-off run was longer and the remaining planes got off all right. However, various mishaps reduced their number and what had been intended as a rather splendid "ER" ("Elizabeth Regina") appeared over the front line as a somewhat skimpy "E." However, the thought was there. For the first time I was glad that the Firefly had a shorter range than the Sea Fury: take-off limitations meant we carried insufficient fuel to reach Korea safely from Japan, and we thus stayed onboard to watch the fun.

It turned out that there was indeed more fun to come when the Sea Furies landed at Seoul to refuel for their return. The airplane had a neat habit of folding one wing at a time, so that a quick flick of the wing folding mechanism would cause one wing to go up and then down, giving a kind of salute. The

CO of 807 Squadron thought it would be a rather neat idea to salute his American allies and so, as they taxied past the control tower, he gave the signal and each airplane lifted and lowered its wing in sequence. Very impressive until it came to the pilot of number four who, carried away by the excitement of the moment, flicked the wrong lever. Up came the undercarriage, down went the Sea Fury, and the whole parade came to an ignominious halt with number four resting sadly on his broken propeller.

Remaining days in Sasebo passed swiftly. Little to do except stand the occasional watch during the day, lots of drinking in various "Clubs" at night, floor shows, geishas, pretty Japanese girls who were nice to us (and little else) in exchange for expensive watery drinks. I spent a lot of time with John and Fritz, discovering thereby the serendipitous trade off which has cemented relations between the Royal and United States Navies ever since U.S. Navy Secretary Daniels decreed that the latter's ships would be dry.

It worked like this. We would invite our American friends on board for dinner and would ply them with strong liquor before, during and after. A few nights later we would get a very diffident invitation, saying that, although there was no possible way they could ever repay our hospitality, they would be honored if we would drop by for dinner and a movie. Once in the know we responded with enthusiasm. Dinner for the occasion was normally excellent steak, followed by as much as we could eat of the most wonderful ice cream any of us had ever tasted. To someone brought up on English ice cream, small brick-like portions in any flavor you wanted, provided it was vanilla, the lushness and lavishness of the American product was a real eye opener. This was a country I had to see more of, if only for the ice cream. Then the movie. We were used to dated product, mostly black and white, and then only if the projector did not break down. They had the latest from Hollywood, glorious technicolor, and projectors that seemed possessed of extraordinary stamina. If ever there was a case of perfect comparative advantage, this RN/USN dinner trade off was it.

Fully replenished and properly rested, we went back on station to find what was, paradoxically, an intensified war. Peace talks had been progressing favorably, and there was every possibility that an armistice might shortly be signed. However, since the treaty would likely provide for a pull back from positions occupied at the time of signing, both sides were pressing for last minute advantages. The Commonwealth Brigade was asking for stepped up close air support, more of the same: rocket and bomb attacks on targets one hoped made sense. After one trip attacking a village surrounded by ammunition dumps, I came back with the most damage I had suffered to date: a bullet in the engine four inches from the fuel filter and main coolant pipe, one through my elevator and one through the main spar, any one of which could have done serious damage. We also attacked some bridges and left a wonderful pattern of near misses: bombs everywhere, except the vital crossing. The problem was we were not trained nor equipped to fly combat missions at night, so the Chinese would bring North Korean labor in after dark and repair all the damage we had done during the day.

An interesting change from dropping bombs on little villages was a visit to the Commonwealth brigade sector of the front line, probably designed to encourage them by proving that we really existed. Reg Simmonds and I flew to Seoul and then went by jeep up the Main Supply Route towards the front. After a lengthy drive during which we were mingled with extraordinary amounts of war material in transit, we arrived at the headquarters of 25th Brigade, met various of their officers and were treated to an excellent dinner. The food was terrific, and we seemed to spend a lot of time eating it. After breakfast the next day we had a tour of the area, ending up at the front line.

From my diary:

". . . we reached the crest overlooking the valley of no-man's land. Notices said 'You are now under enemy observation.' Our guide pointed out the various

> features while an air observation plane wheeled slowly overhead and to our left a Sherman tank pounded away at an enemy held hill. We went along to look at the tank and were allowed to fire its gun which went off with a most satisfactory noise."

Later we visited an artillery unit and fired their guns. Being bigger, their noise was even more satisfactory. A lunch was served on a terrace shaded from the sun by camouflage netting. It was a funny kind of war. Real shells were flying back and forth, lives were lived in deeply dug bunkers, everyone was aware of the enemy over the next hill, but in between it all there seemed to be a very active, if monastic, social life going on. It was unlike what I knew about World War II, which was mostly a war of movement; much more akin to the static trench warfare of World War I. Of course, our view of things was somewhat biased by the fact that we were handled very carefully: it had cost a lot of money to train us and losing an aviator (other than as a result of an air operation) would presumably be frowned upon by the higher powers.

On our way back to *Ocean* we spent a while at K14, a USAF base, waiting for our transport plane. We had lunch in their mess; the meal was served cafeteria style and we all stood in line with trays which the mess cooks filled with whatever we wanted from the food tables. The line was a long one, everyone chatting away quite noisily. Suddenly, from way up in front, I heard a stentorian and very British voice shout out, obviously aimed at me: "I say, old chap, weren't you my fag at Blundell's?" Deathly hush, broken only by the dropping of the occasional food-filled tray as everyone turned and stared at me, those nearest edging away as if I had some kind of plague. Not quite the time to enter into a detailed discussion of the nuances of American - as opposed to British - English. It was indeed Eades, whose fag I had been for a year, and who was now an RAF exchange pilot with the USAF. At least the chance meeting gave me a reason to go to the head of the line, but I'm sure there were many among the U.S. Air Force 4th

Interceptor Wing for whom that day provided solid evidence of the horrible decadence of their British allies.

Back on *Ocean*, things had become more interesting. We attacked a number of different targets including some caves in which we suspected there was a nest of NKA machine gunners. One of our planes was shot down there a few days before. He managed to ditch and was brought back by an American helicopter. His name was Hick and our Captain sent a polite signal to the rescue unit: "Thank you for picking our Hick up." Later a pilot called Bacon suffered a similar experience and we were able to thank the same folks for bringing home our Bacon.

We shot up a train with some new looking boxcars, and found an NKA army post:

> "I saw a whole platoon, about twelve, running for shelter along a path. Again they were exactly spaced out at five-yard intervals, all very military. They must have been People's Volunteer Army (PVA) since they wore khaki uniforms and had red stars embroidered above their hat peaks. They were firing their burp guns up at us as they ran, so I felt no pang of conscience when I fired back, despite the disproportionality of their 9 mm and my 20 mm."

There were rumors floating around that we were going to be asked to perform some kind of a night flying mission, and shortly after we got back from this patrol Pants and Reg Simmonds left for Seoul to flight test a Firefly that was to be our prototype night fighter. It was fitted with air-to-air radar and a new gadget called IFF: "Identification, friend or foe." Any contemporary pilot reading this would recognize the gadget as a transponder. Reg was full of importance, our ace radar operator.

I think it was Voltaire who said that one of the advantages of a military life was the time it allowed for reading, and such was certainly true of my days on *Ocean*. I enjoyed the Osbert

Sitwell trilogy: *The Scarlet Tree, Left Hand, Right Hand,* and *Laughter in the Next Room.* I think Sitwell's father, Sir George, reminded me a little of my own parent: "It is strange," Sir George once said, speaking of their large, multi-room dinner parties, "that there always seems to be more laughter in the next room." My father at the time was conducting a lonely letter writing campaign in an attempt to generate public interest in the Korean conflict, which was already beginning to deserve its eventual label as "the Forgotten War." In one letter he contrasted the banal generalities of the BBC with the much more detailed reporting of the American Armed forces network which left its listeners "in no doubt as to the grim bitterness of the struggle and the harsh losses being suffered" by the men in Korea.

MICHAEL READING ON *OCEAN*

"I think it was Voltaire who said that one of the advantages of a military life was the time it allowed for reading, and such was certainly true of my days on Ocean.*"*

Evelyn Waugh, still one of my favorite English writers, had just brought out *Brideshead Revisited*. This I still consider one of the great works of contemporary British fiction. I read it for the first time on *Ocean* and have re-read it several times since. There is a character in *Brideshead*, Anthony Blanche by name who, unusually for the time the book was written, was characterized as an unabashed homosexual. One evening he takes Charles, the protagonist, out to a pub for drinks and orders Brandy Alexanders, a rather garish cocktail. Raising the glass to his lips, Anthony toasted Charles, "Yum, yum, yum, down the red road they go. My goodness, how the boys all stare!"

Pants and I were at the Officers' Club one night and he asked me whether I had read anything good recently. I told him how much I was enjoying *Brideshead Revisited*. Without pausing for a moment, he ordered two Brandy Alexanders, and when they arrived, looked at me over the top of his glass and repeated Anthony's Blanche's toast. Rapidly deciding that the best response to a pass from one's boss was to ignore it, I ordered the next round. Nothing more was said but, in the future, whenever we were out together, he always would turn to me and ask if I wanted a "Yum Yum". He was a wonderful man and an excellent leader; I became very fond of him. It has struck me recently how hard, lonely and dangerous the life of a homosexual must have been before the laws softened up, and everyone came out of the closet.

Most evenings when in harbor, I would spend some of the time with my new friend Fritz Finger and shipmates of his from the USS *Trathen*, a destroyer escort. Once we invited several of them to dinner and I remember one of them, a very young Ensign, new to the area, becoming quite upset when he saw who was serving his food. We asked him what the matter was. "He's Chinese," he whispered hoarsely. "So?" "But they're communists. We're supposed to be fighting them." We tried to explain that our cooks and stewards came from Hong Kong, belonged to families who had been serving the Royal Navy for generations, and probably felt just as strongly about communism as he did. Nothing would convince him: Chinese were communists and that was what he was there to fight and, in any event, they'd probably poisoned his dinner.

It was either that night or a similar one that the *Trathen* sent its captain's gig over to pick up Fritz after a rather late and liquid evening. Quite a wind had got up which made it rather difficult for the boat to lie alongside *Ocean's* companionway. Fritz, standing half in and half out of the gig, was determined to honor protocol. He saluted the Officer of the Watch, he saluted the bow, he saluted the stern, he saluted the place the ensign would have been if it hadn't been so dark. He saluted anything he could lay his eyes on, all the time swaying gently in the quickening wind. Each time he saluted the coxswain of the gig would plead, "Mr. Finger, you must get on board, I can't hold this thing much longer." Finally, after snapping off a crisp one at the moon, Finger turned sharply seaward and stepped off the platform. Unfortunately, the gig was now some six feet away and my new friend disappeared beneath the oily surface of Sasebo harbor, leaving only his Ensign's cap floating to mark the spot. They soon had him out, and he reappeared at the Officer's Club the following evening little the worse for wear.

Back to sea for our fourth patrol, and despite all the rumors swirling about, the war's end did not seem any nearer. Our first day off the Korean coast was marked by a tragedy that, at the time, seemed totally unwarranted and sixty years later still does. We must digress for a moment to go back to earlier discussions about why airplanes fly. It is essentially lift that gets the airplane into the air, and lift is a product of the shape of the wing, the angle at which it meets the oncoming air flow, and the speed of the airflow over the wing. The air-speed at which an airplane will begin to fly is its take-off speed. And for an airplane taking off from a moving aircraft carrier the take-off speed will be a combination of the wind over the deck and the forward movement of the airplane. The wind over the deck will be a combination of the natural wind over the ocean and the wind produced by the forward movement of the ship.

Ocean, like others of her class, had a design speed of 25 knots, but for those on board it always seemed as though she had reached her limit at about 22 knots. Although no one told us at the time, Korea translates as "Land of the morning calm," which meant that pilots waiting to take off at dawn should expect very little natural wind over the deck. A Firefly with a full load of weaponry needed about 95 knots to get airborne, so with 22 knots from *Ocean*'s best efforts, and little help from the morning calm wind, even a Rolls Royce engine needed assistance to get us airborne, which is why most of our operational take-offs were either catapult or rocket assisted.

A problem with the catapult meant that take-offs on the day in question had to be rocket assisted. A theoretical take-off distance had been calculated which should provide sufficient deck for an aircraft with a certain all-up weight to become airborne using Rocket-Assisted Take-Off Gear (RATOG). However, this was a minimum distance, and made no allowance for error of any kind. That day although there was plenty of room on the deck, for some reason the first airplane to take off was pulled out of the deck park and taxied forward so that it started its run at the minimum distance, thus compounding the lack of wind problem.

The first off, a Sea Fury, did all the correct things and his rockets fired appropriately, but still he vanished over the bows and seemed to take a horribly long time to reappear. Undaunted, the bridge signaled the next one to take off, another Sea Fury piloted by Jan Mulder, a popular young Dutch exchange pilot. Mulder pressed his firing mechanism too soon, which meant that the rockets had fizzled out long before they could do any good. The airplane went straight over the bows into the sea and disintegrated. Mulder bobbed to the surface too close to the ship's side for comfort—he had to kick himself off a couple of times as it went by. Amazingly our helicopter found him and pulled him to safety, still conscious and with only a small cut over one eye.

As if nothing had happened the line of aircraft waiting to take off moved slowly forward. Two more Sea Furies took off uneventfully. Then it was the Fireflies' turn. Again the lead airplane was ranged up to the theoretical minimum take off point. Paddy Evans, the pilot, gunned his engine until the brakes wouldn't hold any longer, started his roll, pressed the button at the right point, but only three of his four starboard side rockets went off. He was nearly airborne when he disappeared over the bows and those who could see reported that he was some way off when his wheels touched the water, causing another spectacular water spout which those of us still waiting to take off could just see. The American plane guard destroyer rescued Evans, but he died on board shortly afterwards. Ken Thomas, his observer, the only married man in the squadron, was never found. At this the mission was finally canceled. Brodhurst, piloting the plane just ahead of me, and the next pilot scheduled to take off, who had seen both crashes, threw up after getting out of his plane. I could understand why; it must be a little unnerving to be strapped into an airplane which, propelled by insufficient and unreliable high explosives, appears to be heading inexorably towards violent contact with the ocean.

We buried Paddy at sea that evening; our three escorting destroyers gathering close by to share the moment. It was almost dark, and we could only just read our hymn sheets. His body, covered by a Union Flag and carried by eight seamen, was placed on a chute over the stern. We prayed and sang and then, when it was truly dark, the remains slid gently down into the wake. The Captain dropped a wreath, we sang "Abide with me", and then the guard fired three volleys. Finally, a bugler played a mournful Last Post, followed by a stirring Reveille. It was all very moving, and of course, a totally unnecessary loss of life.

Even before that there was little love lost between the aircrew and "Flyco," (the bridge level from which flying operations were controlled). "Wings" (commanding all *Ocean*'s flight operations) was Commander Steven Brooks, a short, pompous little man who always appeared more concerned with form than substance. He was aggressively striving for promotion to Captain and clearly saw the closing days of the Korean War as a significant opportunity.

Unfortunately for him, his subordinates did not always share his ambitions. We were pleased one night, when exploring the back streets of Sasebo, to be told by an enterprising Mama-san that hers was a very clean house, "Captain Steve was here." A probably apocryphal story, which became a kind of sea-going myth, had Steven, who was never seen other than in an immaculately tailored white uniform, busily performing upstairs in a "Geisha" house when the United States Navy shore patrol came crashing in the front door. Hastily throwing on his uniform, he jumped out of the window straight into a "honey bucket" placed there to provide basic sewage drainage, Sasebo's back streets lacking any more modern alternative.

FUNERAL AT SEA (HMS *OCEAN*, 1953)

"It was almost dark, and we could only just read our hymn sheets. His body, covered by a Union Flag and carried by eight seamen, was placed on a chute over the stern. We prayed and sang and then, when it was truly dark, the remains slid gently down into the wake."

Poor Captain Steven had to return ignominiously to *Ocean* wrapped in a rather grubby kimono. I doubt it ever really happened that way, but many of us wanted to believe it had.

Thankfully, that was my last day on *Ocean* for some time, since the orders had finally come through for our night fighter detachment to be set up ashore. Some background is called for. "Bedcheck Charlies" (United States Air Force code name) were elementary but very effective NKA planes that were used at night to bomb Allied installations just south of the front line. They had frustrated all attempts on the part of the United States Air Force to intercept them and had caused considerable damage. Most "Bedcheck Charlies" were PO2's, wooden-framed, fabric-covered, open cockpit Soviet training aircraft. Their advantages in the night war over Korea were several: their ability to fly at low level down Korea's narrow valleys made detection difficult, a problem compounded by the poor radar reflecting properties of the plane's rudimentary construction; their 80 knot speed made interception by high performance jet aircraft difficult if not impossible; and even if interception did take place, their slow speed and narrow turning circle facilitated escape.

Over a two-week period in early 1953 several targets were attacked by Bedcheck Charlies, and caused minor material damage, but considerable frustration to the defense. PO2's continued to strew their small bombs pretty much at will around the Seoul and Inchon areas. Indeed, the pace if anything increased, raids coming in almost every night in June 1953. On the night of June 9th, nine PO2's came close to hitting the Presidential Mansion. The following night PO2's, started several fires in Seoul and a blaze that destroyed five million gallons of fuel in the tank farm at Inchon. The defense was frustrated: one PO2 was destroyed, but at the cost of the F94 jet fighter, which had throttled down close to stalling speed in order to make the kill and subsequently crashed. During this attack, radar, guns, and aircraft were swamped with contradictory reports, causing the only UN interceptor that did actually become airborne to be fired at from all directions by its own troops.

BEDCHECK CHARLIE

"Bedcheck Charlies" were PO2's, wooden-framed, fabric-covered, open cockpit Soviet training aircraft. ... their ability to fly at low level down Korea's narrow valleys made detection difficult, a problem compounded by the poor radar reflecting properties of the plane's rudimentary construction"

Given a lull before the next full moon, Fifth Air Force took two steps to find a solution to the "Bedcheck Charlie" problem. First, the Kimpo tactical air direction was given authority to control all ground fire, systems were introduced to prevent overload of the information flow, and to focus efforts only on those aircraft whose transponders failed to reply with the correct identification codes. Second, the Air Force admitted failure in the interceptor role and turned it over to more task-appropriate (i.e., slower) piston-engine aircraft. The aircraft selected, in addition to the already deployed Marine Corps AD's, were four Corsair (F4U-5N) single seat fighters from

USS *Princeton* and three Fireflies from HMS *Ocean*, all radar equipped. The plan was to patrol all night along the Seoul-Inchon line to intercept any intruders from the north.

So that was the background for the events that brought us ashore. Everyone wanted to be in on this act: it promised time ashore away from the sometimes monotonous ship-board life; it meant working closely with the Americans and, as I noted at the time, at least it would be a change from strafing ox-carts!

Our night fighter group was attached to the 12th Marine Air Group that operated from K-6, a vast base carved out of the Korean countryside near the little village of Pyongtaek-ni, some thirty miles south of Seoul. The airfield, now known as Osan, is still operational under the South Korean air force. In 1953 most of its seemingly unending array of aircraft were engaged in close air support of the US Marines. The single 8,000 ft. runway appeared to stretch for eternity to those of us more accustomed to a 600 ft. flight deck. But to a carrier pilot used to returning to the reasonable amenities of his ship, which included a comfortable bunk, quite good food, and for the British, a well-stocked bar, K-6 was barren indeed. The runway had been bulldozed out of red earth and laid with steel matting. Dust from the bare soil was everywhere, including the tented huts that provided messing and sleeping accommodation.

We were shown the huts in which we would be living and commented on the lack of any furnishings. The marine showing us around suggested we talk to the supply sergeant. The supply sergeant shrugged his shoulders and suggested we make our own and pointed to some broken packing cases. We asked about nails and tools and he shrugged again. Clearly whatever we arranged would be very much up to us: the Marines must have been missing from parade when the much-vaunted American hospitality was being issued.

Pants said nothing. We got back into our jeep and returned to the airfield where he gave me my marching orders and a signed requisition for the chief wardroom steward on *Ocean*. Half an hour later I was landing on the ship, and twenty minutes after that being catapulted off again, my precious crate firmly strapped into the back seat. Back at K-6, I was met by Pants and we returned to the supply sergeant's office. Quietly placing a bottle of Scotch whisky on his desk, Pants said, "And there's another one waiting if we have something to sleep on tonight."

MICHAEL OUTSIDE HUT AT K-6

"...to a carrier pilot used to returning to the reasonable amenities of his ship, which included a comfortable bunk, quite good food, and for the British, a well-stocked bar, K-6 was barren indeed. The runway had been bulldozed out of red earth and laid with steel matting. Dust from the bare soil was everywhere, including the huts that provided messing and sleeping accommodation. "

A few minutes later a truck pulled up to our tent and the better part of a Marine platoon jumped out. They proceeded to unload a vast amount of lumber and what appeared to be an entire barrel of nails. Soon, as if by magic, we had beds with mosquito netting, chairs, tables, and if not all the luxuries of life, at least a set of furniture that compared well with what our hosts enjoyed. The second bottle handed over, the team disappeared, and we looked with some awe around our new quarters. Dealing with Americans, it seemed, you could get anything you wanted so long as you had the right currency. In Korea, right then, Scotch was an excellent currency.

810 SQUADRON NIGHT FIGHTER GROUP AT K-6

"Our night fighter group was attached to the 12th Marine Air Group that operated from K-6, a vast base carved out of the Korean countryside near the little village of Pyongtaek-ni, some thirty miles south of Seoul."

I should say right away that our time at K-6 was challenging, educational and, for most of the time, really interesting. It was for most of us our first close look at America at war, and although there were some quirks, most of what we saw was very impressive. The particular quirk was the Marine Corps, which seemed to us sailors to be determined to make life as miserable and uncomfortable for themselves as possible. Our US Navy fellow pilots agreed with this. Indeed, to the extent there were lines drawn at all it was the Navy (US and RN) on one side and the Marines on the other, rather than Americans versus the Brits. The Marines seemed to want to create a physical challenge out of the most mundane day-to-day functions, while the navy men wanted just to make things as easy as possible. The Marines seemed to relish dirt and the huge boots to deal with it. The Navy hankered after their clean ships, decent showers, and relatively private heads.

Yes, it was the latrines that really separated the sailors from the Marines. A long trench had been dug into a hillside and concealed from public view by a rather sketchy piece of sacking. There was a rough seat over the trench with some nine or ten holes in it. Normally these holes were occupied by a row of very large Marines, all boasting rather bloodthirsty tattoos and all grunting heavily about their morning business. For those of us who had never defecated in public, and few, if any, of the Navy had, this was all a very traumatic experience. I recall some three days of self-imposed constipation before nature took charge and I had to bare my rear to the elements and the US Marine Corps.

Initial operations were confused by the inevitable problems associated with our respective misuse of the common language. We found it hard enough to get a radio frequency to use, and when we did, we were plagued with ground controllers who either could not, or would not, understand our English “accents”. Finally, however, we started work in earnest - sometimes indeed, too earnest!

From my diary:

"July 22: It is pouring with rain when Reg Simmonds and I get out of the jeep down on the line and by the time we have buttoned on our Mae Wests and helmets we are wet through. It is ten minutes past midnight when I start up.

Following the traffic jeep is difficult and there is a slight delay on the end of the runway because an AD has just landed in the wrong direction. It is twenty-five past when, feeling as though I am casting myself off a high diving board, I open up the throttle and start to roll. Almost right away I am in cloud on instruments climbing to the north. My legs are shaking and I have a tremendous feeling of vertigo. It is a real struggle to rely on the instruments and not follow my instincts. We level out at 3,000 feet and try to contact the ground controller, but he is one of those who make a great play of not being able to understand our 'accents'. Eventually he gives us an east-west patrol line ten miles long, north of what appears to be the Han River, from what we can see through breaks in the cloud. We get the occasional radar contact, but they turn out to be mountaintops.

Down below a battle erupts: red stars moving slowly along searchlight beams, flashes illuminating the far shore of the river. We ask for a fix and find we are right over the bomb line, so decide to head south. More contacts prove abortive. We have been airborne for over two hours and have about another hour's fuel so head for home. We are told that a number of planes are being diverted to K-6 and we must hold. We go into a port orbit and the controller tells us with some agitation that there is an airplane heading towards us from the north at an unknown height. Reg sees it on the radar and then, as I break away, he actually sees the other flash by. The cloud is now very dense and it must have been extraordinarily close. After a further spell of orbiting we are given a Ground Controlled

> Approach into K-6 where they are reporting a 600 ft. base with heavy rain. They talk us right down to the runway.
>
> I suddenly felt so tired that I followed the taxi jeep back in a daze: three hours night flying with two on instruments, hard instrument flight, and the Firefly boasted no such luxury as an auto-pilot. I can hardly stand and, after de-briefing, drop into bed like a log."

Although we were busy at night, there was only so much sleeping one could do during the daytime. My principal memory of that time at K-6 was thus having the freedom to fly almost at will about what was still a war zone. Reg and I would invent some vitally important errand to be run which required flying up to Seoul or down to Pusan. A trip to Seoul involved a low level flight for about twenty minutes along a railway line; borrowing a jeep to drive into town; a few cold beers and lunch at the Commonwealth Officer's Club which boasted not only a friendly bartender, but wonder of wonders, a swimming pool; a quick dash to do whatever the errand was and then flying back to K-6 for the evening briefing.

We found plenty of opportunities to demonstrate how much we still had to learn about the real world (in other words, the world as understood by our Marine Corps hosts). Such occurred one day when, after landing at K-6, I pulled over to the tank farm looking for a gas refill. As Reg and I waited by our plane we noted that about a hundred yards away a youngish-looking pilot had become the center of attraction of a growing crowd of fellow Marines. Sauntering over, I asked someone what was going on. The fellow could hardly get the words out "That's Ted Williams," he spluttered, as if announcing the second coming. "Who's Ted Williams?" I asked, "never heard of him!" The man I was talking to turned around and gave me an incredulous look: "Ted Williams," he replied, "is probably the best hitter ever seen in Major league baseball – and you've never *heard* of him?" Other bystanders crowded over gazing in disbelief at a couple of foreigners who'd never heard of Ted Williams who, it turned out, was indeed a remarkable baseball player, who had volunteered to be a Marine fighter pilot and proved extremely successful due, it was believed, to his uncanny eyesight. (He tested 20/10.) We enjoyed our brief moment of fame – the guys who'd never heard of Ted Williams!

One day we were asked if we could provide a plane to fly down to Pusan to pick up the payroll for K-6's Korean workers, the usual armored truck having broken down. I volunteered and was told that I would have to take a ROK (Republic of Korea) officer to guard the money. When we got to Pusan I found a truck waiting with what seemed to be enough paper money to pay the entire ROK army. Inflation had devastated the Won which was about to be exchanged for new Wan (or vice versa) on a 1,000 to one basis, but my cargo was the old currency, near worthless until exchanged for the good stuff at an official money changer. Looking at the pile of money, and the Firefly's rather cramped back seat, I decided that the best thing would be to put the ROK officer in first, and then pack the money around him. This crammed the rear cockpit so full that only the little man's eyes could be seen over all the grubby old paper. I started up, climbed to about six thousand feet and headed north. It was a lovely day, not a cloud in the sky, and I decided that life would be complete if I did a few rolls on the way home. I had, I am ashamed to say, forgotten entirely about the precious cargo in the back. Three to the left, three to the right, maybe a couple of hesitation rolls; I forget. I was cleared into K-6, landed and taxied up to the ramp where a truck with a guard of ROK MP's was waiting. I noticed that they all seemed to be looking rather anxiously at the back of my plane, and when I got out I could see why. The poor ROK officer had obviously been horribly ill before he finally fainted. The inside of my rear window was coated with green vomit or brown currency (or maybe the other way around) while my unconscious passenger was slumped down in the middle of a truly revolting mixture of money and breakfast. Fortunately his English wasn't up to explaining what had happened, and I wasn't about to try. We wrote it all off to normal airsickness and the ROK MP's were put to work cleaning up the officer, the plane, and the currency. It may have been the first time the Koreans had been paid in laundered money, but I doubt the last, at least in those days.

Despite constant rumors of truce, the war continued to wind on, each side battling for a few inches of ground that might provide an advantage when hostilities ceased. At night the pyrotechnics over the lines were quite beautiful if you could disregard the damage being done on either side. At five thousand feet we wound our way back and forth over the flares and artillery, kept alert by frequent alarms, but never catching sight of the elusive "Bedcheck Charlie". Indeed, with one notable exception, no one saw any of the little biplanes after we arrived, but no further damage was done to the oil tank farms. On that basis at least, we were doing our job petty well.

The notable exception to the lack of enemy contact was one of the U.S. Navy F4U pilots, Lieutenant Guy Pierre Bordelon. Bordelon appeared to have an almost uncanny luck in finding the little North Korean airplanes. Although each of his engagements took place on the enemy side of the lines, meaning that no wreckage was available to permit verification, he was credited with five kills. Each of these was confirmed by the same ground-based Air Force radar operator who would later testify that, yes, he had indeed seen the two contacts merge and that only one survived. The United States Navy, with no Korean War fighter ace to brag about, was hungry for good publicity and Bordelon provided it, scoring his fifth "kill" just before the truce was signed. For this he received a Navy Cross.

Bordelon's reputation as the Navy's only Korean War "ace" stood him well for the rest of his time in the service. He later achieved passing fame as the spokesman for the astronauts during some of the earlier space missions. However, none of the other K-6 pilots American or British, entirely bought the story. Nor, I suspect, did James Michener who wrote the following in his carefully researched novel *Space*:

> "There was, for example, the Air Force pilot . . . who returned to base morning after morning claiming that he had overtaken one of the plywood night invaders and had blown him out of the sky. No one

could inspect the ground behind enemy lines to identify the shattered plane, but the high command was so eager to create the illusion in Washington that it was dominating the skies that it gave this windbag a medal with two clusters."

Michener, a Navy man loyal to his service, made Bordelon an Air Force pilot, but the rest is familiar enough.

It was a normal afternoon around our hut: some of us were sleeping, the rest reading or talking, when one of the US Navy pilots came by and told us that the truce would be signed at ten o'clock the next day. After so many days of waiting it came as rather an anti-climax. Indeed, much more important at the time, it seemed, was a heated argument Reg and I were having as to whether it was possible to get ice cream from the PX (Post Exchange = commissary) to our hut without it melting. Later that evening we got a little drunk and sang songs, but it was all rather half-hearted. It didn't have the flavor of a real victory night, perhaps because it wasn't a real victory, particularly for those of us who, actively involved at the time, lived long enough to see the sixtieth anniversary of the truce go by with no peace treaty in sight. However, the South Koreans were generous enough to invite some survivors to Seoul to celebrate that anniversary, including my good friend Reg Simmonds. By that time, I was American so they probably would have had problems finding me, had they wanted to. But more importantly, whatever they were giving out, he deserved it more than me. I never lost sight of the fact that a fellow who sat patiently in the back of a plane while I landed it on a 600' deck had a level of sustained bravery that vastly outweighed whatever snippets of courage I might have been able to summon from time to time.

No one trusted the North Koreans and their Chinese patrons to keep the truce, so we kept up our nightly patrols along the cease-fire line, quiet now that the shooting had stopped. Without the excitement of possible combat, however remote, life became rather boring and I think we all started to get on each other's nerves—six of us in a small hut. Pants went back to the ship to become "Little F" (the number two officer in the air department, responsible for all flight deck operations) and Martin Boissier, a bossy Dartmouth (Naval College) RN took his place. He and Bob Greenshields, the Senior Observer, tried to tighten things up, which we resented.

I checked some US Navy pilots out in the Firefly. They all wanted to do it since it had the same engine as a Spitfire! I had my heart in my mouth each time they went up in case I'd forgotten to tell them something vital. However, they all made it back in one piece.

The deal was that they'd fly the Firefly and we would get to fly the F4U (Corsair): something I really hankered after at the time. I thought I was next in line but was told that an Air Force F-86 pilot was ahead of me. I went to listen to his briefing, during which they spent a lot of time talking about the torque effect on takeoff with a really high-powered engine turning a really large propeller (my experience at Eglinton still fresh in my mind, I knew of what they spoke). The jet jockey, who rode the world's hottest fighter plane in daily combat over the Yalu wasn't overly impressed by someone who drove behind a *propeller*, for God's sake, and paid little attention.

The F-86, being a jet, of course evidenced no torque effect. The runway at K-6 had been scooped out of a hill so that there were banks of red earth on either side. The F4U with the F86 pilot at its controls, started off down the runway, and then began to veer to the left. Using full throttle, the jet jockey tried to lift it off before it hit the bank. He failed and the F4U did a neat roll onto the bank that, unfortunately, broke the pilot's neck. U.S Fifth Air Force banned any more F4U rides, by anyone, even me!

With the truce came a prisoner exchange and I flew up to Seoul with Peter Moranne (a radar operator newly included into our night fighter group) to greet the lone Royal Navy captive. Peter had enjoyed a really rough evening the day before, drinking rye whisky with some American friends and looked and felt like death. His uniform was tattered and mud stained and he had a nasty cut over one eye. He came into the mess hall where the Red Cross was feeding the returned prisoners. Most of them were wearing newly issued clean uniforms and looked quite fit, although a little lean. A huge Australian doctor saw him and became very concerned. "My oath, look what the bastards have done to this poor bloke, someone give him a hand." A pretty American Red Cross girl gave him a gorgeous welcoming smile, a big plate of eggs and bacon, and a cup of coffee. The coffee he managed to get down, but the eggs and bacon were too much, and were pushed away as a wave of nausea swept over him. No one was tactless enough to ask him questions; obviously the memory of what he had been through was too painful. Perhaps later, when time had healed the scars, not then. He threw up in the back of the plane on the way back to K-6 and I made him clean up the mess.

After the truce came the fun part. We paid a lot of calls on other air bases, going to the various units' officers' clubs, socializing with kindred spirits. Possibly the best and most exclusive officers' club in Korea was Rorke's Drift, where South African Air Force F-86 pilots would entertain those few outsiders lucky enough to be allowed to cross the crazy plank bridge which spanned the Drift, to drink with the extraordinary pilots inside. (One must remember that this was long before the days when apartheid made white South Africans international pariahs: the world was quite happy to have them fighting as part of the United Nations in Korea.)

It was Peter Moranne and Dave Ashby who first discovered the South Africans at K-55. They came back to K-6 much the worse for wear and told us about a bare hut with a round bar behind which an SAAF sergeant with a huge mustache poured powerful intoxicants at any hour of the day or night. There was, they said, a dartboard but little more. They had been drinking with an older pilot called, what else, Dad, who appeared at the bar wearing nothing but a mosquito net and an enormous pair of British army boots.

Peter took me back to Rorke's in a jeep and we spent a very lengthy evening there with bulky people carrying names like Doc, Jumbo and Scotty. Peter tried to call the Pope on the field telephone but couldn't get through so went to sleep in the seat of a handy jeep instead. We were given beds in someone's tent and chased away the next day's dry mouth with a lot more cold beer. After lunch we realized that we would be back very late, but Peter drove the jeep at a speed which must have represented a course record for the rocky Korean roads of that time and we just made it by 3 p.m. I was supposed to be flying but there was a general opinion that neither of us was up to it. In my case this was reinforced by the fact that I had traded my naval beret for Doc's green jockey cap. After a lot of coffee and hard talking I convinced Martin that I was in fact capable, and Peter and I took off at midnight, feeling like death.

To someone reading this in today's world, it must seem surprising that a young lad of twenty-one was allowed to strap himself behind a two thousand-plus horsepower engine and careen around the countryside at three hundred feet with a blood alcohol level that likely today would disqualify him from taking a moped to the supermarket. But that's the way it was: authority was tolerant, and most of us assumed we were leading charmed lives.

By August things were winding down. Peter and I flew down to Pohang to say goodbye to three of the Princeton F4U pilots (Bordelon, the fourth, was probably off getting another medal somewhere). We played dice, had a few beers and some lunch and then spent the afternoon on the beach. It was a truly beautiful day, and we swam and lay around just as if we were on expensive vacations except that there was a helicopter flying up and down the beach keeping a lookout for unfriendly frogmen, and every now and then a flight of F8F's would scream in to land. There were a lot of parties back at K-6 too, and everyone spent considerable time telling us how wonderful we, the Brits, were. Part of it was the fact that we were the only source of good Scotch whisky in the camp, and part that we weren't nearly as stuffy as they'd been led to believe.

Finally, on the last day of August, we flew back to the ship. We loaded our baggage into the planes and then flew up to Seoul where we had to be inspected by one of the truce teams: three "neutral" officers in fancy dress uniforms. They looked at the planes but weren't permitted to look in them. They wrote things down in a book and then allowed us to go back to *Ocean*. We landed on and the ship turned to head back to Japan. It was another splendid day: Korea to the left, some islands to the right and, later, a heaven full of stars. The wind off the sea felt good and I was glad to be back.

FIREFLY LANDING ON *OCEAN*

"We landed on and the ship turned to head back to Japan. It was another splendid day: Korea to the left, some islands to the right and, later, a heaven full of stars."

By September we could feel that summer was nearly over, as was our tour of duty in the Far East. We still had to continue our patrols since we were only in a condition of truce that might prove temporary (writing this well over half a century later, the truce continues, as temporary as ever.) There was, however, much less tension and we operated on a peacetime routine: exercises with other ships, simulated attacks on our own, and for the aviators, training in non-flying aspects of the ship.

We also had to go back to South Korea from time to time to ensure that the truce was being observed. In mid-September we went over to do a road and rail reconnaissance. I had a Swiss UN Observer called Hans Baumann in the back. As we went off the catapult, I asked him if he was all right. "Yess—that wass a kick in ze pants, hein?" And after we landed, he watched the others coming in. "Jeezes Christ," he said, "It's murder!"

While at Kure, Reg Simmonds and I visited Miyajima, a sacred island in the Inland Sea. It was actually a Japanese resort and we swam, played tennis, and viewed the pagodas and other attractions. What made it interesting was the fact that it was the place where eight years earlier, Kamikaze (suicide) pilots had spent their last few days on earth. They were given everything they could possibly desire: gifts for relatives, worship at holy shrines, beautiful scenery and sport, the most gorgeous geishas, and abundant sake. We met a man who worked there who had been due to fly off on his first and last mission when the atom bomb went off at Hiroshima across the bay. On the way back we went through Hiroshima by train. It was eight years after the bomb, and the place, though still devastated, looked no worse than the mess we had left behind in Korea or, for that matter, the mess the Germans had left in Plymouth or London. As we drew near the station the conductor shouted "Hiiiiir—osh—ima!" It was rather mundane considering the international significance attached to the name.

Finally, at the end of October, it was time to leave and sail south to Hong Kong, Singapore, and home. A fly-past of twenty-eight airplanes was, we were told, probably the last real flying *Ocean* would ever see. Ten Fireflies and eighteen Sea Furies took off and formed up five miles astern of the ship. We flew over at 800 ft. and then headed for Kure, then Iwakuni. Most of the aircraft landed at Iwakuni to be picked up by HMAS *Sydney*, our Australian twin that would relieve us. (see cover painting). A few, including three Fireflies, one of them flown by me, came back to the ship. The last arrival was indeed *Ocean*'s final deck landing. She was later converted into a Commando Carrier, using helicopters – nice work, but without arrester wires and tail hooks, it doesn't really count as naval aviation.

MOST OF *OCEAN'S* AIR GROUP, TAKEN THE DAY OF THE FAREWELL FLYPAST OVER KURE, JAPAN

"A fly-past of twenty-eight airplanes was, we were told, probably the last flying Ocean *would ever see."*

It was much later that I learned about the recognition given *Ocean*'s air group for its work in the Korean War. Our Captain and a couple of other ship's officers had been "mentioned in dispatches," but only one true decoration (Distinguished Service Order) had been awarded, this one to Pants Bloomer. Whether this was for his overall leadership of 810 Squadron, or for his work in assembling our little night fighter group with scant resources and little notice, I don't know, but all of us who had served under him felt that he deserved it and that we had helped him earn it. Almost better was the knowledge that "Captain Steven" got nothing.

KOREA AT NIGHT

"There is a current satellite photograph of Korea at night. It shows Japan—all bright lights, South Korea—the same, China and Mongolia—quite a lot of light and North Korea (still under the guidance of its "Dear Leader")—near total darkness."

Prior to the truce my brief war had involved some forty-eight missions into or over the combat zone, ten of them at night. The thirty-eight daytime missions had each required a deck landing, all of them completed safely. In fact, after my initial poor start, I never again bent either airplane or ship. I had dropped a lot of high explosives on people who had never done me any harm, but who surely would have had they had the chance. Some of them I killed, and rare in aerial combat, in several cases I had seen them die. The Korean landscape after three years of war was so totally devastated that I came away convinced that anything would be better than what we had inflicted in that wretched country's defense. Yet, when I visited there some thirty years later, I had to admit how very wrong I was. There is a current satellite photograph of Korea at night. It shows Japan—all bright lights, South Korea—the same, China and Mongolia—quite a lot of light and North Korea (still under the guidance of its "Dear Leader")—near total darkness.

I think we did a good job for the Koreans, and I remain quite proud of the small part I played. Moreover, as Winston Churchill had noted a half-century earlier, "Nothing in life is so exhilarating as to be shot at without result." However, writing this some six decades later, I must admit to feelings of guilt about those I killed or injured: was it necessary? Should I have taken pride in it? Will I at some point have to face a Judgment Day and, if so, will I be forgiven?

On passage from Kure to Hong Kong we had no aircraft on board, and *Ocean*'s Captain took advantage of this to make us act as assistants to the watchkeeping officers, having in mind the idea that this would be good for our careers and, in any event, we mustn't lose sight of the fact that as far as he was concerned, we were supposed to be seamen first and aviators only second.

I really enjoyed these watches, and especially the early

morning duty when one could watch the sun come up over the South China Sea to our east. I wrote a poem one day to memorize the beauty of it all. Readers must forgive the slight note of pomposity: I was only twenty-one at the time.

Look eastward now, and see the sun
Paint crimson colors on the tips
Of clouds and watch the wave tops spun
By early morning wind that dips
The spume away from green and drops
Again, to make another trough.
Dawn is a sight at sea that stops
The heart; and eyes are not enough.

Beauty must die, but never here;
The sun is hid by thunderheads
And darkness makes the waters bare.
The sea comes up, but now it sheds
Its gentle cloak and soon becomes
A thing of fear; sharp lightnings crack
On heaving waves, while thunder drums
A music wind and sea shout back.

Petal soft rainfall spatters now
The water with its many rings
As shadows from a leafy bough
Dapple the ground, and many things
Are beautiful, but none so rare
As horses white all tossed in spray,
Nor countryside has seemed so fair
As seascape on a tropic day

Written while on the South China Sea,
September 1953

On the way from Hong Kong to Singapore a rumor went around the ship that they were going to ask pilots to volunteer to fly for the French in Indochina. France at the time was entering the final phase of the bitter colonial war that would end in tragedy a few months later at Dien Bien Phu. Those of us who had unashamedly enjoyed their rather one-sided exposure to battle hastened to volunteer. I admit to being one of the dozen or so who lined up outside Captain Steven's cabin until we were told it was all an unfounded rumor. Had we known the full horror of the final agony we might have been less enthusiastic. On the other hand, we were young men, and young men know they are immortal. If they didn't believe that, we probably wouldn't be able to have any more wars, and what would that do to the armament industries?

My mother and father, who had been standing on Plymouth Hoe with many other ship's company relatives, came back to the dockside to greet us after we passed by the breakwater. They were pleased to see me home but only now that I am a parent myself do I realize how very relieved they were to get me back from my small war safe and sound. On the other hand, I think they were sad that I would be off again in the New Year, this time to America.

Chapter 8

A FIRST TIME VISITOR LEARNING ABOUT AMERICA, UP CLOSE

There were six of us on the Cunard Line's *Mauritania* when she pulled out of Southampton on a cold drizzly January day in 1954: Harry Smith and I were the pilots; the others, Peter Pritchard, Jock Goldie, Reg Simmonds, and Tom Ford were Observers. As part of the NATO build up following the Korean War, the United States had agreed to equip its allies with various weaponry. The Royal Navy's share of this generosity was a Squadron of "Skyraider" Airborne Early Warning (AEW) planes. Designed rapidly at the end of World War II to counter the threat of low flying Kamikazes, AEW planes carried a high-powered radar which could pick up intruders a long distance from the fleet and, using what in those days was a highly sophisticated communications link, transmit the radar picture back to the command center. Part of the deal was that, in order to be sure that this equipment was used properly, the aircrews should be trained in the United States. Hence our trip to New York, Cabin Class on a luxury liner at the British Government's expense.

On a couple of evenings a few of us changed into our naval mess dress, short jackets, stiff shirts and black bow ties, and bribed a friendly steward to let us through his pantry into the First Class quarters. More spacious, perhaps, but they didn't seem to be having a much better time than we were. Indeed, there was little to do on board except eat and drink and even that paled as we got into northern latitudes and the ship, lacking such modern conveniences as stabilizers, began to roll in the swells of the North Atlantic in mid-winter.

The sky was cloudless when we arrived in New York. All of us there for the first time were on deck trying to take in several different attractions. There was the famous skyline, living up to every expectation, on one side. There was the Statue of Liberty on the other. And ahead of us was a group of fireboats squirting large amounts of water up into the air to honor a visiting Head of State. Finally, on board, there was a vast gaggle of reporters who had come with the pilot tug to interview the important visitor who, it turned out, was the President of Turkey.

RMS *MAURITANIA*

"There were six of us on the Cunard Line's Mauritania *when she pulled out of Southampton on a cold drizzly January day in 1954."*

In our case the dreaded immigration was quite easy; as visiting military people on diplomatic visas we didn't even have to have our passports stamped, but we did cause some confusion by wanting to have them marked as a souvenir, demonstrating how rare it was in 1950's Britain to find a traveler who had actually been to America. The only serious question asked was whether we were, or ever had been, members of the Communist Party and, since none of us had been (at least so far as I know), we were allowed in.

Our hotel was the Wellington, which is still standing on Seventh Avenue. What it's like now I don't know, but I hope they've refurbished it since, as it was pretty shabby even in those days. My room on the 19th floor was rather poky and off an airshaft, but there was a special faucet for ice water in the bathroom which I thought a great luxury.

Peter Pritchard and I set off down Seventh Avenue to Times Square where we tried various bars, finding everything rather expensive compared with London. We went into Jack Dempsey's and met the owner, a huge fellow sitting at a table with four tough-looking blondes. He gave us an autographed picture of himself knocking out Jess Willard to become the world heavyweight-boxing champion in 1919. We acted suitably impressed.

After that our first night in New York turned into a very long one, with only kaleidoscopic memories of a series of encounters in a number of saloons before we stumbled into bed at six in the morning. There was amazing music in Greenwich Village and a very drunk girl who fell off her bar stool making a lunge at Peter. There was a singer in another bar with an incredible décolletage and, in yet another bar, a beautiful black girl with platinum blonde hair. We were offered innumerable sensory attractions in Harlem, $10 for the night and three different nationalities. And throughout there was the dichotomous reaction to our foreign-ness. Everyone we spoke to was intrigued by our speech; the British invasion of the United States had yet to begin and visitors like us were rare. Some thought we were Ivy Leaguers with phony accents. Those who agreed we were genuine British agreed with little else: Why do you trade with China? Why can't you defend or support yourselves? Why are you still imperialist?

Why did you get out of India? Why don't you get out of Africa? Who invented television, the automobile, the airplane, etc., etc.? It was all rather trying, even though interspersed by the occasional Anglophile who had nothing to say except how wonderful we were. It was dawn when Peter decided he wanted to go to Flatbush because he liked the sound of the name, but we couldn't make our money go into the subway turnstile (a nickel!), so sensibly went to bed instead.

Apart from a horrible headache and mouth like sandpaper on account of the excessive central heating, I decided when I was woken two hours later that I could really get to like New York. First impressions were universally favorable. The enormous numbers of cars, thousands—possibly millions—of them, proceeding in great rivers in all directions. The fact that every now and then, for no particular reason, one came upon a wisp of steam rising out of the sidewalk. The voices of the telephone operators, all of who said "You're welcome" whenever you thanked them and whose friendly assistance made us think they must be blonde goddesses if encountered in person. But most important, New York was awake, seemingly at all hours. Used to a London that, with the exception of a few private clubs, rolled up its sidewalks at around 11 p.m., we were fascinated by the fact that in this wonderful city you could apparently get anything at any time. Want something to eat at three in the morning? There would be a hamburger joint on the next block. This was living.

By this time, I had realized what many of my compatriots seemed so sadly to have missed; America is not just a big place full of people who might have been British had they not been sadly led astray by malcontents in the eighteenth century. It is a large lusty and very independent country that seems perfectly happy to remain that way. We (the British) may do things one way and they (the Americans) may choose to do things totally differently, but they certainly don't spend their lives hankering to adopt what we might consider the right way. My experience with Americans in Korea had introduced me to some of their charming idiosyncrasies, and now I was meeting them head on in the middle of Times Square and had better get used to them.

Mr. McStoker worked for the British consulate in New York; his job was to make sure that we got to the right places at the right time. After a coffee and Alka-Seltzer breakfast he took us onto the subway and showed us how to work the turnstiles. At the U.S. Naval headquarters for New York a Mr. Peterkin cut our orders—it seemed that, no one in the United States Navy, from the lowliest sailor to the mightiest Admiral, could go anywhere without a properly "cut" set of orders. Clutching ours dutifully in our hands we went back to our hotel, collected our baggage, and set off to the Pennsylvania Station. This, before its untimely destruction in the 1960's, was a vast church-like structure with a lofty roof supported by massive pillars. There were lots of shops and services and the whole place functioned like a small town. We were most impressed by the vending machines where you could get almost anything: different flavors of ice cream, candy, drinks, cigarettes, etc. Baggage storage was even coin operated; it all seemed fantastically *avant-garde*.

Reg and I walked up to Times Square and diffidently asked a ticket agency whether we could get seats for *Can Can*. Walter Winchell that morning had confided to his readers that seats were selling for as much as $60 per pair—an unheard-of price. Our luck was in: two on the aisle for the matinee, tenth row of the orchestra, had just been returned and we got them for $5.40 each.

Can Can was terrific. A memorable moment of theater was the opening of a scene where the heroine, played by a gorgeous woman with the odd name of Lilo, greeted the morning in Montmartre with Cole Porter's haunting "I Love Paris." After the show we went to the top of the Empire State building and admired the view. There was quite a haze and visibility was down to about a mile, but we could still see most of Manhattan, a blaze of light, skyscrapers silhouetted in the dusk, every window an illuminated pinprick, thousands of brightly colored neon signs. On either side the headlights of the homeward bound cars on the great elevated highways looked like giant red caterpillars crawling away from us.

Earlier, at Pennsylvania Station I had been puzzled by the apparent lack of trains. Now, after collecting our luggage, we found that they were tucked away in a very inferior position, down dingy little staircases and along rather poky little platforms. Although we were traveling first class Pullman, we were less than impressed by the rather dirty and very hot and stuffy carriages.

We woke up the following morning as the train barreled down the narrow neck of land which leads to Cape Charles and which might be Delaware, Maryland or Virginia or sometimes all three at the same time. It was frosty and very clear and, apart from their color, the people going about their early morning farm chores might well have been in rural England. However, as we went further south, the proportion of blacks in the work force seemed to increase markedly. At Cape Charles we left our train, and boarded a ferry to Norfolk, Virginia.

I needed to use the bathroom and, spying a likely looking entrance, headed to it. It was clearly a men's room but, as I got closer, I could see that it was labelled something like "Blacks Only". Fortunately, I soon discovered another likely door labelled "Whites Only". I was unaware of the fact that President Truman had desegregated the military some five years before my first coming to America, which explains why my arrival in Virginia (a southern state) was also my first exposure to the still vexing question of skin color in American life. (New York had long been ahead of the game and therefore didn't count.) Sadly, I have to record that, apart from the odd bathroom signs I am referring to, America's race problems did not cause us much lack of sleep at the time. We tucked them into the backs of our minds as just a few more of America's charming idiosyncrasies.

Norfolk Naval Air Station, which was to be our home for the next few months, was a vast place, designed to provide shore facilities for the carriers of the United States Navy's Atlantic Fleet. One of its many activities was the Fleet Airborne Electronic Training Unit (Atlantic), acronymed in the American way to FAETULANT. Faetulant was going to teach us how to operate the APS20 radar. Later, up at Quonset Point

Rhode Island, we would learn how to fly the AD4W "Skyraider." The first part of the course, however, only concerned the Observers who would sit in the back seat and operate all the bells and whistles. Although Skyraiders did have a repeating radar scope in the front seat, and we would from time to time have a go at playing with it, neither Harry Smith nor I intended to do anything so mundane as to become a fully-fledged radar operator. Thus we, or certainly I, assumed a rather detached air towards the whole process.

The second night we were there we decided to see what Norfolk had to offer in the way of entertainment– little, or so it seemed, other than a lot of bars and some burlesque houses. After a fairly lengthy sampling of the former, we decided to try the latter. And here we must make a small digression.

In England at the time, and we had also assumed in America, there was a comfortable tradition for young men on their own to round off an evening of fairly serious drinking by taking in the last show at the neighborhood burlesque house. But there the similarity between the two countries ends. England, we knew, had very tough laws regarding what the girls could do, but was pretty relaxed about what the audience got up to. In America, as we learned to our cost, it was the other way around.

The Lord Chamberlain, an appointed functionary who had regulated what went on in English theaters since the time of Charles II, had decreed that women could appear naked on stage provided (a) that the essential parts were covered with something, however small, and (b) that they stood absolutely still. Not a single quiver was allowed to stir the shapely flesh on display, or else the show would be closed, and the performers arrested; hence, what were known as *Tableaux Vivants*, more or less living statues. The curtain would go up and one would ogle a dozen or more young ladies wearing as little as it is humanly possible to wear, who would stand there absolutely motionless while the band played appropriate music. Britannia was always a favorite: the leading lady with a helmet and a minuscule shield but nothing else, surrounded by equally undressed nymphs, all to the sound of Elgar's

"Pomp and Circumstance".

Peaches Page was a popular stripper in Portsmouth (the largest British naval port). Posters advertising her arrival would say, "Hello boys—I'm looking forward to seeing more of you. I hope you're looking forward to seeing more of me." One evening a group of us went to see her after having imbibed a fairly significant amount of beer at the Keppel's Head. Our seats were in the balcony and we had come well prepared. As the curtain came up on the fair Peaches and her attendant court, we released homemade parachutes, which floated gently down onto the stage, each with a little burden attached. The girls, well trained, remained frozen until, as each parachute landed, the white mouse parachutist started to scamper around the stage. Girls screamed and then, the Lord Chamberlain notwithstanding, broke and ran. A lot of shapely pink flesh charging off in all directions added zest to an otherwise rather boring evening. The police arrived, but no arrests were made.

English audiences were less disciplined than the performers, and one of the favorite audience gambits was to constantly maneuver for a seat nearer the stage, to see more of what there was to see. At the Windmill Theater, London's premier home of the *Tableaux Vivants*, it was not uncommon for the more athletic members of the audience to make a dash for a newly emptied seat in the front row, gracefully hurdling across the intervening members of the public. No one seemed to object; indeed, a particularly ambitious leap was considered good sport.

Not so, as we have noted, in America. In Norfolk, in any event, the performers in the burlesque house seemed totally unrestrained as regards to either movement or apparel. By the end of her act the lead stripper was clearly down to no clothes at all, and shimmying at a pace that left even the audience exhausted. America certainly seemed to take seriously its claim to be the home of the brave.

TABLEAU VIVANT

"The curtain would go up and one would ogle a dozen or more young ladies wearing as little as it is humanly possible to wear, who would stand there absolutely motionless while the band played appropriate music."

That night in Norfolk, just as things seemed to be really warming up, four audience members got up to leave, vacating seats in the very front row. Bingo! Peter Pritchard led the charge, but the rest of us weren't far behind. Over the seats we went, oblivious to increasingly angry protests from the audience. With cries of triumph we settled down in our seats from which we could view more than man (at least 1950's man) should ever be permitted to see. But it didn't last long. Suddenly the show was interrupted by blasting whistles and a crowd of sailors with white armbands identifying them as Naval Police came charging up to the front of the house and hauled us out of our hard-won places. Explanations fell on deaf ears; we were off to the naval brig and charges would be preferred in the morning. Fortunately, somebody finally realized that we were foreigners—something to do with some foreign navy for God's sake! —and we were released with stern warnings never to try anything like that within the Norfolk City limits as long as we lived. Over half a century later it would not surprise me if a diligent sleuth (assuming he had that much time to spare) would discover that I had an outstanding arrest warrant in Norfolk, Virginia.

Things took a sudden and remarkable turn for the better a few evenings later when Reg and I were sitting in the Norfolk Officer's Club bar. From the far side of the room came a mighty shout of greetings. It was our friend Fritz Finger. His ship had come home from Korea and was now attached to the Atlantic Fleet with, so far as I could gather, not a significant amount to do. He was amazed to see us and immediately invited us to join his party, many of them officers from the *Trathen* we had got to know in Sasebo.

Fritz and some other *Trathen* officers had rented a house out on Virginia Beach. For reasons then somewhat obscure its occupants called the place The Teahouse of the January Moon. Reg and I were invited to become honorary tenants and did.

Next door to the Tea House a naval family was just moving in. It consisted of the father, a Chief Petty Officer, the mother, a ten-year-old son, and a daughter whose age both Fritz and I decided was quite immaterial. Thus, there started an extraordinarily complex three-way relationship. As we got to know her (which we did quite rapidly), Fritz and I both concluded that Anne was the most attractive witty, fun to be with, you name it, woman we had ever come across. However, she was not inexpensive: she liked to eat well and could drink like the proverbial fish. Indeed, I had never before come across the phrase "hollow legs," but if legs could indeed be hollow, then Anne's were hollower than most. In addition, the girl needed wheels; no cheap date, she was not about to be bussed from A to B. However, when you saw the heads turn when she walked into the Officers Club with her war paint on, it was all worthwhile.

Since neither Fritz nor I had a car or the wherewithal to buy one, serious measures were needed. Pooling our resources, we went down to the local office of a company called Hertz which was just beginning to market the revolutionary idea of a chain of car rental places where one would be able to pick up a car in one place and return it in another. They wanted, a cash deposit of $150 to rent a car for the weekend. (Credit cards were rare in those days.) The cost involved both a daily rate and a mileage charge. We told them that we would be driving to Richmond and would probably drop it off there. Then, in a spirit of friendship and accommodation that was truly heartwarming, we took it in turns to enjoy Anne's company.

ANNE ALLEN

"Fritz and I both thought that Anne was the most attractive, witty, fun to be with woman we had ever come across. However, she was not inexpensive: she liked to eat well and could drink like the proverbial fish."

If it was Fritz's night, he would take the car and the girl and we would agree ahead of time that I wouldn't go where he might be found–on my night, vice versa. Occasionally there was a big party at the Tea House and she would go with both of us. She handled the affair in a very sophisticated manner, not giving either of us cause to believe that she was fonder of the other. She also kept the whole thing very under control—at least with me at the time and, as Fritz assured me afterwards, also with him. Every week or so we would call the Hertz people in Richmond to tell them that we had been delayed and their car would be up there shortly. No one at Hertz seemed to mind too much but we both knew that the day of reckoning wasn't far off.

One of the British contributions to the Tea House mess was liquor. Through some complicated bilateral arrangement, we were officially carried on the staff of the British Embassy in Washington. As diplomats (sic!) we were entitled to bring in duty free liquor. Un-taxed Scotch whisky was about $1.50 a fifth, which even in those days was a bargain. We had been about a fortnight in Norfolk when the word came through that our first batch of liquor was waiting for us at the Embassy, could we pick it up. Tentatively we asked the boss of the base communications squadron if we could get a plane ride to Washington. He said it was very doubtful, there was a long waiting list, and why did we want to go to Washington anyway? The moment we had explained the reason for the trip, Reg was on a special flight to the nation's capital.

So, liberally supplied with liquor, wheels and a most desirable woman, time sped by. On my Anne nights we would often finish the evening, or rather the night, with breakfast at Ward's Corner, a supermarket complex that advertised proudly that it never closed. A store that never closed? Coming from a country where all the stores closed at 6 p.m. sharp, noon on Saturdays, never open on Sundays, this was almost too good to be true. I delighted in going in there at 3 a.m. and buying steak or some milk, just to test them. They had a bar billiards table and we would go in there, buy some beer and a hamburger, and play billiards, all only a few hours before dawn. Some nights I wouldn't bother to go back to bed, just shave, have some coffee and go down to the flight line for the morning trip. Sometimes I wondered how the indefatigable Anne managed to hold down her job, whatever it was, but I didn't lose much sleep over it; I didn't have much to lose anyway.

The work for the two of us who were pilots wasn't very demanding. Indeed, no one seemed to mind if we did nothing at all which, since that was all I was capable of most of the time, was a good thing. Our training took place in radar equipped P2V Neptune airplanes; two-engined land-based patrol planes with an endurance of almost a day. Fortunately, they thus had a bunk in the back so that crew members could get a quick nap. Fortunately too, neither Harry Smith, nor I, was twin-engine qualified so there wasn't much we could do legally to help with the piloting. As soon as we got on board I would make a beeline for the bunk, pull a blanket over my head, and sink into a deep sleep. Someone was usually nice enough to wake me in time for lunch, after which I would sit down in front of one of the radar screens and twiddle a few knobs to try to look useful.

For someone who kept his ears open America did provide rich educational opportunities. Once, for example, I was in a tavern with Fritz, a seedy place somewhere between the naval base and the Tea House where we had paused for needed refreshments. There was some rather rancid looking cheese dip and damp crackers on the bar and a sign over it said "Free Lunch." I must have commented on the generosity of the innkeeper because Fritz, who could become quite emotional at times, grabbed me by the lapels and urgently hissed in my ear "Don't ever, ever, forget that there is no such thing as a free lunch." I guess it was one of the things they taught at Babson (a business school where Fritz had passed a couple of post-high school years), but the more I thought about it, the more sense it made to me. In fact, if you think about it, "No such thing as a free lunch" is the most basic of all economic precepts.

Another seminal occasion during our stay in Norfolk also involved Fritz. His ship was berthed at the Convoy Escort (CE) piers where there was a small bar which, on Wednesday nights, served beers for a dime. Since what little money we had between us was dedicated to entertaining Anne (Hertz had not yet become serious about retrieving its car), making a dime beer last the better part of the evening and casually watching the tavern's TV set represented a cheap way of passing the time when Anne was unavailable.

It was on one such evening that we watched what might have been a turning point in American political journalism. It was the beginning of a drama that would transfix the public over the next several weeks and, strangely enough, become by far the most memorable part of my first visit to the United States.

Joseph McCarthy was an obscure Republican Senator from Wisconsin until, in 1950 or thereabouts, he discovered the headline grabbing power of anti-communism. His technique was a simple one: to accuse a broad cross-section of a given community of being communist or communist sympathizers. "I have in my hand," he would say, brandishing a piece of paper that no one ever actually got to see, "the names of 205 Communists in the State Department." His numbers and names would vary from speech to speech, but the thrust was always the same: there were traitors in our midst, and Joe McCarthy was, at the right time, going to expose them.

One of the many pleasures of America, as I saw it, was the *New York Times*, a strong and principled paper which really did do its very best to live up to its motto and furnish its readers with "All The News That's Fit to Print." Even today, I cannot start the day without the New York Times, and this addiction first took hold in Norfolk in 1954. And at that time, clearly of paramount importance to the *New York Times* and its readers was Joe McCarthy, then Chairman of the Senate Permanent Subcommittee on Investigations. In January a Gallup poll had found that 79% of Americans had an opinion about Joe McCarthy, and that over two-thirds of those holding an opinion (but not including the *New York Times*) viewed him favorably. Clearly, Americans were concerned about communists in important positions. However, as the poll made clear, many of those who admired what he was doing were less appreciative of the way he was doing it. Yet few among America's leadership, including Dwight Eisenhower, the Republican President, seemed willing to challenge the demagogic senator.

Which brings us back to the bar on the CE Piers during the last week in March 1954. *See It Now* was a highly regarded weekly news show featuring famed reporter Edward R. Murrow. Murrow had made his name reporting from London during the Blitz and was probably as trusted by his audience as Walter Cronkite would be a decade or so later. Murrow, deciding that those who opposed McCarthy's methods could no longer keep silent, had prepared a program that used newsreel clips of McCarthy in action to devastating effect. The impact was enhanced by the timing; when the show first aired, late on a Wednesday evening, McCarthy was locked in combat with a broad cross-section of the country's political, military, journalistic and business establishments.

We watched the show with a sense of mounting excitement. Even our dime beers went untouched. We were witnessing a man destroy himself on network TV; clearly history was being made, not only in a political sense but, possibly more importantly, because a medium was coming of age. Murrow followed up his first show with another deemed even more devastating. But the real job had been done the first time. For McCarthy from then on it was all downhill. At the time I was still young enough to believe in the perfection of the British political system, but even so, I did harbor some doubts as to whether a similar situation, should it arise somewhere among Britain's governing classes, would ever be exposed so brutally by our beloved British Broadcasting Corporation.

SEN. JOSEPH MCCARTHY vs. EDWARD R. MURROW

*"*See It Now *was a highly regarded weekly news show featuring famed reporter Edward R. Murrow... Murrow, deciding that those who opposed McCarthy's methods could no longer keep silent, had prepared a program that used newsreel clips of McCarthy in action to devastating effect."*

We still had some unfinished business in Norfolk. First, the Hertz company was becoming increasingly demanding. Our stories about pressing diversions on the way from Norfolk to Richmond were beginning to wear thin, and ugly letters were coming in insisting on the return of the car and the payment of what had become a staggeringly high list of daily and mileage charges. Finally, we gave in: the car went back to its original base in Norfolk, and we were presented with a bill for some $350 that, in those days, was an enormous amount of money. I was able to raise about $100, Reg made me a loan, and Fritz put the arm on his father, who I gather was not pleased. Despite that, Fritz and I remained close for many years until his death in the late 1960's, which came much earlier than it should have done. He was a fine friend, and I still miss our lengthy transatlantic phone calls.

Secondly there was Anne. We had never found out what she did; there were vague references to some kind of school and Fritz and I had assumed that she was taking undemanding courses at some neighboring Junior College. How else, we asked ourselves, would she be able to stay up until the small hours, consume inordinate amounts of good Scotch whiskey, and still hold down whatever occupation was claiming her attention? It was fairly late in the relationship that I arrived at the Allen house one evening to pick her up. Anne wasn't back, but her mother was there. Anne would be a little while, she explained, she had to stay late in the library to do some homework. Homework? Her mother was quite unfazed as she confirmed what she assumed we had always known: daughter Anne was 16 going on 17 and a junior in high school. I was deeply impressed: if this was what the American nation could produce by way of school children, just wait until they grew to be adults! However, my recognition of the extent to which I had contributed to the delinquency of a minor (with, I must add, the willing assistance of the young lady's parents), did make saying goodbye a little easier.

Narragansett Bay is a large inlet in the small coast of Rhode Island. It leads up to Providence, the state capital, and is anchored on the eastern side by the town of Newport. Quonset Point was created by the Navy during World War II on filled land on the western side of the bay. It was designed to permit the largest carriers of the time to berth right next to the taxiway so that aircraft could be driven up and then hoisted directly on board. In 1954 it was used principally for Skyraider training. We were due to spend six weeks there so that Harry and I could learn to fly the Skyraider and the observers could obtain practical experience using their Norfolk-acquired radar skills in the new plane.

The Skyraider was a truly immense airplane. However, although it was large, it was a beautiful machine to fly and, as we would find out later, an absolute dream to deck land. Also, to our British eyes used to the Spartan vagaries of our domestic aircraft industry, it was remarkably luxurious. Everything appeared to be in the right place, easily accessible, obvious as to its intent, and, strangely for a warplane, pleasing to the eye. It had an electric elevator trim, boosted aileron controls and, with a lavishness we could only associate with America, was endowed with an autopilot.

SKYRAIDER AD4W

"The Skyraider was a truly immense airplane... it was a beautiful machine to fly and...an absolute dream to deck land."

It was not until mid-May that we started flying at Quonset Point, first some dual in Harvards and then solo in the Skyraider. New England in May was a wonderful place to be flying. The pace was quite leisurely but since each trip was fairly long I managed to put in over forty hours during the four weeks we spent there. Once I had got the hang of the plane it was fairly uneventful flying with plenty of time to look around. It was commissioning time for all the many yacht clubs on Long Island Sound and I recall watching enviously from about 1,500 feet above, as legions of sail and powerboats put to sea to test themselves and the waters for the first time that year. It never occurred to me then, nor should it have, that little more than a decade later I would be launching my own sailboat into those same waters.

Newport is connected to the western shore of Narragansett Bay by a high suspension bridge. Returning to Quonset one had to call in and report “over the bridge for landing.” Then, on down wind, one had to report “gear down and checked, three in the green,” meaning that there were three green lights to indicate that the undercarriage was firmly in place. To us folk reared in simpler disciplines, it all seemed rather exotic.

There was a lot of time to spare between flights, and soon we were again caught up with all the drama of the battle between Joe McCarthy and the United States Army. Any time we were free we would scrawl a message on the ready room blackboard: “gone to watch Joe,” and hightail it up to the Officers’ Club where there was a TV set which appeared permanently tuned into the conflict. Although we saw it mostly as high comedy, contrasting as it did so strongly with the statelier processes of British public life, it also had the same attraction as would any raw struggle for power, with clearly defined good guys and bad guys, and outstanding villains and heroes.

The villains were McCarthy and his sidekick, Roy Cohn, who had accused the Army of blackmail. The one clear hero was Army counsel Joseph Welch, an austere New Englander who, over a long and tortuous series of public hearings, amply demonstrated the truth of the Army’s claim that Cohn had wielded incredible pressure from McCarthy’s Subcommittee in order to attempt to obtain a long list of favors for his good friend G. David Schine, who had been abruptly drafted into the army. It was Welch who used wit, the most potent of weapons where demagogues are concerned, to bring out what, in the 1950’s, was publicly unmentionable. A photograph of Schine produced in evidence turned out to have been doctored by someone on Cohn's staff. Welch asked who had done it, and no one seemed to know. "Was it a pixie?" Welch asked. McCarthy: "Will the counsel define . . . what a pixie is?" Welch: "Yes, I should say, Mr. Senator, that a pixie is a close relative of a fairy." His most famous comment, made when once again McCarthy stepped over even the most liberally drawn line, was "Have you no sense of decency, Sir, at long last? Have you no sense of decency?"

We watched, in fascination as the system, working as it was supposed to, gradually destroyed the Senator, but those of us who had watched Ed Murrow six weeks earlier had already seen the writing on the wall. McCarthy, disgraced, died of drink three years later, leaving behind a new phrase in the language and a trail of wrecked careers. Roy Cohn went on to a checkered profession as a lawyer, always teetering just on the wrong side of the law. He died quite recently of AIDS, but was already immortalized by the amazing Nathan Lane in the play *Angels in America*. I'm not sure what happened to G. David Schine.

The recreational options afforded by Quonset Point were limited. There was, on the right hand as you went north (nothing but water to the south) the ancient town of Providence with Brown University and little else. To the left (southwest) was New York. We never even considered Providence. Maybe a few years later we might have considered Newport, but in those days there was no bridge across the eastern entrance to the bay, and getting to Newport was complicated, getting back worse.

Money had become short (Hertz had taken its toll), and thus our visits to New York had to be carefully planned. Reg and I divided our time between the theater and Greenwich Village, the latter as frugal tourists rather than, as in our earlier visits, hedonistic bacchanites.

We saw *Pajama Game*, with its wonderfully witty score, Alfred Drake in *Kismet*, a big sumptuously staged musical, and *Tea House of the August Moon*, John Patrick's comedy set in

Okinawa under American occupation which, I then realized, had inspired the name of our home from home in Norfolk. We spent a lot of time in the Village—no cover charges in those days and a cheap beer would go a long way. Eddy Condon's was then the favored place for good jazz, featuring a trumpet player with the engaging name of Wild Bill Davidson and Ralph Sutton, an excellent pianist.

We returned to England in May 1954 in the same high standard that we had left: Cabin Class, this time on the Queen Mary, a vessel of some antiquity which had probably seen its best days as a troop ship during the war, and subsequently as the means of reuniting thousands of British brides with their GI husbands. She now sits, rusting graciously, in Long Beach, California where, I understand, you can be married in the suite used regularly by the Duke of Windsor, his predatory Duchess, and their 1,200 pieces of luggage.

The journey was, predictably, stormy; why did transatlantic passenger liners try to disguise the fact that the quickest route from New York to Southampton took one north of Labrador for most of the trip? We did all the conventional shipboard things, and eventually arrived at the landmark Needles, off the westernmost end of the Isle of Wight. It was great to get back and, much as I was attracted to what lay to the west, it never dawned on me that I would ever cross the Atlantic again. (In case any readers find me lacking in imagination, they must remember that passenger jets were still a gleam in some designer's eye, and crossing the Atlantic by air involved propeller planes that were slow, noisy and, by today's standards, horribly expensive.)

I regard it as a truism that, out of any group of half a dozen Englishmen coming to America for the first time, one will hate it, constantly carping as to why a people who appear to deserve so little end up with so much, and always whining about things not being the same as they are at home. Peter Pritchard was one of those. Four will remain neutral, hoping always that they will be able to find a decent beer or a good cup of tea, and quietly pining for home. And there will be one who falls in love with the place, and in our case, that was I (and to some extent, Reg).

I felt comfortable with America and Americans, possibly due to my early reading but more likely overwhelmed by the sheer exuberance of place and people. I was particularly taken with American women who seemed to approach life with a warmth and vitality not noticeable among most of my British women friends. I don't think I realized at the time how deeply I had fallen in love with the place, but I had, and I have remained a constant lover ever since.

Chapter 9

LEARNING WHILE FLYING IN THE PEACETIME NAVY

The Royal Navy established 849 Squadron, its first operational Airborne Early Warning unit, in 1953. By the time I joined it at the Culdrose Royal Naval Air Station in 1954 it consisted of a headquarters unit and four flights (A, B, C, and D) which were attached to various carriers. Reg Simmonds and I became part of C Flight, commanded by Lt. Cdr. D. T. Andrews, known mostly as Andy, but sometimes as "Boy". He was a wonderful fellow and my time with C Flight was one of the happiest I spent with the Navy.

Culdrose was no exception to the rule that Royal Naval Air Stations would always be sited a long way from anywhere. It was located in hilly country just outside the little town of Helston, which anchors one corner of a triangular and extraordinarily picturesque piece of Cornwall jutting out into the English Channel and known as The Lizard. The other corner is bounded by the Helford River. In between are a dozen or so tiny villages, many of them sheltered in steep little valleys leading down to the sea. The villages carried wonderful names like Mullion and Porthowstock (pronounced Proustock), St. Mawes and Goonhilly Down, Mousehole, and Tintagel, home to the legendary King Arthur's castle. Each boasted its own little pub and it all added up to marvelous beer drinking country. The area has a long history of wrecking and smuggling and a healthy disrespect for the laws of England. While I was at Culdrose its complement of officers, particularly aircrew, added further legends to those already established by the native Cornish.

"C" FLIGHT of 849 SQUADRON

"...my time with C Flight was one of the happiest I spent with the Navy."

Our work at Culdrose, while interesting, was really only preparation for joining a carrier. It thus paled compared to our extra-curricular activities. Nevertheless, we began to work as a team, both inside and outside the airplane. Reg Simmonds and I had already spent much of our flying careers with each other, and so needed little time to learn to work together. However, the Skyraider carried a three-man crew (two in the back), and for the first few months we lacked a permanent third man. We did do a lot of flying, learning the local area, practicing fighter intercepts, and tracking submarines.

Culdrose had its share of fog at certain times of year, and the Skyraider's powerful radar provided it with a unique homing capability. The Helford River, which was about a hundred yards wide at its mouth, narrowed to about fifteen at which point it led directly to Culdrose's northwest-southeast runway. During times of low visibility, Reg would find the river on his radar and then give me directions so that I could follow it blind, at about fifty feet above the water, until I could see the runway. Reg and his fellow radar operator in the back had minimal external visibility while, on the way in, particularly during the latter stages of the approach, all I could see were trees and houses flashing by on either side. But the whole thing was under our own control and we preferred it to some remote person looking at a radar screen on the ground. Also, the last landmark on our way up river was the Three Tuns Inn, a Helford institution and Andy's home away from home. It gave one a comforting feeling flying final approach on a cold winter's day to know that down there was a cheerful fire and a friendly pint or two.

Our training also included the occasional session of Airfield Dummy Deck Landings (ADDL's), which were required to get us accustomed to the deck landing characteristics of the Skyraider. It was a very friendly airplane, and we anticipated little trouble. Instrument flying too was important; the Royal Navy was moving into an all-weather, twenty-four hour a day configuration. New jet-powered night fighters were coming on line and 849 Squadron was an important component of the new and more technically demanding doctrine.

"C" Flight of 849 Squadron consisted of six pilots and twelve observers, equipped with five airplanes. It was a small group and a remarkably homogenous one. Most of this I attribute to Andy who was a great party man and managed to attract kindred spirits to his group.

Our favorite off-duty gathering place was the Bell Inn in Helston, run by two spinster sisters who had a long a warm relationship with the Navy. The bar was heavily decorated with memorabilia, including many squadron photographs, everyone lined up in front of their airplanes, preparatory to going off to war. Jan and Belle, the owners, remembered many of them, with sorrow or joy, and when warmed up probably could demonstrate more knowledge of the Service than we had. There was a fine and friendly bunch of Wrens, and what I recall as endless warm summer evenings spent roaring around the Lizard in fast cars packed overly full of couples whose principal concern was getting in one more beer before the pubs closed.

BELL INN

"Our favorite off-duty gathering place was the Bell Inn in Helston, run by two spinster sisters...Jan and Belle, the owners, ...when warmed up probably could tell us more about the Service than we could.

Since I was only a couple of hours drive from Cornwood, I would also go home for weekends whenever duty allowed. My latest vehicle, a Sunbeam-Talbot was a fast and steady car, and I took pride each trip in knocking another minute or two off my previous record. My passengers, often Reg, must have had nerves of steel.

MICHAEL IN THE SUNBEAM-TALBOT

"My latest vehicle, a Sunbeam-Talbot was a fast and steady car, and I took pride each trip in knocking another minute or two off my previous record. My passengers, often Reg, must have had nerves of steel."

My parents appear as somewhat shadowy figures in this part of my narrative, largely because after I joined the navy my visits home were brief and usually uneventful. An exception to this was my time based at Culdrose, when Little Stert was easily reachable by car. We normally had weekends off and friends enjoyed sharing the comforts of my home. This was especially true of Reg who (when his nerves could withstand the trip), welcomed a family environment, but primarily, I suspect, a decent meal with dessert enhanced by Devonshire cream, still produced by my mother, with Ruby's help, using methodology little changed from the sixteenth century

Culdrose's Station Flight had a Sea Fury that was designated for instrument training, but which also provided a welcome change for those of us determined not to lose touch with our aerobatic skills. As an added, but seldom discussed benefit, it only took about twenty minutes to fly from Culdrose to Cornwood. Andy, a benevolent man, would sign me off for an hour of "Aerobatic refresher," without being too specific regarding what it was or where it was to be done, and I would fly down to Little Stert and alert whoever was there by doing a few aileron rolls dangerously close to our roof top, leaving the scene by flying down the Yealm Valley and over the viaduct. Most impressed by all this showing off was our housekeeper Ruby, who would announce proudly to whoever would listen that "Master Michael was doing his Flairy-gary stuff over the house today." I don't know where she got the phrase "Flairy-gary", but it seemed to fit the descriptive need quite well.

Albion was one of a class of eight carriers laid down in 1944 in anticipation of a continuing war with Japan. At the end of the war construction was halted but then continued on four of them when the Navy realized they would be needed to meet the needs of the next generation of jet aircraft. Three of the class: *Albion*, *Centaur*, and *Bulwark*, were completed in 1953 and 1954 and, together with older (and larger) *Eagle* and *Ark Roya*l would comprise the Royal Navy's carrier fleet for the next decade. The fourth of the class, *Hermes*, was completed much later and incorporated a number of improvements.

The angled deck was a British invention but, as with so many other of their bright ideas, they lacked the funds to exploit it to the proper extent. *Albion* and her two sister ships had what they called a "modified angled deck" which in practice meant that they had welded some steel onto the port side of the flight deck and painted a canted angle onto it. However, to the aviators she represented a significant advance: no longer faced with the wire barriers that stretched across a conventional flight deck, a pilot who missed all the arrester wires on landing could just go round and try again. Stress levels were notably reduced. The angled deck was timely; prior to the introduction of jets there was a lot of engine in front of the pilot, available to absorb at least some of the impact. In early naval jets, on the other hand, the pilot was right out in front and thus would be pretty much the first object to come in contact with the barrier in the event he missed all the wires. Decapitation was a likely outcome.

On our first cruise with her *Albion* lacked two other major British contributions to carrier operations: the steam catapult and the mirror landing system. We were still reliant on the older, and less reliable, hydraulic catapults to get us airborne, and our "Batsman" to guide us safely onto the deck. However, our confidence was vastly increased by the fact that, if any of us made a mistake during landing, there was no longer the inevitable costly sound of bending metal as the airplane crashed into the barrier.

Albion was about as new as a ship could be when we flew on board in September 1954. Completed only the previous May, she had been engaged in trials of various kinds and the builders' people were still fussing about. Compared with *Ocean*, somewhat battered by several years of war and post war service, she was clean and comfortable. Moreover, even though we were still lowly Sub-Lieutenants, our four berth cabins aft were effectively air-conditioned; even on the hottest days in the Mediterranean I don't recall ever being too warm. However, we were still directly under the flight deck, although at the place where aircraft landed rather than right under the catapults.

HMS *ALBION*

WITH SKYRAIDERS ON "MODIFIED ANGLED DECK"

"Albion... had what they called a "modified angled deck" which meant that they had welded some steel onto the port side of the flight deck and painted a canted angle onto it."

We spent our first few days on board her cruising up and down the English Channel, showing our new ship off to the press, getting the flight deck crew used to flying operations, and regaining our deck landing skills. Then it was off to the Mediterranean for most of the winter.

HMS *ALBION* IN GRAND HARBOR, MALTA

"Albion *was about as new as a ship could be when we flew on board in September 1954.*"

Our principal base for the next six months was Malta. Sometimes we would disembark our airplanes to Hal Far, the Royal Naval Air Station there, but most of the time when we were only in port for a day or two we would stay on *Albion* in Grand Harbor. Reg and I flew with a succession of different observers in the back seat until, in mid-November, Ron Harrison appeared on the scene.

I never found out much about Ron's background nor, I think, did I want to. Senior to both Reg and me, he came to us with a reputation for reckless behavior and low morals, and my first sight of him did nothing to create a sense of confidence that he would enhance the abilities of our little team. Harrison's physical appearance was such as to justify the more acceptable of his several nicknames: El Squalido. He was a big heavy man whose rather flabby body was surmounted by a large moon face of extraordinary pallor. How wrong I was in my judgment; never assess a book by its cover.

Harrison became not only one of my closest friends; he was also an amazing radar operator. He and Reg had an uncanny ability to pick up the smallest "enemy" contact under the most difficult circumstances and bring our "friendly" fighter aircraft right up behind it. I was mostly just along for the ride, my main job being to get them off and bring them back safely, but I shared in the aura provided by two of the most professional airborne fighter directors in the navy.

Most of our time at sea was spent working with our ship's fighter and strike squadrons. Apart from 849 'C' Flight, *Albion* carried 898 Squadron of Hawker Seahawk jet fighters and 813 Squadron of Westland Wyverns. We have already mentioned my ambition to fly Wyverns; now I am not embarrassed to express my relief that I had been denied this privilege. Apart from the fact that its complex turbo-prop engine seemed always to be breaking down, the airplane had an unenviable reputation for killing people. I remember a Wyvern pilot friend of mine ending up rather messily in the rear end of HMS *Eagle*'s island superstructure. He was dead when they got him down to the sickbay.

The Russians were thought to be using submarines to keep a close watch on us, so we also conducted anti-submarine patrols. *Albion* at that time carried no specialized anti-submarine squadrons but the Skyraider's powerful radar could pick up a periscope or snorkel at a considerable distance. The plan was for us to bring a nearby frigate up to do its worst with depth charges, since we ourselves carried no ordnance. Although the all-weather nature of our job was challenging, there wasn't enough of it to get the adrenalin flowing and, apart from getting on and off *Albion*, (and even that was becoming rather routine), the flying was somewhat monotonous. However, back in Malta we made up for it, professionally and socially.

Professionally I took advantage of the fact that there was a seldom used Sea Fury at Hal Far, that an indulgent Station Flight commander allowed me to fly from time to time. By 1954 Sea Furies had been superseded by the jet Sea Hawk. However, converted to civilian use, Sea Furies remain popular even today as "unlimited" class competitors at the Reno Air Races. The plane was a dream to fly and I happily took one up whenever I could, accumulating some ten hours, mostly playing aerobatics among the clouds over the neighboring island of Gozo.

Socially, Malta in the 1950s was a most entertaining place. Although independence was already clearly in the cards, the natives were very friendly and, in most cases, almost embarrassingly loyal to the crown. During WWII King George VI had visited Malta to bestow the George Cross on every islander for heroism during the intense Axis bombing of 1941. Later the newly married Queen Elizabeth lived there for a while with her young naval officer husband, Prince Philip. Malta's preoccupation with royalty was obvious – nearly every bar you went into had on its wall a framed letter from Buckingham Palace in which some secretary acknowledged how pleased Her Majesty was to have received the owner's loyal expression of good wishes on her accession or birthday or visit or whatever.

1955 was a wonderful year. There was a lot of flying to be done around Malta, and on and off *Albion*. She was a really splendid ship and we were all becoming very attached to her. Many years later, my naval career well behind me, I acquired a beautiful 41' Hinckley sloop for cruising Shelter Island waters with my family. Her name, registered with the U.S. Coast Guard, is *Albion*.

✈✈✈✈✈✈✈✈✈✈✈✈✈✈

We would be called on to do a lot of night flying from *Albion* and our next challenge was learning to land on an aircraft carrier in darkness. One evening Andy arranged to have a tug turn our ship so that her stern pointed towards one of the battlements of Valetta Harbor. Then, as night fell, he took those of his pilots who were not yet night qualified (including me) up on the battlements, and had the ship turn on its deck landing lights. These consisted of a faint line of white lights down the middle of the deck and some blue ones at strategic

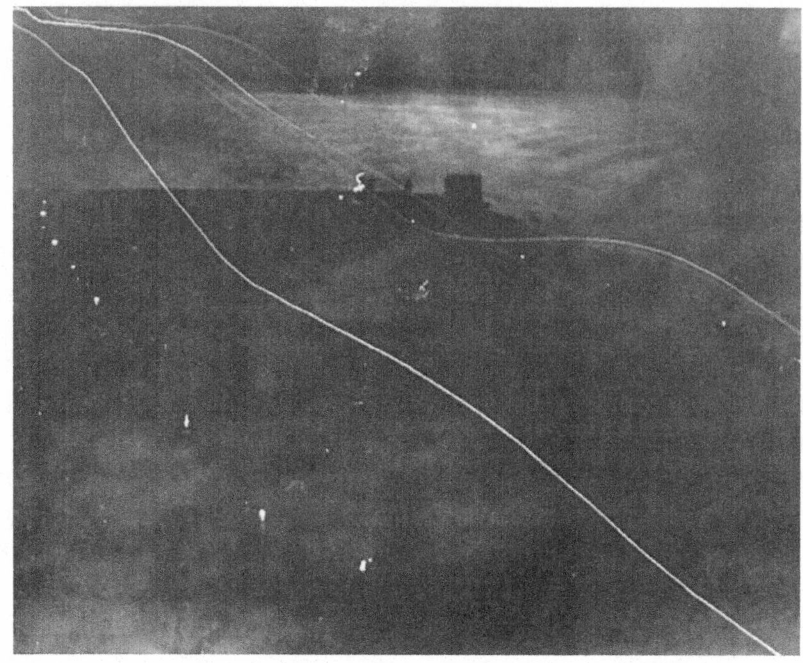

MICHAEL IN SKYRAIDER NIGHT LANDING ON *ALBION*, 1955

"Unbroken lines are the airplane's navigation lights. Other lights are: "deck landing lights...a faint line of white lights down the middle of the deck and some blue ones at strategic intervals on the sides. Small, shielded floodlights provided additional rather sparse illumination so that, from the final approach, you could see a little bit of what you were about to land on. Having a bright moon helped too."

intervals on the sides. Small, shielded floodlights provided additional rather sparse illumination so that, from the final approach, you could see a little bit of the deck you were about to land on. The batsman had fluorescent wands. Everything was at a very low intensity so that, hopefully, snooping enemy submarines wouldn't see us. From the wall where Andy had us standing we had an excellent view of the ship as she would look during a landing. It was a very thoughtful way of introducing us to a rather hazardous experience. When we went to sea and some of us tried the real thing it wasn't nearly as bad as people made out; we each did four landings and got a "qualified to deck land at night" endorsement in our log books. It was a significant rite of passage.

At the end of March Reg Simmonds, Ron Harrison and I brought the Royal Navy's spring exercises to a premature close before they had started, by taking off after midnight in a gale in the Bay of Biscay and finding the Home Fleet on its way out to intercept us ("us" in this case being *Albion* and her escorts). I guess the staff of the Home Fleet, our "enemy," thought they could safely go to bed since there was no way we could be closer than 200 miles and a dawn search by their aircraft would surely find us. Instead we flew out for an hour and a half in seriously bad weather, found the "enemy" and tracked them until dawn when we directed a strike which, had we been in a real conflict, would have sunk the lot. *Albion* should have been on her best behavior that night, but even she had to pitch and roll quite a bit among the Bay of Biscay's stormy seas. That was a night that all three of us felt we had truly earned our flight pay. It was thus with some relief when, the exercise over, we all returned safely to Culdrose. If I had possessed a better sense of my own history, I might have wondered for a moment how this period compared to my first days on HMS *Indefatigable*, in January 1951. I was back on the Bay of Biscay, but at least I wasn't still scrubbing decks, indicating some degree of progress.

Like the angled deck, the mirror landing system was another British invention whose full development required the deeper pockets of the United States Navy. The original idea was first tested by its inventor, Lt. Cdr. Goodhart, by having his Wren secretary prop the mirror of her powder compact on his desk, with her uncapped lipstick in front of it. He then walked across his office, keeping the reflection of the lipstick in the middle of the mirror, and ended up with his chin on the desk. In practice the mirror was gyro stabilized and mounted on the port side of the ship so that it always maintained a constant angle in relation to the horizon. Instead of the lipstick there were bright lights mounted aft of the mirror which reflected back as a perfect glide path. A rack of green lights, mounted horizontally either side of the mirror provided a datum (a fixed point). If the pilot kept the glide path lights (the "meatball") in line with the green lights, he would catch the third wire and make a perfect landing. In those days we still had a batsman to keep an eye on things and, at least for propeller planes, give the mandatory "cut" or "wave off." But apart from that he was out of work. One of the early mirrors was mounted on HMS *Bulwark* and we spent most of May on that ship, testing it, by day and night. We also showed it off for the press and the BBC.

In the fall, and back on *Albion* we were off to the Mediterranean again, spending some time in Naples and working with the Italian Navy. Reg and I went by train to Rome and did all the right Vatican and St. Peter's stuff. On the way back to Naples I unscrewed a plaque from the railroad carriage that said, "It is dangerous to lean out of the window" in five different languages. I had a mechanic fix it to the side of the cockpit of my Skyraider and was rather proud of it. We went on to Pompeii and looked at all the dead people and ruins dug up from under the earthquake. Prior to the eruption of Vesuvius, the town was a vacation resort for wealthy Romans, a sort of archeological Hamptons, and it was said that the gods sent the earthquake to punish them for all their misdeeds.

We did some exercises with the American Sixth Fleet during August, and then headed back out of the Mediterranean via British-owned Gibraltar. Franco, who was still running a fascist Spain at that time, was going through one of his periodic snits about the British presence on his doorstep (something the Spanish had never really accepted ever since they lost Gibraltar in 1704 following the War of the Spanish Succession).

There were silly rules about access, one of which was that only officers would be allowed across the border without some special permit. The ostensible reason was to preserve the virtue of Spanish womanhood, an argument that those of us familiar with the general run of local talent found somewhat unconvincing. Several of us were out one night when we ran into our highly skilled and valuable Chief Petty Officer radar technician. We told him we were going across into Spain, and would he like to come. He pointed out that, not being an officer, he couldn't leave Gibraltar. Not to worry, we replied, and hailing a passing taxi, stuffed him into the trunk. No problem crossing the border and a happy few hours spent drinking cheap sherry and watching even cheaper girls doing strange things with animals. Coming out of the last bar around two in the morning we heard a rather odd noise coming out of the trunk of our faithfully waiting taxi. Opening it up we found the wretched Chief, completely overlooked, curled up in a fetal position, gasping for air. The situation called for rapid application of stimulants and we all piled back into the bar, woke the sleepy girls, and within an hour had our precious radar expert back in the land of the living.

We left the Mediterranean and joined *Centaur*, our sister ship, for exercises in the North Sea, participating in the annual NATO large-scale maneuvers designed to defend northern Europe from the threatening Soviet hordes. The weather was rough and we spent a lot of time flying around at low levels, at night and in fog. However, all was worthwhile when we came into Copenhagen for a "flag showing" visit. I was appointed fleet social officer, in charge of all entertainment. The most popular recreation for the enlisted sailors was a tour of the Carlsberg brewery, which consisted of some half hour during which the men looked impatiently at shiny copper pipes and vast yeasty smelling vats, and two or three more hours in which they drank Carlsberg until satiated or insensible. The experience would later stand me in good stead.

The Danes were incredibly hospitable, kindness we repaid with a rather splendid cocktail party. Among the guests were some wondrously congenial English hospital nurses who took a couple of us back to their apartment where they provided all the comforts of home a lonely sailor could ask for. Back at sea we left *Albion* for the last time after a lengthy and energetic farewell party, taking off with throbbing head and shaky hand into what appeared to be endless cloud. I was fortunate to have Andy's wing to fly on, otherwise I think my bones would even now be decorating the bottom of the North Sea, along with those of the unsuspecting Reg and Ron. My logbook reads "Arrived Culdrose, heavy rain, 300' cloud base." I have never been so glad to see the ground. Harrison and Simmonds slept through the entire thing.

Back at Culdrose we had little to do before going on our Christmas leave, during which I had planned to join my family in Switzerland for a ski vacation. One evening Reg and I drove to Penzance to see a movie after which an incident occurred that had a powerful influence on my future lifestyle. We were coming home along the coast road when, rounding a corner we came upon a very nasty car crash that had obviously happened only moments before. It was a small car and it was totally upside down, with stuff dripping out and, from the faint sounds we could hear, someone alive underneath. Reg and I and a third person managed to lift the wreck enough so that we could see what was there; it was two men, horribly mangled, neither with any chance of living. I had never seen such a mess. We could move the car no further, and could hold it where it was no longer, so gently put it back and waited for the wrecking crew. The men were artists, well known locally as the Cornish Potters. Alcohol was involved and both were dead before the ambulance arrived. It would be wrong to claim that I never drank and drove again, but from that point on I had a harrowing notion of what the combination could do.

I finished 1955 in London, where I joined the traditional pre-Christmas Fleet Air Arm gathering at Shepherd's (located in the Market of the same name, and a favorite watering hole for fellow naval aviators), together with one of the congenial nurses from Copenhagen. Life could hardly get better, but it did.

Chapter 10

LEARNING ABOUT THE MAGIC OF AN ENCHANTED EVENING

"Some enchanted evening
You may see a stranger
Across a crowded room."

South Pacific,
Music by Richard Rodgers,
Lyrics by Oscar Hammerstein

My parents, brother Tony, cousin Dorothy and I went skiing in Davos, Switzerland over the Christmas/New Year week, (1955/56). We arrived on the morning of Christmas Eve, and after renting our equipment signed up for a brief ski-school refresher. We had some lessons and skied a bit in the afternoon. That evening we had dinner at a hotel near the station that had a little dance floor and an accordion band. The five of us were enjoying a drink after dinner when Dorothy pointed out that, while my mother and father had each other's company, and she and Tony were together, I was all alone. Someone said that they were sure I could take care of myself, which I took as a challenge.

Looking across the room I saw two women sitting by themselves. One rather plump one was drinking a liqueur, while the other was drinking tea. The tea drinker was a breathtakingly beautiful blonde. Demonstrating an unusual amount of *sang froid*, I casually sashayed across the room. “Would you care to dance?” I asked the blonde. There was a long pause while the plump one leaned over and whispered something, which I was informed afterwards, was a warning to take care because I looked shifty. The blonde eventually gave me a dazzling smile and said “Certainly”. She was tall, almost my height, slim and with the most beautiful voice. Her name was Joan; she was American, and I immediately fell deeply in love with her, and remained so for the rest of her life. In later years, when people asked me where I met Joan I would say,“I picked her up in a bar in Switzerland”.

The evening went by in a daze. We danced some more, laughed a lot, seemed to get on well, but it would be a tough chore to separate her from her friend Sue. They were traveling together in Europe, had just been to a wedding in Germany, and had decided to spend a few days in Switzerland. Sue didn’t ski, but Joan did a bit and was determined to do better. Sue was the self-appointed guardian of Joan’s virtue, and wasn’t going to let her out of her sight.

By an amazing coincidence we found that we were in the same ski school class. Later, I discovered later that it wasn’t such a coincidence: Joan had determined that she was under-challenged in the next lower class and had had herself promoted to mine. We skied together, had lunch together, got together in the evening, but the only time I was able to shake the ever-present chaperone was when we were skiing, and it is not easy to make the slightest dent in a woman’s moral armor while she is wearing skis.

A night or so later I gave a cocktail party in my hotel room, inviting my mother and father, Tony and Dorothy, Joan and her friend and, to fill out the numbers, the accordion player from the hotel bar who played “Arrivederci Roma” with lots of flourishes. I made a devastating martini but we had no ice so I took a suitcase outside and filled it with snow. The porter wanted to know what I planned to do with it and I told him I was taking it home as a souvenir. He gave me a funny look—

maybe stealing Swiss snow was a Federal offense. We filled the washbasin up with snow and chilled the martinis. At the time it all seemed very sophisticated and extraordinarily romantic. All I wanted to do was impress this splendid creature God had so generously dropped in my lap. Looking back, I'm not sure a suitcase full of snow was the best way to do it, but my love was tolerant.

I discovered all the vital things about her. She came from Cambridge, which I learned was outside Boston, where she lived with her mother. She had two brothers, one of whom, as she put it, worked for Henry Ford. In his spare time he was a pilot in the U.S. naval reserves. The other had something to do with copper. The way she described them they seemed very rich and rather awe-inspiring. Her father had died some years earlier. She had been teaching school in Boston, but her family had suggested she take a vacation in Europe. Deciding to stay longer, she had given up her job and started working for the American Army School system in Germany.

On the last day of the year we went up to the top of the Parsen, eight of us I think. Our instructor, with a gay cry, "Follow me!" disappeared over the crest of the mountain, as did the first two or three of his pupils. Joan was next. "My goodness," she said, "I can't do that; they're going over a precipice."

"Of course, you can," I urged her. Gingerly she poled herself over the edge and began accelerating down what was, in fact, a rather steep slope. Instinctively she reached out to grasp hold of the nearest fixed object, an orange pole marking the trail. Her upper body stopped, but the bottom half went on, until the whole of her subsided in a heap. I thought it was funny until I realized that she was quite badly hurt: a torn ankle ligament as it turned out. Clearly, she could not ski down the mountain, but clearly too she could not go back down by train on her own. The instructor asked for volunteers. Another man, an obviously nasty piece of work called Michael Isaacs, tried to get in on the act, but I got there first. Joan managed to limp back up to the top with me carrying her skis, and then we set off back down in the little mountain railway. It was quite crowded, and we had to stand. No skis, no Sue, a crush of people pushing us together! Wow! She had the most delightful fragrance, but what really got to me was the voice—a very soft and melodious New England accent. If I was in love before, by now, ten minutes later, I was totally infatuated. Many years had gone by when a good friend of mine, who had kindly offered to read a draft of this book, asked me "What happened to the Father, Mother, Brother and cousin Dorothy who had so happily set off with you on your ski vacation?" And the best I could reply was "I have no idea: from the moment I met her, I paid attention only to Joan, no one else existed." Looking back, all I can think is that my family must have been extraordinarily indulgent or very forgiving. But it didn't take long for them to join me in our love for Joan.

Later that night the odiously bossy Michael Isaacs insisted on her coming to his room so that he could look at the swollen ankle. I seethed with jealousy when she agreed, only to have my adoration further inflamed when she insisted that both Sue and I come along too. Afterwards all either of us could recall about his room was a pair of scarlet long-johns hanging behind the door. They, I think, spelled the end of the pushy fellow.

Bravely she danced in what must have been a very painful condition. We drove around town in a horse-drawn sled, Sue still tightly in tow, but there was opportunity under the ratty old bearskin rug for a tentative cuddle. Back at the railroad hotel, where they were staying, we dumped the friend and sat on the stairs until the early morning. I kissed her and decided, then and there, that this was the woman I was going to spend the rest of my life with. She in turn told me that I was the most remarkable man she had ever met. I could hardly believe my ears—under the circumstances it was hard to believe, but it was a splendid thing to hear at that moment. From then on I was like putty in her hands and so remained.

Poets can find a thousand or more ways to describe their first true love and what they find so unique about that person, but to the ordinary mortal the task is near impossible. If I had to say what first attracted me to Joan and kept me bound to her body and soul for over forty years, my normal command of language would totally fail me. I suppose I might have said that she was very beautiful, and she made me laugh – both true, but woefully inadequate. It probably sounds weak and foolish, but I think the main reason that I loved her was because she loved me, and if asked she would probably have said the same about me. You could say it was a mutual passion with no obvious means of support. Others might put it all down to pheromones, and I would too if I knew what they were.

This is a book about learning, not a romance novel, so it seems appropriate to follow the advice of that great American philosopher, Mr. Yogi Berra: "When you come to a fork in the road, take it," and the fork in the road here is firmly marked, so we can take it. We'll continue in the more demanding direction of learning, and require readers (disappointed as they may be) to allow their imaginations to construct the path of true love as it follows the bumpy road appropriate for two young people: a British naval aviator and an American school teacher; one an Anglican, the other a Catholic; one barely graduated from high school, the other with a BA and a teaching degree; etc, etc. True to form, the love story will not be a smooth one, but we'll try to stick to the chosen mandate (education) and only allow ourselves to wander off into the fields of romance when such is necessary in order to construct an understandable story.

✈✈✈✈✈✈✈✈✈✈✈✈✈✈✈

Culdrose was cold and wet and rather depressing after Switzerland and Joan. My friends were very impressed with this new woman in my life; I carried a photograph of Joan on skis in which she looked a lot like the movie star Grace Kelly (I thought her much more beautiful) and my good friend Paddy Lynch was always insisting that I pull it out and show people. When he first saw it, he commented, "Great looking girl, Coles—what's she like between the sheets?" I was aghast—she would never do anything like that. How we would ever reproduce ourselves if we married had obviously not occurred to me. I was still living in an age when there were naughty girls who did and nice girls who didn't, and if you couldn't tell the difference your mother surely would be able to. Joan fell so obviously into the "nice" category that there was never any need to consult my mother. There was general agreement that anyone that beautiful must be a millionaire's daughter (British popular opinion at that time was still convinced that millionaires accounted for a considerable proportion of the American population.) Never having asked, I could neither confirm nor deny that; I only knew that I missed her terribly already.

JOAN COLLINS, 1955

"I carried a photograph of Joan on skis in which she looked a lot like the movie star Grace Kelly (I thought her much more beautiful) and my friend Paddy Lynch was always insisting that I pull it out and show people."

On short notice we were sent up to Eglinton in Northern Ireland where, three short years earlier, I had learned to land on a ship. True to form, Eglinton proved to be colder and even wetter than Culdrose. We were supposed to participate in some anti-submarine training involving 815 Squadron, which was equipped with Avengers (TBF's). Real submarines would approach from the Atlantic, and we would have to pick them up on our radar and steer the Avengers in for the kill. All well and good except that most of the flying involved extended legs out over the North Atlantic, at night, and never more than 500 ft. above the waves. The Skyraider only had one engine, and we placed considerable faith in the workmanship of its manufacturer, the Curtiss-Wright Company, and its employees.

To give us some chance of survival in case of engine failure we had been given "wet suits": rubber coveralls that went over warm underwear and sealed tightly around the neck and wrists. Newly introduced to the Navy, these garments were supposed to keep us alive in sub-zero water whereas, we were told, the life expectancy without them was some twenty minutes.

We arrived at Eglinton on a rainy day (all days are rainy there) and we were told that we would share the 815 Squadron Ready Room. Since it was quite small and all the best chairs were occupied and no one seemed inclined to move we hung around the door waiting to see if anyone was going to invite us in. Suddenly Ron Harrison spotted a mouse sitting quite still in the middle of the floor. "Christ," he said, "look at that f---ing mouse" (always one for gracious introductions was Harrison). Then, using what must have been a size twelve wetsuit boot, he gave the little creature a sharp and well placed kick. The tiny beast caromed around the walls like a nicely planned pool shot and eventually came to rest not far from where it had started. By this time, however, it was on its back, wee paws in the air. This was very obviously one very dead mouse. Harrison's rather pleased expression gave way to dismay when he was subjected to a stream of four-lettered abuse; the mouse, it seemed, was the 815 Squadron pet, laboriously trained over several months so that it would come when called and eat, sleep and play in the middle of the ready room. All that work, and what appeared considerable affection, now lay inert in front of its trainers. Our hosts were a generous group, but it took several gallons of Guinness dispensed over the Eglinton wardroom bar to compensate for the dead mouse and to bring our relationship back to a civil working level.

It was a typical wet, northern Irish day when Joan's letter arrived. I had never seen her writing before, but even without the German stamp I would have known it was from her, and over the next few years the writing, with its strong slightly backward sloping strokes would become a major part of my life, heralding letters that always started my heart thumping like a runaway motor. (Readers with short memories may need reminding that all this was happening when e-mail was a dream in the mind of some student at MIT. In those days people wrote letters on pieces of paper, placed them in envelopes, stuck on a stamp, and gave them to the Post Office. I don't know how many trees died to satisfy our grand passion, but I guess by the time of our wedding we had made a hole in a small forest.) I hurried back to my room and wrote a reply that I hoped would convey my enormous enthusiasm without appearing sloppy.

So began what must have become one of the longest and most consistent romantic correspondences in history. Soon we were writing each other every day, sometimes twice, and so it continued all the time we were apart for the three and a half years until our wedding.

I had known Joan a bare ten days or so, but her presence changed my existence in many ways, not the least of which was a near total forsaking of the somewhat dissolute life-style which I had formerly taken for granted. With an occasional modest exception, I think I can claim that from that point on I was as pure as driven snow, temperate enough to please the most dedicated Baptist (or nearly so), and frugal as only a man with few assets to his name can be when contemplating a move whose expense was so enormous as to defy all quantification. I was determined to marry Joan.

By the end of March, 1956 I had, including my time at Quonset Point, nearly two years in AEW work. From my point of view things were winding down, accentuated by the fact that Andy had gone off to other duties, his place taken by a much less convivial fellow called Fuller, while Reg had disappeared to Yeovilton to take a night-fighter course. I still flew with Ron, but others came and went to take Reg's place, none as good, and I missed him. Paddy Lynch was still around, but my main reason for visiting the Bell in Helston was no longer to be part of the crowd around the bar.

We are talking 1956 here, and a long-distance telephone call was quite an important event, requiring considerable operator inputs. Overseas was quite unthinkable; only foreign ministers or the most powerful of business tycoons ever placed a call overseas, and it took a lot of time and effort to do so. Trying to call Joan from the lone pay phone in the Culdrose Officers' Mess was difficult and caused a lot of irritation with others waiting to use it. Indeed, it was only a year or so earlier that the rule requiring approval of one's commanding officer before making an overseas phone call had been rescinded.

I thus had an arrangement with Jan, the landlady of the Bell. I would go up to her bedroom and use her only phone to place the call, then go down to the bar to wait. When the call came through, normally after about half an hour, I would hear the international operator: "Is that Lieutenant Coles? I have Miss Joan Collins on the line–go ahead Miss Collins." When we had finished talking the operator would call back and tell me how much the call had cost and I would pay Jan. Soon we found that it was pretty much the same operator each night; I guess he listened into some of our calls which did get a little steamy at times. Then, instead of telling me Miss Collins was on the line, he would sing some romantic song, most often the old Edith Piaf "La Vie en Rose". Our regular phone calls became quite an event–to me, to the operator, and to the folks in the bar at the Bell. To anyone who wanted to know what was going on, Paddy Lynch would say, "Show them the photo," and I would proudly drag out my by now dog-eared picture of Joan on skis, still looking like Grace Kelly, but still much more beautiful, and everyone would ooh and ah. But, although we knew we would write to each other and talk on the phone a lot, we never knew when we would see each other again.

Throughout this period, I had been debating my future. I had no idea if Joan would marry me or not and had not yet plucked up the courage to ask her, but I knew if I was to have any credibility I must be able to offer something in the way of economic security. There were two ways to do this: a serious long-term career in the Navy, or a radical departure into something in the civilian world. Both had their drawbacks. The Navy offered stability and all my performance reviews indicated that I had reasonably good professional prospects. But the Navy was a miserable life for wives, as I had seen too often when stationed at some of the more God-forsaken places that Her Majesty chose to put her naval air stations. I just couldn't imagine Joan living like some of the other navy wives, in a dank cottage outside Londonderry with poor sanitation and permanently damp wallpaper. Of the civilian world, on the other hand, I knew little. I had no idea what I might do, whether I could do it, and how I would go about getting it. The options looked bleak, but every time I looked at Joan I knew that love somehow would conquer all.

In the meantime I had taken what seemed a sensible step by applying to become a flight instructor. As it was when I learned to fly three years earlier, all military instructing was done by the Royal Air Force, and the RAF took their training very seriously. No one could teach an air force or navy pilot to fly unless he had first passed a quite grueling course at the RAF's Central Flying School (CFS). The emphasis there was not only on technical skills, flying and ground school, but also on teaching techniques. The latter were considered as important as the former. Unlike the more Darwinian approach of the American system, the British took the attitude that if someone wanted to fly and had the basic aptitudes, a good instructor should be able to teach him. I happen to think it a good system that turns out excellent pilots. I thoroughly enjoyed my time at CFS.

I had several motives for wanting to go there. First, I think it was a sensible career move; passing the CFS course meant that one had above average and well-polished flying skills. Second, I was not yet jet-qualified and was beginning to get in a propeller driven rut. A flying instructor had to be a jet-pilot, and this was one way of getting there. Third, it meant that for two years, at least, I would be in one place, and that place would be on dry land. I would thus be able to place my pursuit of Joan on a more solid footing. Lastly, I believed it would be a qualification that should help me if I decided to leave the navy at the end of my eight years and go on to try my luck with the airlines. So I went to the Central Flying School, but first I had to learn to fly jets.

The jet-powered airplane then currently employed as a trainer was the de Havilland Vampire, a splendid little machine. However, the Navy, in its wisdom, had decided that conversion to jets would take place using Gloster Meteors (of which they had none) instead of in Vampires (of which they had plenty.) They employed a firm of civilian contractors to teach us how to fly Meteors, after which we would do a quick switch to Vampires. The oddity of this arrangement was enhanced by the fact that the Meteor had two engines while the Vampire had but one, requiring a conversion from single to twin engine as well as from piston to jet. And, to further complicate the situation, readers need to realize that flying with two engines is, paradoxically, a lot more difficult than flying with just one. The marvels of the military mind, I thought at the time. Looking back with the cynicism provided by advancing years, I must also admit that possibly the whole transaction may not have been quite as squeaky clean as the way we liked to believe our government operated, in those days at least.

The Meteor course did not start until early July, and I had finished at Culdrose in early June, so I was able to take three weeks leave. Joan and I decided to meet in Copenhagen, which was great, but her friend Sue would be coming too, which was not so great. Also, I must hasten to add here, going back to Copenhagen had absolutely nothing to do with memories of my last visit there. The weather was beautiful and we did all the right sightseeing, but one afternoon it rained. What to do? Based on my last visit to Denmark's friendly capital, I knew just the thing and, calling the Carlsberg brewery, discovered that, yes indeed, they would be open to the public that afternoon for conducted tours. "Why on earth," asked Sue and Joan, "would we want to look at a brewery?" Vat after vat, pipe after pipe, they asked the same question and I gave the same answer: trust me. Finally we came to a door which, when opened, disclosed a big hall with a long table on which were little flags denoting each nationality on the tour and dozens and dozens of bottles of Carlsberg beer. Our tour companions each took a decorous sip or two and went their ways out into the rain. Joan, Sue and I took to the task more seriously. As I recall, when we left an hour or so later the sun was shining. If it wasn't, it should have been.

On mid-summer's eve we went to the Tivoli Gardens, Denmark's great playground, which boasted the tallest Ferris wheel in Europe. The three of us got into one of the little cars and went round and round with the wheel. When it stopped we were at the very top, with a breathtaking view over the whole city. Joan was next to me, with Sue opposite.

I leaned over and whispered in her ear (Joan's, not Sue's) "Will you marry me?"

Sue's ears perked up "What's he saying? I didn't hear."

"Nothing," said Joan, "just a funny remark."

Not the most successful proposal in the world, and certainly one for which it took an inordinately long time to get an answer. But still, in the history of such things, midsummer's eve, the top of the Ferris wheel, in Denmark's Tivoli Gardens is probably as enchanting a place as any.

Mid-summer in Denmark there is little or no darkness. We eventually shook off Sue, who went home to bed, and Joan and I talked and danced at a nightclub called Adlon that finally put us out at about 4 a.m. It was daylight and the only place open was the zoo, so we went there and admired the elephants. I don't know what we said to each other, except that I know she didn't say "yes" to me, but it was still a remarkable night: midsummer in Copenhagen, 1956, Ferris wheels, dancing and elephants; the time I first proposed to Joan, and she hadn't said no.

From Copenhagen we went to Oslo, where the ever-vigilant Sue left us, after making sure that Joan and I were safely ensconced in different hotels. In fact, there being some convention going on, hotels were hard to find. The visitors' bureau found Joan a bed in a nice private home but could find nothing for me other than a convent. The nuns were extraordinarily solicitous; I gather I was the first man ever to spend the night there, and I didn't embarrass anyone.

We went on to Bergen, nearly on the Arctic Circle, and then caught a boat over to England. It was very rough and Joan needed comforting, but wouldn't allow me alone in her cabin with the door shut. Hence passing passengers were treated to the sight of Joan, her face a pale green color, lying on her bunk while I knelt uncomfortably on the floor, my feet sticking out of the open cabin door. I was beginning to learn the complex implications of a Catholic education.

Passing through London on our way down to visit my parents, we called on my uncle Tim (a prosperous wine importer). He was highly taken with Joan and sent his secretary out for champagne. Joan was very impressed with him when he casually tossed the empty bottle over his shoulder with unerring accuracy into the wastebasket. I didn't like to steal his thunder by pointing out that it was a trick he practiced almost daily. We had lunch at the Berkely Grill, and as we parted around three, he gave her his highest accolade: "She's a fine old girl for her food and drink," he said. After a brief visit with my parents we headed back to London, then I made my way to Wales and Joan back to Germany.

Chapter 11

LEARNING TO BE A FLYING INSTRUCTOR

There were six of us in the Meteor conversion course at St David's. I forget all of them except Brian Jones, who was a delight to see again. Now married, he too was leading a quieter and more sober life, but his home provided a welcome respite from the rather basic amenities of the mostly unused World War II airfield we were living on.

The Meteor, which first flew in 1943, was one of the very early jet aircraft. A few were used operationally during the war, including attacks on the V-1 "flying bombs" which really needed a jet to catch them. Legend has it that particularly bold RAF pilots would fly close to them, tuck their wing-tip under that of the V-1 and flip it over on its back so that its gyroscopes all got mixed up, causing it to crash. Meteors established world speed records of over 600 mph in 1945 and 1946, and were subsequently exported to many different countries.

The Meteor not only introduced me to the vagaries of jet propulsion (slow to accelerate and decelerate, prone to "flame out" if you opened the throttle too suddenly, unbelievably smooth and quiet, and masses of power for aerobatics), but also gave me my first and only exposure to twin-engined flight.

The problem with two engines is that if one stops the other tends to push the airplane into a turn, which may lead to a roll and a spin, all of it requiring fairly rapid corrective action: the greater the power, the greater the asymmetrical engine problem.

METEOR JET
WITH LANDING GEAR DOWN

"The Meteor, which first flew in 1943, was one of the very early jet aircraft."

The Central Flying School of the Royal Air Force was a remarkable institution, and anyone who has been lucky enough to pass through its rigorous six month training program will find themselves not only a markedly better pilot but also, as a teacher, benefitting from a considerable improvement in technique, regardless of whether the subject being taught is aerobatics or algebra.

During my time there the school taught its instructors-in-training in two locations, both in some of the most beautiful parts of Gloucester. South Cerney trained experienced pilots to be able to undertake *ab initio* instruction, taking pilot candidates who had never flown before and bringing them up to a skill level sufficient for them to perform relatively demanding maneuvers in basic training aircraft. Little Rissington (deemed the home of RAF flying instruction) taught South Cerney graduates in more complex, often fairly high performance, front line aircraft, again instructing already experienced pilots to a level where they could be excellent teachers.

The Royal Air Force (with the Royal Navy following along) was a great believer in Standardization: flying instruction was based on a well-developed and disciplined line of “patter”. Rather like an actor in a West End play, students were not allowed to “Improve” the script with their own words and phrases; ideally a young trainee in Canada being instructed by a CFS graduate would hear exactly the same patter as he might get from a similarly trained teacher in central England. At South Cerney and Little Rissington we were learning the patter and how to apply it, in the air and on the ground, in basic trainers and in quite advanced jets.

In addition, pilots under CFS training were learning in a similarly disciplined way how to prepare a student before a lesson to be given in the air, and how to de-brief once it was over. The basis of teaching, therefore, was the old “Methodist Minister’s sermon” formula: “tell ’em what you’re going to tell ‘em; tell ‘em; then tell ‘em what you told ‘em”. I’m prejudiced enough to think it was all very effective.

After my proposal Joan and I managed to get together for a couple of times; she came over to a summer ball at Yeovilton and then later for a similar event at Ford, in Sussex where, having successfully learned to fly the Meteor, I was now learning to fly the somewhat simpler Vampire. We also spent some time with my family at Little Stert. Everywhere we went she was a tremendous hit with my friends and family, and apart from her understandable reluctance to commit to matrimony with someone whose prospects were as unstable as mine, our affair was moving along absolutely swimmingly.

Then came September and the new school year had started in Germany while the Central Flying School was requiring 100% of my time. Calls and letters continued, but there was no point on the near horizon when we could be sure of seeing each other again. But I was enjoying CFS, doing well, learning a lot, and really noticing the improvement in my flying skills. South Cerney, where we were based, was a pleasant enough place and the Jones' and I took advantage of its proximity to Oxford and London.

At the end of October we finished the first part of CFS, mainly concerned with teaching people the basics of flying in the piston-engined Provost, the successor to the lamentable Prentice in which I had gone solo four years earlier. We moved a few miles across Gloucestershire to Little Rissington where we would concentrate on more advanced flying in Vampires. It was just about then that the whole international situation blew up.

Some background is necessary. About three months earlier Egypt's dictatorial Colonel Nasser had nationalized the Suez Canal, owned at the time by an Anglo-French consortium. Egypt's action, running counter to the prevailing norms of international behavior, greatly angered the British and French, and particularly Britain's Prime Minister, Anthony Eden. A crisis atmosphere quickly took hold in both injured countries, and preparations were made to counter the Egyptian action, by military means if diplomacy failed. However, despite British assurances that the "wogs" would be unable to run it, ships continued moving gracefully up and down the Canal, and each day that went by reduced the sense of international outrage and increased the possibility that any Anglo-French military move would be met with international censure. Tension piled upon tension when the Hungarians attempted to throw off the Soviet-sponsored Communist regime that had dominated their county since 1945. The world appeared increasingly unstable, but fortunately economic pressure, skillfully applied by Washington's Eisenhower administration, together with the willingness of London and Paris to accept the inevitable loss of face, brought the matter to a peaceful conclusion. (Anyone interested in learning more about this seminal event in recent British history should read "Suez, 1956" in my book *Naval Occasions 1939 through 1956*, available through Amazon.)

Going about my business over the cool green fields of Gloucestershire all this seemed a long way off. However, Joan was in southern Germany and if what was going on in Hungary spilled over the borders she would be in the line of fire. My calls showed increasing concern, while she remained totally confident; things, she said, were not nearly as bad as they seemed from the press and besides, a lot of the United States army lay between her and the Russians.

Of further concern at this time was the fact that Joan, who had not said "No" to my proposal, had yet to bring herself to say "Yes." She did, however suggest that I might want to take the instruction in the Roman faith, required in those days for a heretic wanting to marry a Catholic.

I found a Catholic naval chaplain called Father Heamus conveniently near Little Rissington, who agreed to put me through my religious paces. He was a splendidly rotund fellow, in appearance rather like Friar Tuck in the stories of Robin Hood. He also had a well-developed taste in wine. Indeed, unlike most of his ilk, he was a popular presence in any wardroom mess since he always willingly took on the rather onerous task of Wine Secretary, leaving behind him around the country a series of cellars that remained for some years the delight of his messmates. We would sit in front of the fire, sampling some excellent claret and talking about the Catholic faith which, in that context, seemed much more benign than the menacing threat that our Elizabethan forefathers had fought so valiantly to repel.

One afternoon he asked me why Joan would choose to marry a non-Catholic. I said I thought it was because she loved me—I didn't dare tell him she hadn't yet agreed to. He said that wouldn't do, there had to be a Vatican approved reason, and we could choose from three. First, had I made her pregnant? My goodness no, I replied, restraining myself from telling him I hadn't even got to first base. Then, he asked, was she the only Catholic living alone in a small community where there was little chance of meeting young men of her own faith? No way, I replied, thinking that even with Father Heamus' liberally elastic interpretation, Boston probably wouldn't pass muster as a small, Catholic-free community. Oh dear, he sighed, then there's only *aetas aetatis* left. What's that? I asked. (My Latin lessons long forgotten.) He told me that it was a dispensation permitted if, as he put it, the girl was getting a "bit long in the tooth," and I was her last chance at matrimony. We'll take that one, I said. When I told Joan later she appeared amused but, judging by the way she never forgot it, she may have felt me a little on the disloyal side.

While all this was going on, we finished our CFS course with a bang—literally. One must remember that it was only nine years earlier that United States Air Force Major Chuck Yeager, flying the Bell XS-1 at Edwards Air Force Base in the USA, had demonstrated that supersonic flight was possible. The United States Air Force had introduced its first transsonic fighter, the F-86, in late 1951 in Korea, and in 1954 the RAF had acquired the British-made Hawker Hunter a rather mean looking airplane that remained the staple fighter in several European air forces for over two decades.

It was thought useful experience for flying instructors to have flown supersonically; even then the numbers of British aviators with that training was quite limited. There was no trainer version of the Hunter, so I felt the RAF showed touching faith when, after half a day spent studying the instruction booklet, they strapped me solo into this lethal piece of machinery and merrily sent me on my way. The first flight was forty-five minutes getting the hang of the thing, and then landing it at what seemed at the time to be an incredible speed. The second flight lasted about the same time and is recorded in my log book as "Mach run—bang at 1.15." That meant I had been 1.15 times the speed of sound—in a dive. There was little to tell other than the position of the needle on the mach-meter and a slight bump on the controls, but I was told it made a healthy bang on the ground. For the final flight I put the plane through its paces, aerobatics and another bang, followed by an instrument approach. All very tame in today's world where passenger-loaded Concordes in their time casually went supersonic every day across the Atlantic, but quite exciting for a young lad in early 1957. I have a colorful certificate in my logbook saying that I am a member in good standing of the Mach 1.0 Club.

HAWKER HUNTER

"There was no trainer version of the Hunter, so I felt the RAF showed touching faith when, after half a day spent studying the instruction booklet, they strapped me solo into this lethal piece of machinery and merrily sent me on my way."

We qualified as flying instructors at the end of January 1957. I continued to be rated an above average pilot, and had distinguished myself by winning a big trophy for getting the highest grades in ground instruction. I recall this came about because I undertook to coach a fellow student who was not the brightest of intellects. As a result I learned the stuff much more effectively than if I had studied on my own. To my credit, he passed also, providing me with a useful educational rule: you can learn almost anything better if you find a way to teach it to somebody else.

My posting was to the Royal Air Force station at Valley on the island of Anglesea in North Wales, but first they gave me a couple of weeks leave. Joan wanted me to meet her family, an idea that terrified me on account of both its social and economic significance. Socially I had visions of all these forbidding New Englanders, the formidable Mrs. Collins in the lead, surrounding me and demanding to know how I had the temerity to even look at their daughter/sister. Economically, I knew I could make it over the Atlantic and back, but that there would be precious little left over to spend when I got there. Fortunately, the Bank of England bailed me out of financial embarrassment: due to Britain's continued post-Suez economic woes, travelers were still only allowed to take with them some fifty pounds when traveling on vacation. This I explained to Joan by letter, suggesting that maybe when I got to New York she could finance me in the form of a loan, which I would pay back when she returned to London. She did indeed carry me, tactfully and unobtrusively, during my stay in America. It was the most productive borrowing I ever undertook. So far as I can recall, I never paid her back, though I still nursed hope that she thought it a worthwhile investment on her part.

After a few days in New York, visiting Joan's brother, we drove up to Cambridge where I stayed at the Brattle Inn, near where Joan's mother lived. While staying in Cambridge Joan took me for a walk which, given the future, demonstrated on her part either remarkable prescience or a devilishly

Machiavellian turn of mind. Coming out of her apartment on Memorial Drive we turned left, then right over the Lars Anderson Bridge. "Why look," she exclaimed ingenuously, "it's the Harvard Business School." After reading Herman Wouk's book *Sincerely, Willis Wade*, in which the Business School played quite a significant role, I was generally familiar with its purpose, and was thus not completely unprepared when she suggested we look around. Our path was no accident; unerringly she led the way up a flight of stairs and thence to the Placement Office where a wall full of notice boards carried what seemed an enormous number of job offers. "Why look," she said, "management trainee at Ford, $6,000, financial analyst at Raytheon, $6,500. . ." Since I was at the time making a bare $3,000 per annum and very much doubted that I would do better in a yet to be determined civilian capacity, it all seemed rather far-fetched. Joan was sensible enough to leave the thought hanging, and we moved on. Some of my children even today refer to that little expedition as "The Walk."

Joan's sister-in-law, wife of the Navy pilot, who I had wrongly assumed would naturally be on my side in any dispute regarding tricky matrimonial issues, suddenly got herself involved in what, until then, had been a dispute-free situation. Full of bluster, she approached Joan's mother saying "You have to put a stop to this relationship!" followed by a list of reasons why: I was a foreigner; I didn't have a proper job; I wasn't a Catholic; I wasn't properly educated (no college degree), etc. etc. Joan promptly put the woman in her place, which naturally was akin to throwing more gasoline on the blaze of my passion. So much for the sister-in-law. My relationship with her husband, Joan's brother, always seemed to move along smoothly: after all, what else should I expect from a fellow naval aviator?

Ten days in America with Joan reinforced what was by then a dual love affair but, although I was really excited by the idea of spending the rest of my days married to Joan, it had not yet occurred to me that America might become my home. Indeed, quite the opposite; while urging Joan to marry me I had told her that she must never expect me to give up flying. It may have been this that gave her pause, because as I boarded the plane back to London, I realized that despite every manifestation that my grand passion was reciprocated, she had yet to give me a simple "Yes" to my now six month old proposal. Worse, now she was back in America and I duty bound in England, there was no clear time schedule ahead of us. I was thus heavy hearted as I returned back across the Atlantic.

Chapter 12

LEARNING BY TEACHING

Anglesey is barren island stuck off the northwest coast of Wales. Separated from the mainland by a narrow passage, the Menai Straits, it is connected by several bridges. Its main claim to fame is the terminus of the main rail route to Dublin, which ends at Hollyhead where passengers could board a ferry across the Irish Sea. To encourage non-Irish traffic the railway company had developed the island with a huge hotel and a noteworthy golf course. In addition, a number of wealthy merchants from Liverpool had built summer houses, taking advantage of splendid sandy beaches. In the summer it was quite beautiful; in the winter it was very desolate. The Royal Air Force had built Valley, a large airfield where, at the time I was there, they were taking pilots who had completed basic training in Provosts and bringing them up to "wings" standard in Vampires (jets). All naval pilots went through Valley, comprising about half the student body. Naval pilots such as I accounted for about a third of the instructors.

The de Havilland Vampire was one of the world's very first jet fighters; the prototype first flew in 1943. It entered service in the final days of the war in Europe and remained one of the RAF's principal fighters until it was retired in 1956. It was really a very neat little plane; the pilot sat in front of the engine, which sucked its air in through wing-root inlets and pushed the exhaust out of the back. The tail was supported by twin booms, which meant that the cockpit/engine nacelle was quite tiny. The plane was like a little toy, but flew beautifully. The engine, a product of the very early years of jet aviation, had a centrifugal compressor, meaning that the air was pushed into the combustion chamber by a fan rather like the one in a vacuum cleaner. Later jet engines, including the one used in the Hunter, and most of today's, were axial flow, which involved a very complex set of turbine blades which were more susceptible to damage from errant birds, but were much more efficient. Early versions of the Vampire were prone to "wet start" which meant that a lot of unburned kerosene would gather in the combustion chamber and then go up in flames with a rather alarming whoosh. To be sure that there wasn't some unburned kerosene lying around to imperil the next start, the ground crew had to stand the little plane up on its tail to let any spare inflammables drain out.

With the adoption of high-speed jet-powered airplanes, air forces had discovered that it was nearly impossible for the pilot to bail out in the traditional way, by climbing out of the cockpit onto the wing and then diving over the side. The ejector seat had been developed to deal with this; the pilot sat on a kind of artillery shell which, when he pulled the correct lever, blasted him and his seat and his parachute out of the airplane so that, when clear, he would automatically separate from his seat and the chute would open. The Vampire, however, was too small to incorporate an ejection seat so we were led to believe that a more traditional form of exit would work. Fortunately I never had to put it to the test; however, I must have been relieved by the knowledge that the pretty Wren officer who had shouted "jump" during our parachute training four years earlier would not yet be out looking for a new line of work.

DeHAVILLAND VAMPIRE FB5

"The plane was like a little toy, but flew beautifully."

What we are talking about here is the FB5, a single-seat fighter-bomber that our students used for all their solo work and which the instructors flew when leading formation flights. There was also the T11, however, a two-seat trainer version in which the instructor and student could sit side by side. This had a large enough cockpit to squeeze in two ejector seats installed, we believed, because even the glibbest manufacturer could not convince the air force that one person, let alone two, could escape unaided. There was a problem, however: the cockpit was just wide enough for the ejector seats, but they took up so much lengthways space that anyone who bailed out would find that he had left his knee-caps behind on the instrument panel. So, in addition to all the normal straps and paraphernalia, we had to wear ties around our legs that fastened back onto the base of the seat. The idea was that you pulled the handle and the thing shot up into the air neatly snapping your legs back and out of harm's way. Again, I fortunately never had to try this in practice.

I enjoyed instructing. It is always exciting to be able to teach someone a worthwhile skill, and particularly so if the skill is one you relish for its own sake. I loved to fly and, leading three students in a tail chase among the cumulus clouds in the empty air space over the Irish Sea, I couldn't believe this was something deemed remunerative work. Lesson completed, we would come in as a flight of four, echelon back from the leader (me), the students getting appreciably better with each flight. The technique, commonly known now as a "military break" was then a new one: we streaked in over the down-wind end of the runway at about a hundred feet, then broke off at ten second intervals into a high hard turn, throttled back, speed-brakes out, so as to lose enough speed to permit a constant rate curve back onto the runway. As the students got better, we would take off in pairs and come back the same way, landing in two-plane formations.

Most of my students were naval. Several of them, having come through the regular commission (Dartmouth) channel, were fairly close to me in age. Some of them had been classmates of my friend Richard. There was a very attractive fellow with the wonderful naval name of Hornblower, Michael Hornblower, who went on to a brilliant career; Michael Fitzpatrick who would later be an usher at our long-delayed wedding; and David Pentreath who demonstrated outstanding leadership commanding HMS *Plymouth* during the Falklands Islands campaign.

Other naval students were on short service commissions, like I was. They were midshipmen or sub-lieutenants, younger than the Dartmouth men, but with the same amount of flying behind them. I spent a lot of time with a young man called Prime. He had trouble coping with the Vampire and the squadron commander asked me to see if I could give him a hand. They felt he lacked self-confidence and that I might be able to make him feel better about his flying. Why I'm not sure, and with hindsight I wish they hadn't. He was a nice young man, but very nervous, and I spent a lot of time sitting next to him, teeth clenched and willing myself not to take control, while he consistently just missed doing whatever it was he was supposed to do. But gradually he did get better, passed all his check rides, and was duly given his wings. He went on from Valley to the Operational Flying School, flying Sea Hawks, I believe. Some months into the course he crashed and was killed. I went to his funeral and met his parents. He was an only son and it was all very traumatic. I expected chilly treatment and was surprised and overwhelmed when his mother thanked me effusively for having "saved" his flying career. Apparently, he had been writing increasingly despondent letters home about how badly things were going, and then had been assigned to me, and everything started to look much better. Had I made him think he was better than he actually was? Should I have washed him out at some stage? I will never know, but certainly everyone would have been a lot better off if I or the system had been tougher: the Primes would still have a son, the Navy would have saved the cost of a good airplane, and I would have avoided what still represents a burden on my conscience.

Nevertheless, as winter moved into spring, life at Valley wasn't too bad. I missed Joan terribly, although we wrote every day, and sometimes twice. She was talking about coming back in the fall, and it looked increasingly as if it might be for good. I tried to learn golf but was never very good at it. The married students were quite hospitable, and there was an active social life in the officer's mess.

I was in the middle of a normal day's teaching at Valley when I got a disturbing message from my brother. Our mother, who then was in her early 50's, had been admitted to hospital, near where she was staying with her sister in Buckinghamshire. She was diagnosed with pneumonia. I was worried because I had never known my mother with a day of sickness. But I was also tempted: was this an opportunity to show off my pull with the Air Force by borrowing an airplane (for compassionate reasons) and flying down to see her? And to my amazement, it worked: wheels spun and messages zinged and within a matter of an hour or so I was, with my commanding officer's blessing, in a Vampire on my way to an airfield conveniently located near the hospital.

My mother, always rather cynical where any achievement of mine was concerned, exhibited no excitement when I strode into the hospital ward in my flight suit, apart from her usual high level of parental worry. On this occasion she was convinced I'd stolen the Vampire and that there would be hell to pay when the Air Force found out.

She was callously dismissive of my concerns about her: her doctor brother-in-law had already assured her she wasn't going to die, so what was all the fuss about? Indeed, the whole affair worked much more smoothly than I had suspected the military would ever be capable of. The only moment when I did feel a tinge of worry was when I discovered that, by some odd turn of fate, at the time I was flying from west to east (Valley to Buckingham), HRH The Duke of Edinburgh (the Queen's husband) was (with the guidance of an instructor) flying an aircraft of the Royal Flight from Scotland south to London, and, as was customary, a Purple Airway had been declared. A Purple Airway meant that a member of the Royal Family was in the air and that everybody had to keep out of his or her way and observe radio silence. Everybody, that is, except for me: someone had forgotten to tell me about the Duke before I took off. I was already in the air going back to Valley when I learned about the Purple Airway and, I hate to admit it, was somewhat lost. The normal thing to do would be to get on the radio and ask where I was, but not, of course, if radio silence was being observed. After a few moments careful thought, I decided "To hell with it!" and made the radio call. The fellow who answered appeared enormously grateful to be given something to do, and soon had me pointed in the right direction for home. My mother recovered and lived happily to be 97.

Whenever I think of my mother, I am reminded of Billy Collins' poem "The Lanyard", which I read at her funeral. A lanyard is what boy scouts wear around their necks; the writer came back from scout camp and gave his mother a lanyard he had made there:

She nursed me in many a sick room
Lifted spoons of medicine to my lips
Laid cold face cloths on my forehead
And then led me out into the airy night

And taught me to walk and swim
And I, in turn, presented her with a lanyard
Here are thousands of meals, she said
And here is clothing and a good education
And here is your lanyard, I replied,
Which I made with a little help from a counselor

Here is a breathing body and a beating heart
Strong legs, bones and teeth,
And two clear eyes to read the world, she whispered
And here, I said, is the lanyard I made at camp
And here, I wish to say to her now
Is a smaller gift—not the worn truth

That you can never repay your mother,
But the rueful admission that when she took
The two-tone lanyard from my hand,
I was as sure as a boy could be
That this useless, worthless thing I wove
Out of boredom would be enough to make us even.

Although the poem does sell fathers a little short, anyone who has been fortunate enough to have a loving mother will understand this: however careful the book-keeper, the books will never be balanced.

Sometime during the winter, I had decided to add a little more economic security to my life by applying for a permanent commission in the navy. If accepted, I would career-wise be on a par with those who had come into the service the more conventional way, via the Dartmouth Royal Naval College. I would have to spend time at sea learning how to be a sailor, but I would at least have an opportunity to move into more rarified levels of command, maybe even become an admiral. And, I thought, if accepted, I could always turn it down. I wrote the letter and more or less forgot about it. (There he goes again, you may rightly say; volunteering, with insufficient thought inputs.)

It was in May, just before the Whitsun bank holiday that I was called in by Joe Honeywill, the Senior Naval Officer at Valley. He congratulated me, and told me that I had been accepted for a permanent commission. I thanked him, and said I would think about it, which left him looking rather puzzled. A few days earlier I had got a call from my friend Tom Fitzgerald, asking me if I could join him as crew on a yacht participating in the annual Southampton to Cherbourg race. I didn't know it at the time, but Tom had met the owner in a bar on the Hamble River, and after a few beers agreed to crew for him. The next morning, thinking he might be better off with company, he had called me. At the time it never occurred to either of us why any reputable yachtsman contemplating a prestigious race would be searching for a crew so late in the day and, worse still looking for it among strangers met in a bar.

The annual Whitsun Bank holiday gave me three days off, so I agreed, and on Friday evening Tom and I and the owner (whose name I mercifully forget) set sail down the Hamble River to join in the race. We were late for the start, and it was dark and rather lonely when we left the Solent and set off across the Channel for the ninety-odd miles to Cherbourg. The owner did not seem to care too much for the nitty-gritty of sailing, so Tom and I took watch and watch about. I did eight to midnight and then four to eight. I had plenty of time to think and, for the first time, instead of my usual impulsive behavior, I contemplated my future with a serious analysis.

First, I thought carefully about Joan as a naval officer's wife and increasingly, as I tested what I knew about Joan against what I knew about married life in the off-beat places the Royal Navy chose to locate its air bases, it just didn't add up. We would always be poor, living in accommodation that was usually undesirable by my standards, let alone Joan's, and far from civilization. We would be moved around a lot, and once we had children of school age, either separated from each other or from them if they were to enjoy a stable education. And when I went off to sea there would be long periods when Joan would be on her own, which would either mean back to America, something I could see little chance of affording, or as her mother had graphically put it, she would be ". . . alone with a sick baby in Scotland while he's off at sea!" Although nothing had ever been said between us to this effect, it became clear to me as I thought about it that I could have the navy, or I could have Joan, but I couldn't (or maybe shouldn't) have both.

So then I started thinking about what I would do if I left the navy. Assuming that I finished my original eight year contract I would receive a fifteen hundred pound gratuity, which seemed a lot at the time, and which, I supposed, would keep us until I could find some kind of a job, although what kind of job I had no idea. Looking back on that time later, the sum which I had deluded myself into believing would provide adequate support, during what might prove a considerable period of unemployment, showed how little I knew about the real world outside the comfortable economic cocoon provided by the Navy. However, as dawn came up over the Channel, I realized what I had known all along: I couldn't live without Joan, and whatever it took to be a responsible husband would have to be done.

When the owner came on deck around 8 a.m. everything seemed very clear: I would go back to Valley and tell Joe Honeywill that I didn't want the permanent commission, serve out the final eighteen months of my original contract, marry Joan and carve myself out a career in the outside world of which I knew so little. The visit to Harvard Business School had made little impression on me at the time, and the logical question: which world, hers or mine? had still not occurred to me. Nevertheless, it had been an extremely productive night. And, it is important to note that the conclusion reached was entirely my own; although I am sure Joan was relieved to find that I felt our marriage and my navy to be incompatible, never once did she put that forward as having been her own decision.

It was only later I realized that this moment, during the midnight watch, sailing in the middle of the English Channel, was the first time in my adult life that I had ever looked before leaping, and when making a really significant decision had given serious consideration to my future, and that of another person I truly loved.

Things became a little less productive around mid-morning when the owner announced that we were well to the east of the Cherbourg peninsula, and heading down into the Bay of the Seine. Tom and I both insisted that he was wrong: we had been up all night and he hadn't, we knew the courses steered and the approximate speed and course made good, and besides, way ahead on the horizon we could see towering cumulus which, at that time of year, could only mean land. No, said the owner, we must turn west immediately: he knew where he was, and besides it was his boat. We argued that doing so would head us well out into the Atlantic, spoil any chance of making a land-fall in daylight, and certainly eliminate us as race contenders. Things got a little heated until Tom and I looked at each other and, acting without any pre-meditation, shoved the owner down the hatch, slammed it shut and bolted it. There was a lot of shouting and yelling from below, but we finally persuaded him that we meant business and he was staying there until we reached Cherbourg, which we estimated in about four hours.

True enough, Cherbourg was straight ahead, and we did arrive late in the afternoon, easily the last boat to get there. We let our "skipper" out and he grumpily conceded we had been right. The French threw a splendid cocktail party, where a number of experienced Channel sailors rolled their eyes when they learned the identity of our skipper. Technically we were mutineers. Practically we were relieved to learn that our friend didn't want to sail his boat back for a week or two, so we could with good conscience leave him there in Cherbourg and take the ferry back to Southampton. A useful rule to live by: never go offshore with someone you have only just met in a bar.

Back at Valley I went to see Joe Honeywill and told him that I had decided not to accept the permanent commission after all; I would serve out the rest of my eight years and then leave. There was a long pause. "I don't think you can do that," he said. "You asked for a permanent commission, they gave it to you—I don't think you can just give it back like that. You'd better go away and think about it." I told him that I had thought about it, a lot, and that more thought wouldn't change things. Little did I know it at the time, but this was the beginning of an extended tortuous passage punctuated by people telling me I should go away and think about matters to which I had already addressed considerable attention. For some reason I have yet to understand, the Royal Navy appeared to have a strong desire to keep me in its clutches even though it was down-sizing left right and center and at the same time was making policy decisions that pretty much spelled, over the long term, the end of its Fleet Air Arm and its related aircraft carriers. Actually, I exaggerate: the Royal Navy did change course and begin acquiring aircraft carriers again, but not until 2017, when the newly built *Queen Elizabeth* joined the fleet, but I was 85 then, an American, and anyway a bit late in the game to be of much help to the Fleet Air arm.

The immediate outcome was that everyone seemed to take a deep breath while they decided what to do with me. Over the next year or so I remained in a kind of limbo while I undertook the lengthy task of persuading a reluctant navy to accept my "resignation" of the commission I had barely touched.

The Royal Naval College at Dartmouth, having finally woken up to the presence of naval aviation, wanted all its cadets to be exposed to flying. I think there were mixed motives: did they hope that very few would actually want to do it as a career, the remainder therefore inclining to sensible occupations like seamanship and gunnery, or were they hoping that enough actually would want to fly, so that they didn't have to go outside the mainstream and hire recalcitrant people like me? Whatever the reason, each summer any cadet who wanted to could learn to fly. Not the whole thing, just enough skill to go solo and fly around on his own for a bit. The summer camp was held up at Lossiemouth, one of my favorite places, and the flying was done in Tiger Moths, an unfamiliar plane at the time but soon to become my most favored plaything. This was to be my job for the next couple of months while the powers that be debated my future.

MICHAEL IN HIS TIGER MOTH FLYING OVER SHELTER ISLAND'S BUG LIGHT, MANY YEARS AFTER THE TIME THE EVENTS DESCRIBED HERE TOOK PLACE

"..the flying was done in Tiger Moths, an unfamiliar plane at the time but soon to become my most favored plaything."

I cleaned out my room at Valley, and fellow instructor John Hollingsworth and I set off on the long drive up to Scotland. We stayed there for some nine weeks, during which time we took three classes of cadets and instilled in them sufficient skills so that most, but not all, could fly by themselves.

The Tiger Moth—officially the DH82A—is a very pretty little bi-plane, originally designed in 1930 as a Royal Air Force trainer. It thus has more characteristics of World War I airplanes than its modern equivalents. However, they were a joy to fly and, as was the case with so many of the Navy's more interesting tasks, it was hard to conceive of our day to day efforts as work.

Most of the flying took place at Milltown, where I had first met the Firefly and had carefully avoided dancing with Princess Margaret. When we weren't teaching, we would go off and pretend we were Germany's Red Baron or his RAF predators: Hollingsworth and I would wear long white scarves and dog-fight at anything from ground level up to three or four thousand feet, all the while taking pot shots at each other with water pistols. We had six Tiger Moths and six instructors and would from time to time fly intricate formation maneuvers or go off on our own doing aerobatics, which the Tiger Moth performed superbly. The Navy was introducing its newest supersonic all-weather fighter, the DH 110 and, when people in the Lossiemouth mess asked us what we were up to over at Milltown, we would look very secretive and say that we were testing the DH 82A, hoping that everyone would assume that this was some top-secret new interceptor. But in case anyone thinks we were squandering the taxpayer's money, I should add that most of our cadets did actually learn to fly, some of them signed up for real pilot training, and none of them got damaged.

In mid-September the camp was over, the cadets went back to Dartmouth, Hollingsworth and the other instructors back to Valley, while I headed south. I wrote a formal letter of resignation and mailed it, then sat back to see what would happen.

I found Joan an apartment in London, in the hope that living in Britain might prove attractive enough to make her want to stay there regardless of what happened to me. She arrived safely in November after a rough crossing in the *Queen Mary* and stayed awhile in a hotel on Half Moon Street waiting for the apartment to become vacant.

Joan had not come to London unprepared. Lacking a work permit she was going to find getting a job with a British firm difficult, but she had gone to Washington and applied to the CIA for something in their London Station. I'm not sure that she advanced her cause when, asked whether she could keep a secret, she had replied: "yes, and so can all my friends." However, they had promised to get back to her soon, which we assumed meant any day.

HMS *STARLING*

"Starling *was a rather elderly frigate that, having seen heroic service in the Atlantic during the war, was now being used for training purposes."*

1956 was coming to a close, and I finally had a reply from the Admiralty, and it was not good news. Since I was now a regular navy officer, my resignation would have to go through normal (i.e., slow) channels while, in the meantime, I would have to broaden my naval expertise by learning how to keep watches on a ship at sea. With this end in view I was to join HMS *Starling*, typically operating out of Portsmouth.

So, always the good officer even though whatever career prospects I had were undoubtedly in tatters, I took myself off to Portsmouth to join my new ship. It was another of our tearful good-byes, again made more poignant by the fact that we had no idea of what the future would hold. I was presumably off to sea while Joan was living in a rather seedy furnished flat, all on her own in London, eking out a precarious financial existence by substitute teaching for the United States Army; the CIA had yet to come through.

In fact, things turned out better than we expected. *Starling* was an elderly frigate that, having seen heroic service in the Atlantic during the war, was now being used for training purposes. Naval lieutenants who were specializing in navigation would come aboard for tuition in the finer points of coastal pilotage, position fixing, anchoring, and other tricky matters relating to moving ships about safely. Fortunately, most of this took place during day trips. We would leave harbor around 8 a.m. and get back about 4:15 p.m. Rarely would we go out overnight, and only occasionally while I was on board did we go on any sort of a cruise.

As soon as I got on board *Starling* I told the Captain that I wouldn't be with him very long since I was sure that at any moment my resignation would be approved. He said I shouldn't be too sure, and he was right. In the meantime, I would keep watches like everyone else and I'd better behave myself. In fact, what was amazing was what you could get away with in the Navy once you had made it clear you didn't care. Provided you kept just on the right side of the law there wasn't much they could do to you, most discipline, among officers anyway, being more a product of career concerns than the fear of punishment. On the other hand, despite a notable lack of attention to my duties, I did in fact learn quite a lot about ship handling and coastal navigation which served me in very good stead when, in better days, Joan and I acquired our own boat and went on cruises with our family.

I established a routine that served me well all the time I was in *Starling*. There was a 4:30 train from Portsmouth to London, and it took about ten minutes to get from the ship to the station. So long as I wasn't actually involved in something important up on deck, I would disappear below at around 4 o'clock and get out of my uniform. Then, as we drew alongside and the brow went over, I would sprint across it and high-tail it to the station. Joan would meet me at Waterloo, and we would do whatever we had planned for the evening. There were various options going back, but my favorite was the milk train, so called because it would pick up milk from farms all along the track. It thus stopped and started all the way down to Portsmouth. It didn't leave until about 2:30 in the morning, which left plenty of time with Joan, but most days it didn't get to Portsmouth until 5:30 or 6 o'clock. I would sleep fitfully all the way down, walk back to the ship, slip into my bunk and sleep again until someone chose to wake me up. I must have been a very bad influence, but the other officers were tolerant and, at times, almost envious of my indifference.

The Captain did get some measure of revenge, however; he made me the ship's sports officer. Anyone paying attention will have realized by now my complete distaste for organized athletics, and some of my most miserable hours in the navy were spent on a wet and windy soccer field in Portsmouth trying to referee sailors' football (soccer) matches, a task made more difficult by my abysmal ignorance of the rules of the game.

Winter turned into spring. Joan continued teaching but had in some respects improved her living arrangements. Tom, who had a one-room apartment on Walton Street, told us about a two room flat on the floor above. The building (Number 29—it is still there, although much more ritzy than when Joan lived there) was owned by an electrician who had a shop in front. The two rooms were just that: empty rooms which had seen little use and less cleaning over the previous decade, but which, after hard bargaining with the electrician, could in fact be made quite livable. He cleaned them out, painted them, sanded the floors, and installed a sink in what became the kitchen/dining room and a gas-fire to warm the living room/bedroom. We papered the walls leading up the stairs and, for what I recall was about $10 per week, Joan had not a bad place to live with a rather fashionable address.

28 WALTON STREET, LONDON TODAY

"The building (Number 29—it is still there, although much more ritzy than when Joan lived there) was owned by an electrician who had a shop in front. The two rooms were just that: empty rooms which had seen little use and less cleaning over the previous decade."

There was one notable incident before she moved in which, in a microcosm, illustrated the abysmal state of labor relations in Britain at that time, a situation that only got worse until Mrs. Thatcher arrived on the scene to sort things out. The gas fire, the only source of heat in Joan's living room/bedroom, had to be installed by the government-owned North Thames Gas Board. It was a perishingly cold March, with freezing temperatures forecast for the weekend, but fortunately the Gas Board men were there on the Friday and all looked well for a reasonably cozy occupancy. By 5 p.m. the fire was in and ready to go. The foreman then announced that he would be back on Monday to turn it on. "What do you mean, 'turn it on'?" asked Joan. "Well," he said, "we just have to connect that pipe there to that outlet there and you'll have a lovely warm fire." "Why not now?" she queried. "It's 5 o'clock, Miss, that's our knocking off time. We won't do no more work until Monday." Without saying a word Joan walked over to the door, locked it, and placed the key carefully inside her bra. "Alright, boys," she announced, "nobody leaves the room until the gas is on!" There was a moment of shocked horror and, as I told her afterwards, given the bolshie nature of North Thames Gas Board employees, a very real chance that the whole industry would come out on strike. Then, presumably realizing that this crazy American meant what she said, they grumblingly undid their tools, connected the gas, turned it on, and then meekly asked if they could go home.

I described the flat as livable and, indeed it was with one notable exception: it had no bath and no toilet. There was in fact one of each, but available to the entire building, meaning principally the electrician's employees. They liked to keep their tools in the bathtub and were not overly careful in their use of the toilet. Joan managed to persuade them to find another storage space for their tools, but never quite managed to communicate American standards of toilet hygiene. The bath water was heated by a contraption called a geyser which was gas fired, acting like a miniature boiler. It produced piping hot water, but Joan noticed herself getting rather drowsy as she soaked there. She mentioned it to the electrician, whose first reaction was surprise that anyone would want more than one bath a month. However, he produced a plumber who told her not on any account to use the geyser which might explode at any moment, "and we wouldn't want that, would we ducks, not with a loverly face like yours." I forget how we finally solved the bath problem, but Joan took what seemed the path of least resistance with the toilet: whenever she could she used the facilities at Harrods, which was just around the corner.

Rather unusual in London at the time, the flat was unfurnished, so we searched second-hand furniture stores and eventually managed to get it quite presentably outfitted. But one thing it lacked was a kitchen/dining room table, so in April I drove down to Little Stert and picked up some chestnut planking that my father had cut a few years earlier and was seasoning with the thought that it would one day come in useful. It was time for Easter leave and I volunteered to take mine later, staying behind with little to do but see that no one made off with *Starling* while the captain's back was turned. Paying a small bribe to the ship's carpenter, I borrowed his workshop and tools and spent a week making what I think was a remarkably presentable table. It was about six feet long and three wide with sturdy legs each end. I brought it up to London resting in the back of my car (a convertible, so I could conveniently put the roof down) and assembled it in Joan's flat. It looked very fine. For anyone with a memory that stretches that far back, it was one of the few occasions when the carpentry included in my Blundell's education actually served a practical purpose – or am I being unreasonably harsh?

All this time the battle of words between me and the Admiralty had gone back and forth, escalated now by the involvement of my father, who liked nothing better than to write letters in a good cause, particularly if the cause involved civil servants, Members of Parliament, Secretaries to the Admiralty and other interested parties. A lot of time would elapse between each salvo, but the theme remained much the same: I wanted out, (my desire to leave bolstered by the fact that, by the end of January, I would have completed the service I had promised eight years earlier), while they still insisted that I belonged in.

There was a sub-text, which really annoyed Joan and me: a rather supercilious picture of a young man who had been led astray by a scheming American, but who would eventually see the light and be a good naval officer.

This might be an appropriate point to say something more about my father since he makes no further appearance in this book, other than recognition of his death which occurred peacefully at his home when he was 89, at which time I spoke at his funeral, and what I said then conveys better how I continued to feel about him than anything else I could say here.

> "I was a most fortunate small boy. In those times of five-and-a-half day weeks, I had a father who worked Stock Exchange hours and stayed home on Saturdays. And during weekends and on holidays he was a builder. I assumed that it was for my personal pleasure that he built: at home a swimming pool, a tennis court, a vast sand-box, canoes and motor boats, tree houses, and the world's biggest train set; in the nursery, bridges and skyscrapers; and at the seaside, complex reservoir systems. Later I assumed it was just for my personal safety that he built a truly Luftwaffe-proof air-raid shelter. I thus learned from him that most valuable ability, how to use my mind and hands in constructive work, for my own pleasure and that of others.
>
> He taught me to ski, to play tennis and squash. He introduced me to financial markets. His failure to impart his skills on the rugby field was due to my ineptitude, not his lack of effort. I (and his oldest grandson) remember him well, at the age of 80, skiing off into deep powder high in the Swiss Alps. I recall worrying what we would do if he came to grief, but he never did.
>
> He was always a very private man. Few knew of the services he unobtrusively and efficiently rendered to the Parish, the District, the A25 users, and local

charities. Quietly and skillfully he advised numerous estates and trusts, sharing freely his financial wisdom. He was a man capable of great love, though too often he found it hard to articulate.

Throughout my life, in childhood and as an adult, he was a tower of strength. He played a crucial role in ensuring the long happiness of my marriage. He was always there when needed. I hope that one day one of my children will say of me, as I do of him: 'He was a good man and an excellent father.'"

If I sound cheerful at this time about the verbal battle between us and the forces of naval authority it is because time softens all things and, in any event, I can look back on how it turned out all right in the end. But while it was all going on I did go thorough periods of enormous despair. Joan, on the other hand, remained amazingly strong and confident. Time and again, when I thought all was lost, and I would spend the rest of my working life as a naval lieutenant with dim prospects, she would put her arms around me and tell me it was all going to be all right. And she was right.

Through spring and early summer we were living a somewhat surreal existence. I continued in *Starling*, making my regular nocturnal pilgrimages to London, while Joan was teaching, now on a more regular basis, at an American Air Force school in southwest London. Convinced that I would shortly become a civilian I maintained an erratic and somewhat ill-informed search for employment, but with little sense as to what or where. I answered advertisements, wrote letters, and followed leads given by friends.

The seminal event was probably my interview with Whiteheads & Coles, the stock broking firm my great-grandfather had founded during the previous century. There were no Whiteheads or Coles' in the firm then, but the managing partner met with me and we had a nice chat, at the end of which he offered me a job. "Most of our young men," he informed me, "receive no salary while they are learning our business," thus implying that anyone who was troubled by something so crass as needing to earn a living was really not suited to the stock broking business. "However," he went on, "owing to your family's connection with our firm, and the fact that you are a little older than most of our trainees, we will consider a modest compensation—say four hundred pounds a year." That was all of some $1,100 a year but I rushed back to Joan's flat full of importance to tell her that I finally had a job offer. She heard me out and then asked me to go over the numbers again slowly in case she hadn't heard me right. Then: "That's ridiculous." she said, "We could never live on four hundred pounds a year and in any event, I know you can do a lot better than that." "How?" I asked. "You must go to Harvard Business School," she replied.

The resulting discussion went on for several days and was reminiscent of Macauly's outstanding poem: "How Horatio Kept the Bridge," when those behind cried forward, and those in front cried back. There was no way, I argued, that I could get into Harvard Business School: I had no undergraduate degree, I knew nothing about business, I couldn't afford it, etc., etc. Nonsense, Joan would reply, you're twice as smart as anyone else there, you will get in easily and do wonderfully, and I will teach school to put you through and we can always borrow the rest. Finally, I agreed to fill out the application, which was available in London, and to take an entrance exam that was something mysteriously called a GMAT. An interview with a local Business School alumnus was also required.

The application was quite straightforward. I managed to finesse the lack of an under-graduate degree by pointing out that Annapolis gave degrees and that I was probably the educational equivalent of a United States Naval Academy graduate, (conveniently disregarding the fact that my only post-high school education was confined to learning how to fly airplanes, thus clearly lacking the depth of an Annapolis training). However, I was stumped by a rather big blank space, which asked me to describe my business experience. Nothing, nothing at all. Come on, said Joan, you must have done something that could come under the heading of business. Well, I replied forlornly, I did once help my father take a pig to

Newton Abbot market. That's it, she said briskly, without missing a beat; put down "agricultural merchandising." My awe for this amazing woman and her unbounded self-confidence knew no bounds.

The GMAT's were just like any other multiple-choice test, a hurdle that by now had become second nature to me. Indeed, as I gave the matter more thought, I realized that throughout my life post-prep school. I had been subjected to multiple choice tests of increasing rigor and complexity. Most of these I had managed to pass quite acceptably, and during all of them I had benefitted from the time I had spent with my father doing very similar tests during the wartime blackout. Since so many of the things that had gone right in my life were dependent on luck, I can at this point give a further dimension to my good fortune by saying that I was extremely lucky in my choice of parents.

The Business School GMAT included a kind of personal profile, which included the question: "Do you consider yourself a 'joiner'?" With hindsight, and a better knowledge of things American, I think what they wanted to know was whether I was good in groups. Never having previously been asked whether I was a "joiner," and not quite clear of the meaning, I sought safety in the English usage. Where I came from "joinery" was synonymous with "carpentry," so I answered, truthfully "Yes—I passed my School Certificate carpentry test with distinction." (I might have gone on and mentioned Joan's dining room table, but the form didn't have room.) I have often wondered what the Admissions Office at Harvard Business School thought about all this.

The interview was with a Scotsman whose father had founded a company that made a popular canned dog food sold under the name "Happymeat." The son had been sent to the Business School (by this point in the narrative I think I and my readers know the place well enough to refer to it by its chosen title "The Business School") to learn the skills needed to take over the business, and had come home full of an urge to diversify away from the single product. After some thought he had settled on canned haggis as the diversification of choice.

Haggis is a rather revolting traditional Scottish dish consisting of oatmeal and pigs blood mixed together and then cooked in a pig's intestine, making a bizarre kind of sausage. (If you can finish reading that sentence without becoming queasy you have just passed an important stamina test.) As I understand it, and this may well be apocryphal, the shift to canned haggis was a simple one. The day shift continued to make canned dog food under the Happymeat label. Then, when the night shift came on, nothing changed but the labels. Same cans, same contents, moving off the line and into the unsuspecting market place as canned haggis. I was told it was very well received.

The interview went well, the only tricky question being my current status vis-à-vis the Navy. I assured him that I would present myself at Soldiers Field after Labor Day, all ready to start beavering away at the business books, whatever they might be. Things moved rapidly in those days, and it was only a couple of weeks later that I learned that I had been accepted. Later in my life, people with some knowledge of The Business School and its practices will often question how somebody with no undergraduate degree and no real business experience could ever have been admitted there. I don't know the answer to that either, but I do recall that the two buzzwords at The Business School at the time were diversification and internationalization. My haggis friend gave substance to the former and since The Business School lacked a surfeit of foreign candidates at that time, I was probably a beneficiary of the latter. However, when pushed too hard on the subject of how I was admitted with such a clear shortage of qualifications, I can without blinking respond: "Just lucky, I guess."

Lucky, maybe, but anyone with any feeling for the real world would know that we were dreaming. The Admiralty showed no sign at all of relenting their position that my obligation to serve was a pretty indefinite one (based on their new interpretation that my eight year promise was no longer valid), terminating only when they decided to accept my resignation and, as I discovered belatedly, officers in the Royal Navy had no inherent right to resign their commissions at any particular time. Joan had to go home to prepare for our wedding, and my economic future seemed to hinge very much on my entering The Business School in September. Although all official doors to me appeared firmly closed, I was nevertheless acting as though they would at any moment spring open. I suppose one can put it all down to the optimism of youth.

Joan's departure in June was the absolute low point of that year. All our previous partings had been with the knowledge that it wouldn't be for too long, even if we didn't know exactly when and how. This time, on the other hand, there were so many barriers and, although with her nearby they had all seemed inconsequential, without her around to provide support I sank into a deep funk. I remember too well coming back to her empty apartment after saying goodbye and opening up her closet to see nothing but empty coat hangers. It all seemed so final. But there was still one more disappointment to come: a few days after she left there arrived an official looking letter from the U.S. Government, offering her employment at the American embassy. The CIA had come through at last.

Chapter 13

LEARNING DURING A CIVIL WAR, WITH REAL WEAPONS

The next blow was not long in coming. A few days later I got an official letter from the Admiralty telling me that I was posted to Cyprus to serve on the staff of the Flag Officer, Middle East ("FOME"). This meant nothing to me, so I asked around, eventually finding out that Flag Officer, Middle East was one Rear Admiral Anthony Miers, VC, DSO, known as "Crap" Miers, and reputed to be one of the most fearsome disciplinarians in the Navy. Presumably therefore they were going to beat me into submission. Futilely, I asked myself, apart from wanting to leave (probably deemed a low blow insult in the halls of the Admiralty): "What had I ever done to hurt them?"

From the Navy's point of view Cyprus had another advantage. Since there was a "State of Emergency" there, no civilians were allowed in. Although this would not necessarily apply to Joan, an American citizen, it would be tough for us to get together even had other obstacles not intervened. There would thus be ample opportunity for the deluded young man to come to his senses. However, with benefit of hindsight, I think I am attributing too much cunning to the Royal Navy. I think it was that they just didn't know what to do with me right then. I don't think they had ever been confronted with someone who had applied for a permanent commission, been accepted, then promptly turned it down.

All this time poor Joan had been waiting for news at the end of unreliable telephone lines and agonizingly slow mail, her hopes shifting between the equally remote possibilities that, on the one hand, we would be married as planned on August 23rd or, on the other, that she would find herself a spinster who, apart from an oft-told story about a fiancée stranded on some small Mediterranean Island, had little evidence of her status other than a rather elaborate emerald and diamond engagement ring. But life did have to go on. A wedding had been planned which then had to be cancelled. The principal of the school where she had been hired to teach for the coming school year had to be convinced that her personal complications would not interfere with classroom discipline. The Dean of Admissions at Harvard Business School had to be persuaded that, despite all evidence to the contrary, I was a responsible member of society. All this Joan did with amazing success: I was promised a place for the following year in the Class of 1961 (only later would it be self-identified as the Fabulous Class of 1961, though I knew nothing of this at the time).

Indeed, with all the strain and stress she performed with

breathtaking aplomb, only missing out in one small respect. On the day our wedding was supposed to have taken place a friend took her out to lunch. On the way back they passed the church. The door was open and, coming from the inside, they could faintly hear the chords of Mendelssohn's "Wedding March." She had forgotten to cancel the organist.

Cyprus at the time I arrived there was a reluctant British colony. Set in the eastern Mediterranean it commands the Levantine coast and the entrance to the Suez Canal. Some 130 miles east to west and 50 miles north to south it is a place of enormous beauty and great physical contrasts. The Troodos Mountains dominate the interior with craggy peaks extending up to over 6,000 feet. The lower Kyrenia range along the north coast overlooks southern Turkey and is home to several historical crusader castles. The population then was about four-fifths Greek and one-fifth Turkish. However, it had been ruled by the Turks for about three centuries prior to the arrival of the British in 1878, and a goodly proportion of the resident Greeks had not liked this arrangement, and still didn't.

The British, who controlled various other Greek islands including Crete and Rhodes had, by 1947, ceded them all to Greece. All, that is, except Cyprus. The Greek Cypriots assumed that Enosis (union with Greece) would also take place shortly. Two factors got in the way: first, the Turkish Cypriots were unhappy at the prospect of becoming a small Moslem minority among a Christian majority, and second the British were alarmed at the possibility of losing control of their strategically vital Cypriot bases. Turkey was unwilling to abandon its nationals to the mercies of a Greek government that had no love for its Moslem neighbor, and London, giving little thought to the consequences, made it clear that Cypriot independence was not on its agenda. I thus came to Cyprus with a sneaking sympathy for the Greeks who, like me, were being denied their aspirations by faceless men in Whitehall who, rather than saying soon, or even sometime, persisted in saying never.

CYPRUS

"It is a place of enormous beauty and great physical contrasts. The Troodos Mountains dominate the interior with craggy peaks extending up to over 6,000 feet. The lower Kyrenia range along the north coast overlooks southern Turkey and is home to several historical crusader castles."

Enosis was energetically supported by the Greek Orthodox clerics and in particular their leader Archbishop Makarios. When it became clear that there was no likelihood that their goals would be achieved peacefully, the less moderate Greek Cypriot elements turned to violence through the medium of the National organization of Cypriot Fighters or EOKA. Although at first EOKA tried to further its ambitions by strikes and disruption of public life, it soon turned to killing, first soldiers and policemen, then civilians. And the more violent the Greeks became, the less likelihood was there of any rapprochement with the Turks.

Killings took the form of road ambushes, bombs planted in crowded places, and random shootings. A particularly unpleasant trick was to stretch piano wire across a road at a height designed to decapitate a passing motorcyclist or the occupants of a jeep with the roof down. The normally lackadaisical Cyprus police had been reinforced by a large number of British troops, most of whom would rather be somewhere else and who made no bones about it when dealing with the locals. Nevertheless, relations between the British and ordinary Greeks (other than EOKA members) and Turks continued remarkably friendly considering the circumstances.

The morning after I arrived, I went over to my first meeting at Rear Admiral Miers' office. His Secretary (not a typist, a Supply Branch Commander who took care of all the paper work) ushered me in and, as was proper, I took off my hat and stood at attention. Miers was quite a small man, with a choleric face and bushy eyebrows. He glared at me for moment and then rather abruptly asked me if I was going to commit suicide. After I assured him that such was the farthest thing from my mind he said that was a good thing because everyone on his staff had to carry a revolver when outside the military compound and he didn't want me shooting myself. It was only later when I got to know him better that I told him that I was really rather uncomfortable around small guns (as opposed to the bigger ones on the front of airplanes or the very big ones on warships) and might well have shot myself, but only through incompetence. He terminated the meeting abruptly, telling me to behave myself, and report to his Chief of Staff, who would be my immediate boss.

FOME was responsible for a wide range of matters: all British naval operations in the Middle East, naval intelligence in the same area, and warship movements through his territory. Of most day-to-day significance, however, was running the naval patrol along the Cyprus coast in order to prevent weapons coming in from Greece. To effect this Miers normally had under his command some four or five minesweepers, a destroyer or two, and a flight of four Fleet Air Arm Gannets (the turbo-prop successor to the Firefly, normally used in anti-submarine work.)

All Cypriot fishing vessels, and coastal shipping had to register their movements with the police at each port of entry, who would inform naval operations. Each legitimate vessel also had a registration number, so that a record could be kept as to who owned it and what it was supposed to be up to. The air and sea patrols would keep an eye on all shipping in Cypriot waters and the naval operations staff would keep a plot so that, in theory, at any time we could tell which Cypriot ship was where and what it was doing. A powerful radar on top of Mount Olympus in the middle of the island was also part of the system, but didn't do too good a job on wooden fishing boats. (Remember our problem finding the wooden night intruders flying down from North Korea?) Any ship that was out of place or improperly identified would be boarded and searched by one of the minesweepers. Our job was to manage the process.

To do this we had about a dozen sailors who were divided into four watches, each watch headed by a watchkeeping officer. Watches would run on a four day cycle: first day from 8 a.m. until noon and then 8 p.m. until midnight; second day from noon until 8 p.m.; third day from midnight until 8 a.m.; last day free. The first and second days weren't too bad, but the third one was a long all night haul. Most of the fishing vessels we knew by name and could almost forecast in our sleep where they would be at any given time. Occasionally we would order a boarding just to keep everyone on their toes; sometimes we would tell one of the Gannets to drop a flare to give them something to do and let the Greeks know we were on the ball. I cannot recall our actually finding any weapons.

I wrote earlier that in theory we were supposed to be keeping the Greeks from running guns. In practice it was an impossible job. Guns wrapped in plastic hidden under a couple of tons of fish were hard to find. Guns in waterproof casings attached to the underside of a coastal steamer might be found by judicious tapping on the hull by searchers, but when it appeared to EOKA that the blockade was catching too much contraband, tactics changed and weapons were suspended some ten feet or more under the smuggling boat's bottom by a thin piece of high tensile steel wire, which worked better. How do I know all this? I must get ahead of myself: when the Cypriot conflict was finally settled (but only for a while), Joan, who had finally been allowed into the country, and I were invited to a party given by the American Consul. Joan found herself chatting with two rather swarthy looking brigands who, it seemed, were important members of the new government. They asked her what she was doing in Cyprus and she told them that she had just got married. And what does your husband do, they asked. Oh, she replied proudly, he's in the Navy, keeping the guns out of Cyprus. They asked her to repeat it, making sure they had understood, then called some colleagues over when they all began hysterical laughter, pointing at me and obviously enjoying some enormous joke. When they finally paused for breath they told us that their job had been getting the guns into Cyprus, a task little hindered by our efforts.

Apart from the fact that during my early days in Cyprus Joan was some 4,000 miles away and the duration of our separation was ill-defined (to be optimistic), and that some of the more unrestrained Greek Cypriots were trying to kill me, and anyone else who got in the way of Enosis, Cyprus was a wonderful place to be. It enjoyed an excellent climate, marvelous beaches and very impressive mountains and, as I have described, we had one day out of four free. One of my colleagues had a car, an ancient Renault, which I eventually ended up buying, and we would take picnics to the beach at Kyrenia or go snorkeling at Paphos where, twenty centuries earlier, a Roman fleet had foundered in a storm and one could still find shards of their pottery. Or we could drive up into the Troodos Mountains, provided we were careful about not stopping in the wrong villages or taking the wrong roads. Or, again taking appropriate care, we could stroll around the old byzantine quarters of Nicosia. As with Singapore five years earlier, there were no-go areas, and we had always to go in pairs wherever we went. Shopping was rather dramatic, since a favorite EOKA tactic was to corner their target in a store where there would be no escape (I suspect they were not very good shots.) When shopping, one of us would go into the store while the other would stand just inside the door with his gun drawn covering the street. I felt like a latter-day Wyatt Earp, .38 caliber revolver in hand, looking anxiously up and down the street for the bad guys. I must have looked very incongruous, and I doubt whether I could actually have identified a terrorist in time to shoot him before he shot me. I wish I had a photo to show my grandchildren of me, standing on a street in Nicosia, gun in hand, ready and willing (able? - I doubt it) to plug any villain who got out of line. I never had to, and doubt I ever could.

Much of my free time was spent writing to Joan. Our correspondence had now reached epic proportions: at least a letter a day which, when we ran out of news would run to what for the time must have been fairly steamy accounts of what life would be like once we were together again. Unfortunately for the record, but I think luckily for our reputations, none of these letters survived into our marriage. In addition, correspondence with the Admiralty continued, although it didn't seem to get any further than the "young man who will eventually realize the error of his ways" appraisal which had now been going on without effect for over a year. I would see Miers from time to time, and he would ask how things were going, and I would tell him that I was pretty fed up and not to think that just because I was doing my job well that I was resigned to my exile. He seemed to like my bluntness—after all, he hadn't got where he was by being Mr. Nice Guy—and we gradually developed a fairly pleasant working relationship. I was invited down to his house a couple of times for lunch and, as I got to know him better, the fearsome "Crap" didn't appear to that fearsome after all.

One day he called me into his office and said that he had been invited to a Halloween party at the American Consulate; I was reputed to know about things American so what was he supposed to do at a Halloween party? I told him that I thought you were supposed to have some kind of vegetable with a face carved into it. He looked at me as if I had a screw loose then abruptly told me to make one. I had no idea what kind of vegetable, but the only thing I could find that remotely suited the purpose was a turnip. Turnips are rock hard so it took me the better part of an afternoon and a couple of broken knife blades to hollow out the largest turnip I could find and carve a scary looking face in it. I placed a candle inside and was rather proud of the results. The Admiral went off to his party in his official car carrying the carved turnip, candle lit. It was on the small side, so it looked like a shrunken head, but I gather it was much admired by his hosts and he was quite the hit of the party.

REAR ADMIRAL ANTHONY MIERS, VC, DSO, AKA "CRAP" MIERS

"He seemed to like my bluntness—after all, he hadn't got where he was by being Mr. Nice Guy—and we gradually developed a fairly pleasant working relationship. ... all in all the fearsome "Crap" didn't appear to that fearsome after all.... There are few people in my life I look back on with unalloyed admiration, and he is one of them."

Then in mid-November Miers' Flag Lieutenant was ordered home and a replacement was needed. The Admiral was going to retire in January, so there was little point in sending someone out from England for less than three months. He asked me if I would like the job. Possibly it was my lack of sycophancy, or possibly it was the turnip; whatever the reason, the strict disciplinarian had actually taken quite a liking to me.

Miers would clearly fall into the *Readers' Digest* category of "Most Unforgettable Character I Have Ever Met." He was by trade a submariner and during the early years of the war had commanded HMS *Torbay* in the Mediterranean. At some point in his career, possibly while in *Torbay*, he had been court martialed for getting irate at a sailor while on the conning tower. He had punched the man, who had fallen down three decks and broken some bones. This was not considered acceptable behavior, but top-class submarine commanders were hard to find, and the event did not seem to unduly harm his career. Possibly too it was this occasion that fueled his fearsome reputation for discipline.

Also while in *Torbay* he had taken her into Corfu, then occupied by Italians, surfaced in the middle of the harbor, sunk a number of enemy vessels by gunfire, submerged and escaped. It was a legendary event and won him a Victoria Cross, Britain's highest award for bravery. Later he was the subject of a war crimes enquiry. While off Crete during the German invasion he had sunk a motorboat containing a number of SS troops. Faced with the choice of continuing his patrol with a dozen of Hitler's trained killers on board the already cramped submarine, he took what he deemed at the time to be the sensible path. He threw them off his boat and, to prevent them from reporting his position, shot them. Afterwards this was the subject of an official investigation and he was exonerated. Many years later a journalist re-surfaced the matter as an example of unpunished Allied war crimes. Since Miers was at the time dead, the publicity did no one any good and caused his widow a lot of grief.

Following his time in the Mediterranean he was sent to Pearl Harbor as a liaison officer with the United States Navy's Pacific submarine forces. While on leave in Sydney he met and married Patricia, a beautiful Australian woman, several years his junior. Now a Rear Admiral, Cyprus was the last job in his eventful career.

A Flag Lieutenant is a sort of junior Admiral's aide. His job is to act as a personal assistant and make sure that everything about his day-to-day routine that is supposed to happen actually does happen. Much of the job is social and logistical; the "Flags" is part of the Admiral's official family and thus becomes a kind of alter ego. He is on duty twenty-four hours a day, which can be tiring, but he gets involved in everything the Admiral does, which can be exciting and educational. I took the job (I don't think I had any other option) and, although I don't think I could have stood it for more than three months, it was entertaining while it lasted, and I learned a lot.

I think the part Miers liked most about his job was dealing with the various ships that came under his command. He would always arrange that one of them was near his house at lunchtime, and the officers would be invited to join him and Pat while the off-duty sailors had a picnic and swam from the beach. Pat Miers was very popular with her guests and the lunches normally went off very well, extending at a leisurely pace well into the afternoon. Miers did, however, have an awesome temper, which could be quite appalling if you didn't know that it was really all bark and little bite. Unfortunately, if the slightest thing went wrong with one of his lunches, he would take it out on the nearest person who, while often me, was too frequently his wife. I think Pat was used to the torrent of frequently obscene abuse, words well lubricated by spittle coming like machine gun bullets, accompanied by a purpling face, which made one fear for fragile blood vessels. It was really quite a sight, and seriously upset some of the more chivalrous younger officers who, after a few glasses of wine, saw it as their clear duty to leap to the lady's defense. Part of my job was to exert a restraining influence - striking an admiral was taken very seriously by the Royal Navy - take the fellow concerned to one side and explain that this was all part of the give and take of marriage. Actually, I think that although Pat really loved the man, his temper, when on the boil, did cause her considerable grief.

NICOSIA, CAPITAL OF CYPRUS

The Admiral's office was in the military compound in Nicosia, but his house was down on the beach. It was quite a long drive from one to the other, and we would go at a fast clip in his big official car with armed marine escorts and his driver and orderly sitting up in front. It was all rather grand and, since we never did get shot at, quite amusing. The roads through the mountains were narrow and windy and ideal for an ambush, so they were subject to numerous military patrols and checkpoints. That, combined with the tortuous route, meant that what appeared quite a short distance on the map could take several hours. Miers would become apoplectic when some factotum in London would suggest he "just pop down to Limassol." He would send off a furious signal telling the "stupid bugger" that it would take him three bloody hours to "pop" down there, a signal I would discretely alter to something more palatable before sending it.

MY BROTHER TONY

"My brother Tony was doing his National Service as a meteorologist in HMS Bulwark, *and when she came past on her way back from the Far East I took the barge out on my own to go on board to see him. I think he was surprised to see how I was allowed to use this elegant vessel for my own purposes."*

The Admiral had a barge, a naval term for what was really a rather smart motorboat, and we would use it to go and visit the bigger ships coming through. There was a coxswain to steer and a bowman and a stern man who did complex drills with boat hooks. With the Admiral on board I had to make sure that he received and returned all the right salutes, which made me feel important. I had to wear my best uniform, white tunic and gold buttons with gold braid aiguillettes over one shoulder to indicate that I was his Flag Lieutenant. My brother Tony was doing his National Service as a meteorologist in HMS *Bulwark*, and when she came past on her way back from the Far East, Miers insisted I take the barge out on my own to go on board to see him. I think Tony was surprised to see that I was allowed to use this elegant vessel for my own purposes.

Another use of the barge was to take Pat Miers water skiing. Once he found out that I could water ski too, Miers encouraged me to go along. One day (while *Bulwark* was still in the neighborhood) he was kind enough to invite Tony over for lunch (an extraordinary courtesy: Admirals very seldom go out of their way to entertain mere enlisted sailors!) and afterwards Tony and I both went out water skiing. Sailor in the front, another in the stern, coxs'n at the wheel, and enlisted man Tony Coles behind on the waterskis. I think the whole thing left my brother a little bewildered.

It was toward the end of 1958, a year in which so much had gone wrong that it was almost inevitable that something good had to turn up, when Miers casually dropped a letter onto my desk and told me to read it. From him to the Admiralty it was written in a style which reflected his normally rather salty approach to the English language and, without mincing any words, informed Their Lordships that whoever had been dealing with my situation ought to be shot (or maybe hanged, or possibly drawn and quartered). I was, he thought, a thoroughly pleasant young man of considerable ability who had no intention of spending the rest of his life in the Navy. The sooner those turkeys in Whitehall woke up to the fact that they were wasting everybody's time, the quicker they would be able to send me on my way to everybody's benefit. It seemed to me a rather splendid letter; by far the most sensible thing I had seen to date from any one of high rank, but I suspected it would have as little effect as any of its predecessors.

It was about the time that this wonderful letter arrived that Miers' retirement date came due. He had been made a Knight Commander of the Bath (KCB) in the Queen's New Year's Honors list and would thus enter a well-deserved life of leisure as Rear Admiral Sir Anthony Miers, KCB, VC, DSO, together with his wife, now Lady Patricia. In fact, it wasn't all that leisurely: he went on the Boards of several public companies and charities and we saw him again briefly when we lived in London. He died in 1985 and the Duke of Edinburgh and the entire Board of Admiralty were at his funeral. Apart from members of my family and one or two of my banking partners, there are few people in my life I look back on with unalloyed admiration, and he is one of them.

My last task as his Flag Lieutenant was to ensure that his departure from Cyprus took place in appropriate style. On the day that he and Pat left I took them out to the troop ship on which they would sail home. All his little fleet, two destroyers and six mine-sweepers were gathered to see him off and, as his barge cruised by, me in the back in all my gold embroidered glory, he got all the flags and whistles due his rank. I had become terrifically fond of him and found it all very moving. I saw them into their cabin, made sure all the bags and things were properly stowed. Then I gave Pat a kiss and saluted him. I think it may have been the last time he wore his admiral's uniform while on duty, and thus the last salute he got before retirement. I will always be enormously grateful to that remarkable man.

Miers' successor was Commodore Bromley, formerly his Chief of Staff. A kindly avuncular man, he had none of Miers' vinegary approach to life, and little of his color. Nor did he warrant the services of a Flag Lieutenant. So, I went back to keeping watches but fortunately, since I had never taken advantage of my position's reflected power, I was still among friends.

Soon snow began to fall in the Troodos Mountains. The weather down on the shoreline remained sunny and pleasant, but by early January we had some two or three feet of snow up at the 6,000 ft. level where the army had established a small ski camp. The only way up was by road, so one needed wheels, but once up there you could rent skis and boots from the army and find some quite interesting runs. The whole area was blocked off so that the EOKA people couldn't knock off the skiers and we didn't have to carry our guns although I personally would have relished a photo of myself schussing down a mountain side with my revolver rather ostentatiously strapped to the side of my ski pants. The only snag with all this was that there were no lifts or tows: if you wanted to ski down you had to walk up. Since strenuous exercise was never my strong point, I had to find a better way.

The owner of the little Renault had gone home, and I had bought his car for a modest price, thus giving me the ability (with some wheezing from its tiny engine) to get up the mountain. What I needed now was somebody to act as my chauffeur, and fortune came my way in the shape of a newly appointed army warrant officer who wanted to learn to drive. I gave him rudimentary lessons in starting, stopping and shifting and then told him that the best practice was going up and down hills, since it would require a lot of nimble work with the brakes. Then off to the top of Mt. Olympus we went. He would drop me off at the top and then drive down to the bottom of the run to wait while I skied down. Actually, his progress was slow enough that we both usually reached the bottom at the same time. As I came down, I could hear through the trees the high-pitched grinding of the gears as he ham-fistedly tried to get from third to second, the squealing of the brakes as he narrowly avoided a tree, and the barking of horns as he barely escaped death in the face of an oncoming truck. But both he and the car survived and over the course of the winter on my days off I got in some quite good skiing.

One of the duties of the naval watch officers was to be available in the communications room if a "Top Secret—Eyes of Officer Only" signal came in and needed to be decoded. I was on watch in late January when I was told to be ready for a lengthy message from London. I stood by the cipher machine while seemingly endless pages came over the telex, then spent most of the rest of my watch putting it all into readable English. It was the final draft of the Treaty of London, the product of long weeks of negotiation between British, Greek, Turkish, and Cypriot representatives, which was designed to bring an end to the fighting and a peaceful independence to Cyprus. One provision I clearly remember permitted the Turks to intervene militarily in the event the Greeks ever attempted to impair the Island's independence by resurrecting Enosis.

In 1974, when Greece was ruled by a military junta, they did just that: the Turks invaded, Cyprus was partitioned, and the rest is history. To listen to the Greek community you would think that they were the totally innocent and aggrieved party, but in my view the Turks were entirely within their treaty rights. One of the advantages of colonialism is that the occupying power provides protection for minorities. Withdraw the external administration, leaving behind contentious nationalists, and you have the potential for real trouble.

I was enormously surprised when, with no warning, another letter arrived bearing an Admiralty postmark. With no fanfare or explanation of any kind it simply stated "I am commanded by my Lords Commissioners of the Admiralty to inform you that your letter of resignation dated November 15, 1957 has been accepted effective July 1, 1959." I have often wondered what happened: had the wheels of the bureaucracy finally ground out a sensible decision, or had the obvious contempt conveyed in Miers' earlier letter finally done the trick?

I have always preferred to believe the last explanation. He was, after all, a war hero and only a decade after the end of the conflict their views were not taken lightly. As a holder of the Victoria Cross he would have been expected to hold strong opinions about people who wanted to leave the Service for civilian life before the Service was prepared to dispense with them; indeed, that was why I was in Cyprus. Yet he had written strongly in my support. Whatever the reason, I was certainly not going to ask questions. I dashed off a note to Joan filled with delirious happiness. It was another time in my life that I felt extremely lucky.

My daily correspondence with Joan was now filled with ecstatic joy and exciting plans. Although far apart geographically, daily we became closer. The complex decisions: where and when to be married, with or without families present, seemed to solve themselves with miraculous ease.

The only real difference between us foreshadowed the few differences that would also arise during our lives together: my impetuous desire to get things moving right away, and Joan's wisdom in wanting to think things through before making a commitment. Familiar? I of course wanted Joan to quit her teaching job and come to Cyprus right away so that we could get married and live together on the British base there. She, on the other hand pointed out that what little money we had was to be devoted to Harvard. If she was to quit teaching in the middle of the semester it might prove very difficult to get her job back when she wanted it again the next year. What would we live on? As usual, she was right: she stayed in Cambridge and completed her teaching commitment, then packed a small bag – just big enough for her wedding dress, and took a lengthy overnight trip via London to Cyprus.

Looking back, I can only recall Joan's arrival in Cyprus as representing an act of enormous bravery and optimism. The day her teaching was finished for the summer she packed her wedding dress and a few other essentials and, alone, took the long flight (piston engine, not jet) from Boston to Cyprus. I went to Nicosia airport to meet her and there appeared to be a bit of a hold up: each passenger entering the country had to be sized up by a carefully hidden EOKA turncoat who would give a "yes" or "no" sign to a watching British intelligence officer positioned to determine whether the entrant was likely to be returning to the country to disturb what was still a precarious peace. Once she was through that barrier, we fell into each other's arms, a position neither of us had any desire ever to change. What amazed us both was how seamlessly we were able to resume loving each other after nearly a year of separation, an outcome that says much about the power of the written word.

Our wedding, in the small seaside town of Limassol, was attended by a surprising number of people considering how few naval friends I had there. I suspect some of the aviators from the Gannet flight may have put the word out that one of their fraternity was getting married, and it would probably be a good party. Actually, despite the fact that I now carried a very different persona, it was, and a good time was had by all. Joan even had a bridesmaid, a nice little girl conveniently on loan from one of my fellow watchkeepers.

Our honeymoon began at a small hotel on the beach in Kyrenia, an old Cypriot port that in better days was a convenient point for trading with Turkey. So far as I was concerned, the honeymoon never ended. To get to Kyrenia we had to drive over the Troodos mountains and, for some obscure reason (probably because the little Renault began to cough and choke if I asked her to do too much of this hill climbing) I began to think of my financial situation, which was becoming a little stretched by all the wedding festivities. “Maybe,” I said carelessly as I negotiated a hairpin bend, “we could start using some of yours?” “Oh yes,” Joan replied happily, “My brother Jack gave me $100 before I left Cambridge, if we can find someone to break it we can use that.” Readers already having formed a low opinion of me will be expecting me to say something churlish like “Is that all?” But no, by now if she had asked me to sky-dive for pennies off the highest mountain I would have leapt at the chance. Knowledge of our threadbare financial situation merely reinforced my determination to do well at my new educational endeavor. And for those worried about those pesky school fees, the timely death of an obscure relative did in the end sort much of it out, plus a lot of (effective) letter writing by my father to the grant making department of the Devon County Council (the official political jurisdiction for people, like me, who lived and voted in Devonshire) which came through with surprising generosity, possibly just to get my father off their backs.

The British authorities in Cyprus did not entirely trust

EOKA to keep the peace, particularly when as tempting a target as a wedding was involved. Lurking behind bride and groom in our wedding pictures, the shadowy figure of an armed commando can just be made out, the marksman thoughtfully placed there by the British Army to protect the happy couple.

MICHAEL AND JOAN'S WEDDING, 1958

"Lurking behind bride and groom in our wedding pictures, the shadowy figure of an armed commando can just be made out, the marksman thoughtfully placed there by the British Army to protect the happy couple."

My farewell to the Navy after eight years and a few months appeared quite undramatic; given all the problems I seem to have caused, they treated me very nicely when the chips were finally down. My long awaited fifteen hundred pounds got lost in the bureaucratic shuffle, and I wasn't about to push my luck by fighting for it. The Navy was kind enough to provide us with passage on one of their ships to Malta. There we had just enough time for me to show Joan some of my old hangouts, before we were whisked away to London.

Soon we were on the train down Little Stert to see my parents, the first time since the wedding. On the way, we got up to go to the dining car and Joan momentarily fainted. I mentioned this to my mother when we got home and she, with all the glee of an African elder greeting the bride's first appearance from the nuptial kraal, announced that Joan must be pregnant. Nonsense, I said, we have everything worked out as instructed by Father Haemus during our claret tastings: the green days and the red days or whatever they were, and she couldn't possibly be pregnant. Besides which, if she was, how would I ever get through Harvard Business School? Well she was, and the result was Caroline: next to being married, the best thing that happened to us that momentous year. If Father Heamus' goal had been to propagate the Roman faith, he'd done a pretty good job. Four more wonderful children later, and I don't think we ever did get the green days and the red days worked out properly.

Thanks to a generous wedding present we were able to sail to New York on the SS *United States*, the pride of the American merchant marine. Although intended primarily as a luxury transatlantic passenger vessel, she had been constructed to United States Navy specifications for possible use as a hospital ship during wartime. She was extremely fast and had exceptional watertight integrity. However, despite enormous subsidies, she never really made it commercially. One of her problems was that the heavily unionized New York crew had trouble adapting to the high level of service which passengers used to the British "Queens" and the French Line had come to expect as their due. However, she was new and comfortable and Joan and I were still on our extended honeymoon and asked for little else. Until, that is, it came time for lifeboat drill.

All ocean liners are required to conduct a lifeboat drill within a few hours of sailing, during which every passenger has to go to his or her lifeboat station and be briefed on what to do in case of emergency (all a by-product of the *Titanic* disaster). We must have sailed around mid-morning, and lunch was served as we moved rapidly out into the English Channel. During lunch there was a long announcement about lifeboat drill and, as we went back to our cabin, I was all prepared to gather up my life jacket and follow the crowd to our proper station. To my horror, however, Joan was slipping into a most fetching negligee and climbing into our bed. "You can't do that," I cried "we've got to go to lifeboat drill!" "No one goes to lifeboat drill," she replied, "I'm staying here in my warm bed and you, my love, are getting in here with me." I couldn't believe my ears; I had never heard of somebody not going to lifeboat drill. And this wasn't an accident or a misunderstanding, this was intentional!

There was a brief but intense internal struggle between my duty to go to lifeboat drill and my strong desire to stay right there with my beautiful new wife. And to my everlasting shame it was the spirit of obedience instilled by eight years in Her Majesty's Navy that won out. She snuggled down in our warm bed while I made my way up to the wet and windy lifeboat deck, explaining bashfully to the sailor in charge that my wife was a little tired. When it was all over I rushed back to the cabin, but the moment had passed. There were, we decided, two kinds of people in the world, those who went to lifeboat drill and those who didn't, the divide was an unbridgeable one, and I stood on one side and she on the other. Fortunately there was little else to separate us.

Actually, the *United States* wasn't at all bad, and for me any place where Joan happened to be represented nirvana. The four days of our passage passed quite quickly and since there was no more lifeboat drill to distract us, we spent a lot of time in our cabin. For some odd reason my most vivid memory other than Joan was a well-built young woman who hung around the ship wearing a tight sweatshirt which had "Michigan State" in large letters across a truly immense bosom. Joan explained that this meant she attended a mid-western institution of higher learning and I wondered if there would be any like her at Harvard Business School and then rapidly remembered my new status. Then, on the morning of August 23, 1959, we sailed into New York harbor. There was no Verrazzano Narrows Bridge in those days so again I was treated to the splendid sight of Wall Street, its tall buildings sharply outlined in the morning light, and the Statue of Liberty off to our left. Though I didn't realize it at the time, I was home.

We eventually made it to Cambridge, MA, just after Labor Day – in time for me to join the Class of 1961 (soon to be "Fabulous"), at Harvard Business School. The only cloud remaining on my horizon was my certainty that my lack of appropriate education would soon be found out, and I would be politely told to take my business to some other less demanding school. But that's another story, we'll have to deal with later.

✈✈✈✈✈✈✈✈✈✈✈✈✈✈

Any reader who has proved his stamina by getting to the end of this saga, and who has been observant enough to notice that the subject of learning seems to occur consistently throughout, has the right to ask "So, what do we learn from all this?" And I do think that there are some useful lessons buried here:

- Farming is a cruel taskmaster whose opportunities only appear attractive when covered with a thick layer of ill-informed optimism;

- Large quantities of alcohol do not necessarily make one a better or safer driver, regardless of how skilled you may feel;

➢ When flying be very, very careful when you open the throttle of a 2,300 horsepower Rolls Royce engine;

➢ There is no such thing as a free lunch;

➢ Look before you leap;

➢ If you decide to take up sailing, never cruise offshore with someone you just met in a bar;

➢ Never get into a lock-up situation without an exit strategy, particularly when the military is involved;

➢ Think very carefully before you decide to go to lifeboat drill;

➢ One really happy marriage is a sign of considerable luckiness; two puts you well beyond the outer realms of probability;

➢ And finally, once you have found her, never, ever let her go.

ABOUT THE AUTHOR

Michael Coles, born in England in 1932, was educated there until 1951, when, following the start of the Korean War, he joined the Royal Navy. He served as a carrier pilot on HMS *Ocean*, a light fleet carrier that provided close air support to British Commonwealth forces fighting in Korea under the command of the United Nations.

On return from Korea he spent a further two years in carrier borne flight operations, followed by two years as a flight instructor. He concluded his naval career in Cyprus, on the staff of the Admiral responsible for Royal Navy operations in the Middle East.

On leaving the Royal Navy in 1959 he married the former Joan Collins of Boston MA, and obtained a Master's Degree in Business Administration from Harvard. Following Harvard he joined Goldman, Sachs & Co in New York, and eventually became Chairman of its International Corporation.

After retiring from Goldman, Sachs in 1987 he earned a Master's Degree in History from Columbia University.

During his retirement years he has devoted much of his time to not-for-profit activities, as well as studying and writing naval, military and political history.

Joan, who became afflicted with Parkinson's disease, died in 1999. Michael has since remarried Dr. Edith Langner. They live in Shelter Island, NY and Palm Beach, FL.

Made in the USA
Las Vegas, NV
24 May 2021